WALKING IN WORCESTERSHIRE

31 WALKS INCLUDING THE WORCESTERSHIRE WAY AND MALVERN HILLS

By Julia and Mike Goodfellow-Smith

JUNIPER HOUSE, MURLEY MOSS,
OXENHOLME ROAD, KENDAL, CUMBRIA LA9 7RL
cicerone.co.uk

First edition 2026
ISBN: 978 1 78631 244 0
eISBN: 978 1 78765 270 5

Printed in Czechia on behalf of Latitude Press Ltd on responsibly sourced paper.
A catalogue record for this book is available from the British Library.
All photographs are by the author unless otherwise stated.

Cicerone's EU representative for GPSR compliance is Easy Access System Europe, Mustamäe tee 50, 10621 Tallinn, Estonia. Email gpsr.requests@easproject.com.

Updates to this guide

While we strive to ensure that our guidebooks are as up to date and accurate as possible, changes can occur during the lifetime of an edition. Facilities, accommodation, transport and even rights of way can change, so if you find any inaccuracies in this book or have any feedback, please let us know by email at updates@cicerone.co.uk. Updates will be published on the Cicerone website (cicerone.co.uk/1244/updates), so please check before planning your trip.

To receive free updates, special offers and GPX files where available, don't forget to register your book at the 'My Account' tab at cicerone.co.uk.

Front cover: The view to Berrow Hill on the final stretch of Walk 4

CONTENTS

Route symbols on OS map extracts
(for OS legend see printed OS maps)

- route
- alternative route
- link route/detour
- SF start/finish point
- S start point
- F finish point
- SF alternative start/finish point
- S alternative start point
- F alternative finish point
- route direction

Features on the overview map

- county/unitary boundary
- national boundary
- urban area
- national landscapes eg *Malvern Hills*

>800m
600m
400m
200m
75m
0m

SCALE: 1:50,000
0 kilometres 0.5 1
0 miles 0.5

GPX files for all routes can be downloaded free at cicerone.co.uk/1244/GPX.

ROUTE SUMMARY TABLE

Walk	Title	Start	Finish	Distance (km)	Time	Ascent (m)	Descent (m)	Page
1	Tenbury Wells	Tenbury Wells	Tenbury Wells	10.5	3hr	160	160	20
2	Eardiston and the Teme Valley	Eardiston	Eardiston	18.6	5hr 30min	410	410	26
3	Abberley Circular	Abberley	Abberley	7.9	2hr 30min	325	325	33
4	Martley Circular	Martley	Martley	10.2	3hr	240	240	36
5	Knapp and Papermill Nature Reserve	Knapp and Papermill Nature Reserve	Knapp and Papermill Nature Reserve	10.8	3hr 15min	230	230	41
6	Malvern Hills end to end	Chase End Hill	North Quarry car park	15.7	6hr 30min	980	904	46
7	Great Malvern and Worcestershire Beacon	Great Malvern railway station	Great Malvern railway station	8.1km	3hr	365	365	56
8	Little Malvern and St Wulstan's Nature Reserve	British Camp car park	British Camp car park	9.5	3hr	285	285	61
9	The southern hills	Hollybush car park	Hollybush car park	7.8	2hr 45min	380	380	66
10	Castlemorton Common	Swinyard car park	Swinyard car park	9.7	2hr 45min	165	165	70
11	Birts Street and Castlemorton	Hollybush	Hollybush	8	2hr 15min	120	120	75
12	Upton upon Severn and Upper Ham Meadows	Upton upon Severn	Upton upon Severn	9.1	2hr 30min	55	55	80
13	River Severn and Croome Park	Upton upon Severn	Upton upon Severn	19.9	5hr 15min	145	145	84

Walk	Title	Start	Finish	Distance (km)	Time	Ascent (m)	Descent (m)	Page
14	Old Hills	Callow End	Callow End	3.6	1hr	65	65	91
15	Worcester – rivers and battlefield	Worcester Foregate Street railway station	Worcester Foregate Street railway station	10.8	3hr	60	60	94
16	Pershore, River Avon and Tiddesley Wood	Pershore	Pershore	10	2hr 45min	60	60	100
17	Pershore to Broadway on the Wychavon Way	Pershore	Broadway	27.4	8hr	465	395	104
18	River Avon and Bredon Hill	Eckington	Eckington	16.7	5hr	345		112
19	Elmley Castle and Bredon Hill	Elmley Castle	Elmley Castle	13.5	4hr 30min	475	475	118
20	Broadway Tower and village	Broadway	Broadway	10.1	3hr 15min	335	335	123
21	Evesham and the River Avon	Evesham railway station	Evesham railway station	9.2	2hr 30min	70	70	127
22	Inkberrow and Abbots Morton	Inkberrow	Inkberrow	9.8	2hr 45min	100	100	131
23	Grafton Flyford Hairstreak Butterfly Trail	Grafton Flyford	Grafton Flyford	11	3hr	100	100	136
24	Droitwich Spa and Hanbury Hall	Droitwich Spa Lido	Droitwich Spa Lido	16.2	4hr 15min	120	120	142
25	Bordesley Abbey Meadows and Arrow Lake	Forge Mill Needle Museum	Forge Mill Needle Museum	7	1hr 45min	15	15	148

Walk	Title	Start	Finish	Distance (km)	Time	Ascent (m)	Descent (m)	Page
26	Lickey Hills and Worcester and Birmingham Canal	Barnt Green	Barnt Green	15.3	4hr 30min	290	290	152
27	Clent Hills	Clent	Clent	9.7	3hr 15min	310	310	157
28	Wyre Forest	Wyre Forest Visitor Centre	Wyre Forest Visitor Centre	8.6	2hr 30min	180	180	162
29	Worcester to Birmingham along the canal							
Stage 1	Worcester to Droitwich Spa	Worcester Foregate Street railway station	Droitwich Spa railway station	17.8	4hr 30min	40	25	168
Stage 2	Droitwich Spa to Bromsgrove	Droitwich Spa railway station	Bromsgrove railway station	13.8	3hr 45min	85	45	173
Stage 3	Bromsgrove to Alvechurch	Bromsgrove railway station	Alvechurch railway station	9.6	2hr 45min	140	90	178
Stage 4	Alvechurch to Birmingham New Street	Alvechurch railway station	Birmingham New Street railway station	19.2	5hr	70	80	182
30	North Worcestershire Path							
Stage 1	Shirley to Hagley	Shirley	Hagley	30.2	9hr 30min	665	680	191
Stage 2	Hagley to Bewdley	Hagley	Bewdley	27.2	8hr	505	600	203
31	Worcestershire Way							
Stage 1	Bewdley to Knightwick	Bewdley	Knightwick	31.3	11hr	1065	1060	212
Stage 2	Knightwick to Great Malvern	Knightwick	Great Malvern	17.8	6hr	675	560	224

The canal offers beautiful reflections (Walk 29, Stage 2)

INTRODUCTION

The church at Broadway Court, nestled in a valley (Walk 20)

PLANNING YOUR TRIP

When to go

Worcestershire is a county for all seasons. In spring, the orchards bloom, hedgerows blossom and many of the woodlands are carpeted with Native Bluebells, Wood Anemones and Ramsons (Wild Garlic). In summer, the meadows are in full bloom, with butterflies and bees flitting from flower to flower and Skylarks singing overhead. Autumn is a time for woodlands to become resplendent with their leaves turning from green to shades of yellow, copper and red, and for some of the trees to bear bright, juicy fruit. And in winter, when everywhere else is muddy, you can take to the Malvern Hills or the canals, where the paths are well made and remain passable.

Getting there

Worcestershire is well served by trains from London and Birmingham, and many of the walks described in this book are accessible from stations. There is also a good bus service in the larger urban areas, although it is less frequent in the countryside. Where walks can be accessed by public transport, details are provided in the information box at the start of the walk. These are liable to change; please check online before you rely on them.

Worcestershire also has excellent road access, with the M5 bisecting the county from north to south and a network of roads extending from each of the main urban areas.

Accommodation

There are many places to stay in Worcestershire. For charming towns with the best access to walking country, try Great Malvern, Upton upon Severn, Worcester, Bewdley, Pershore or Evesham. All have plenty of accommodation choices and several walks within easy reach.

Using this guide

If you were to plan a walking route in Worcestershire just using a map, it is likely that you would find blocked footpaths, impassable boundaries, or unsafe stiles or bridges. The number of walks we had to change or give up on while researching this book indicates the continued value of our work. All of the walks included were passable at the time of writing, and where there were overgrown areas, these are mentioned in the route information box. However, conditions on the ground can change faster than updates can be printed. Please check the Cicerone website for updates (cicerone.co.uk/1244/updates) and download the latest GPX file for your route before setting off. If you have difficulty with any of the routes, please let Cicerone know by emailing updates@cicerone.co.uk.

We have organised the day walks in this book by district, with three multi-day walks at the end.

Worcestershire has a lot of lakes, rivers and canals. This is one of the lakes at Croome Court (Walk 13)

Day walks

Most of the day walks in this guidebook are circular. If you prefer linear walks, there are several options, most with good transport links:

- Walk 6: Malvern Hills end to end – north to south or south to north
- Walk 17: Pershore to Broadway on the Wychavon Way
- Walk 29: Worcester to Birmingham along the canal – each of the four stages can be tackled as a day walk
- Walk 30: North Worcestershire Path – each of the two stages can be tackled as a day walk

Multi-day walks

The first of these is a four-day walk from Worcester into central Birmingham by canal, with overnight stops in Droitwich, Bromsgrove and Alvechurch. Each stage can be tackled as a day walk, as they all start and finish at railway stations. Stages can be combined into longer walks; details of the combined distance are included in the route information boxes.

The second multi-day walk is the two-day North Worcestershire Path, from Major's Green, near Shirley, to Bewdley. This can be combined with the third, the two-day Worcestershire Way, from Bewdley to Great Malvern.

It is worth noting that the Wychavon Way was not all well maintained at the time of writing, which is why only one section is included in this guidebook (Walk 17).

Route information

Each route description starts with information you need when planning. We have not graded the walks, so this information is designed to help you assess the difficulty for your own circumstances. It includes:

- the start and finish points, with map reference
- an approximate time (This is only a guide. We have usually used the time calculated by the Ordnance Survey® maps website, unless we thought it would be misleading. It does not allow for breaks, and its accuracy depends on your walking pace.)
- the distance, given in km with miles in brackets
- the ascent and descent, given to the nearest 5m (10ft)
- a description of the terrain you are likely to encounter on the walk, including particularly steep bits, stiles, etc.
- other information relevant to the walk, such as availability of refreshments and toilets, public transport, parking, and (for multi-day routes only) accommodation
- any warnings relevant to that particular route.

GPX tracks

This book is available in the Cicerone app on your phone. View GPS-enabled maps that you can download for offline navigation, check route details and local points of interest, and plan your adventure with confidence.

GPX files are also available to download. See cicerone.co.uk/1244.GPX.

PLANNING DAY TO DAY

Climate and weather

Worcestershire is a Goldilocks county when it comes to weather. In the English Midlands, it is not too hot, not too cold, neither too wet nor too dry, but just right! The exceptions are the hills, which tend to be a couple of degrees cooler at the top than at the bottom and are likely to be windier as well.

Terrain

Worcestershire is characterised by watery plains and rolling hills, with a few notable exceptions. The most prominent of these are the Malvern Hills, which rise sharply from the Severn Plain and often attract snow in winter, which makes them appear more mountainous than they are. This is where you will find the county's highest point, Worcestershire Beacon at 425m (1390ft).

Emergencies

As with elsewhere in the UK, dial 999 or 112 in an emergency and request the police, ambulance or fire service. Several towns in Worcestershire have minor injury units. However, only Redditch and Worcester hospitals have 24-hour accident and emergency units.

ALL ABOUT WORCESTERSHIRE

Geology

The geology of Worcestershire is varied and complex, covering a span of 700 million years. It provides evidence of deposition in shallow tropical seas

The northern hills; Sugarloaf, Table and North Hill (Walk 6)

Worcestershire is peppered with timber-framed houses with thatched roofs. This one is in Childswickham (Walk 20)

and swamps, as well as the collision of continents and the effects of glaciation. The western reaches of Worcestershire form part of the Abberley and Malvern Hills Geopark, and the Geopark Way stretches from Bridgnorth to Gloucester. Detailed information about the area's geology is available at the Malvern Hills GeoCentre, located in Upper Colwall near the Wyche Cutting.

Landscape and geography

The Malvern Hills and Cotswolds National Landscapes both extend into Worcestershire, and several of the walks in this book explore those regions. Previously known as Areas of Outstanding Natural Beauty, National Landscapes are considered of national importance for their landscape features and are protected from inappropriate development.

Most of the county is characterised by low rolling hills and meandering rivers, with a few higher hills rising from the lowlands. Walking is therefore generally fairly easy-going, interspersed with the occasional challenging ascent. In winter the low-lying land can become waterlogged and make for a muddy walk.

Such easy country as this is perfect for grazing cattle and horses, and you are likely to see plenty while walking in Worcestershire, along with the odd field of Alpacas for a bit of variety!

A lot of the walks in Worcestershire pass through pasture. This cow on Castlemorton Common showed no interest in passing walkers (Walk 10)

SAFETY AROUND LIVESTOCK

You should not come across any dangerous cows, bulls or horses in fields with public footpaths, but sometimes a walker is the most interesting thing they will see all day, so even if they mean no harm, they may come over to investigate. Young cattle and horses can be particularly curious about humans crossing their fields, and cows with calves can become protective if they perceive a threat. On very odd occasions, even a lamb that feels trapped can attack, although that is less likely to result in injury than a similar situation with a larger animal.

If animals are on the footpath, you do not have to stick to it rigidly – it's fine to give them some space by walking around them. Walk confidently and quietly and be aware that if you start to run, they may do so, too. If you are walking with a dog, keep it on a short lead unless there is an issue, when you should let go.

If you are attacked by an animal and injured, let the police know immediately by calling 101. If you have any other issues, report them to the local authority or Health and Safety Executive, who can let the landowner know that they need to move the animal in question.

Having said all of that, millions of miles are walked across pasture each year, with very few incidents. Please do not let this note of caution put you off walking in this splendid county.

History

Worcestershire is a county rich in history, with the first evidence of human occupation dating back over 500,000 years. The Ice Ages forced people to leave, but after the glaciers retreated and forests grew, the area was reinhabited. Evidence of occupation in the landscape is minimal until the Iron Age, when several hill forts were constructed in the county, the most dominant of which is British Camp in the Malvern Hills (Walks 6 and 8).

The Romans manufactured salt in Droitwich (known then as Salinae) from its briny springs and built a fort there. Next came the Saxons. During this period, Worcester became an important religious centre of learning, reflected now in the quality of illuminated manuscripts in its library, and great abbeys were founded at Pershore and Evesham.

When the Normans arrived towards the end of the 11th century, they built a castle in Worcester, although there is no sign of it now. There are several earthworks, such as those at Castlemorton Tump (Walk 11), Elmley Castle (Walk 19) and Hanley Castle, but the only stone castle remaining in the county is at Dudley.

In the 13th century, as the name suggests, the Battle of Evesham was

Abberley Church (Walk 3)

fought on Worcestershire soil, and is regarded as one of the early steps towards democracy, with the country's barons trying to claim more power from the king.

The historical events for which Worcestershire is best known are those surrounding the British Civil Wars in the 17th century – another step towards democratic rule. Worcester was a Royalist stronghold, and the Battle of Worcester marked the defeat of Charles II. There is evidence of the war in several places in the county, including sword marks and cannonball pits in the church tower at Powick.

A couple of centuries later, the Industrial Revolution spread across the northern reaches of the county, which became a hub for iron, coal, carpet, glass, nail, needle and fish-hook production, and the home of canals and railways for transportation of goods.

The south of the county maintained its rural character as a centre for plum, pear and apple production to provision the urban centres which were growing rapidly, especially once railway routes were opened up into London.

Culture

Worcestershire is also a rich cultural centre. The composer Sir Edward Elgar was born here, and Jenny Lind, the 'Swedish Nightingale', lived here. JRR Tolkien and CS Lewis were both frequent visitors to Malvern, and you can see how those visits influenced their work – the Malvern Hills provided inspiration for the White Mountains, and Malvern's gas lamps are thought to have inspired that found at the entrance to Narnia.

The county retains a rich cultural life. Upton upon Severn hosts several large music festivals each year, and Worcester Music Festival is the UK's largest donation-only festival, raising thousands of pounds for charity every year. Classical music fans are catered for by the Autumn in Malvern Festival, and every three years by the Three Choirs Festival in Worcester.

Other festivals include those celebrating the agricultural heritage of the county, such as the Pershore Plum Festival and the British Asparagus Festival. Smaller events such as wassailing, an evening of music and drinking to wake up the apple trees and ensure a good harvest in the coming year, are often accompanied by one of the local morris dancing 'sides' (a group of morris dancers).

Malvern Theatres hosts lavish West End productions as well as smaller, quirky shows. Malvern also has the world's smallest theatre, based in an old public toilet – the Theatre of Small Convenience. If you prefer your performances outdoors, the Lenches have an outdoor amphitheatre and the Commandery in Worcester hosts plays in its garden.

There are many more theatres, festivals and performances across the county – check out the Visit Worcestershire or village/town websites for more information.

The waterways that lace across Worcestershire attract all sorts of insects, including dragonflies and damselflies like this one

Plants and animals

Although nowhere in Worcestershire is remote wilderness, you will usually be able to spot a diverse range of plants and animals on your walk. As a largely pastoral area with a lot of land maintained as meadow, Worcestershire is a county of butterflies and other flower-loving insects during the summer months. Many of the walks in this book will take you across colourful meadows buzzing with life.

As a county crossed by major rivers and other waterways, there is also plenty of water-based wildlife to see, such as dragonflies and damselflies, herons, ducks and swans. You are less likely to spot the shy otters that are now resident in most rivers in the county, but might notice signs of their passing, such as spraint, which is often left in a prominent position and is likely to contain fish scales and small bones.

A diverse bird population is also resident in the county. Flocks of tits forage through the trees, Cuckoos call across the hills and Skylarks sing above the meadows. Kingfishers dart low across the water as swans serenely paddle, or, not so serenely, visit the sanctuary at Worcester at feeding time. Red Kites quarter the land looking for carrion, while Buzzards do the same for live prey. Peregrine Falcons, the fastest animals on the planet, nest on quarry ledges and the tower of Pershore Abbey (Walk 16).

Although much of the land is pastoral, there are also opportunities to walk through woods and past ancient trees. Alder was once grown in the wetlands here to use for drainpipes, willows adorn the riverbanks and mixed native woodlands climb the slopes of the hills. And the interest does not stop at native trees. In Great Malvern, wealthy Victorians planted trees that had recently been found by plant hunters as status symbols. Those trees have now matured, and walking through the town and its parks is akin to walking through an arboretum. Exotic trees can also be found in St Wulstan's Nature Reserve (Walk 8), St Peter's Fields in Droitwich (Walk 24) and a couple of formal arboretums: Bodenham Arboretum near Kidderminster, and Arley Arboretum and Gardens near Bewdley.

Worcestershire has a lot of meadows, so you are likely to see butterflies in summer. This Small Tortoiseshell was seen near the River Avon

GLOW-WORMS

On still, dark nights in June and July, if you look closely, you might spot Glow-worms at several places in Worcestershire. Confusingly named, they are actually beetles, although the female never stops looking like a larva. The females climb grasses and emit a greeny-orange light from their bottoms to attract a mate – a delightful sight. Less delightful are their dining habits – they bite their prey to inject digestive proteins into them. These first paralyse and then dissolve the prey. If you ever see a larva on a snail's back, it might be staying safely away from the mucus while the snail slowly dies. Two good places to look for Glow-worms are St Wulstan's Nature Reserve (Walk 8) and the Knapp and Papermill Reserve (Walk 5).

DAY WALKS

The route runs under trees in Lickey Hills Country Park (Walk 26)

WALK 1

Tenbury Wells

Start/finish	Tenbury Wells short-term car park (SO 597 684)
Time	3hr
Distance	10.5km (6.5 miles)
Ascent/descent	160m (530ft)
Terrain	Flat town walk initially. Muddy and partially overgrown woodland walk as you leave town and follow the course of the River Teme. Most of the walk is through orchard and rolling meadows. Several stiles and gates.
Refreshments	Several options in Tenbury Wells; café at Frank P Matthews Tree Nursery (2.3km)
Toilets	At start/finish; Frank P Matthews Tree Nursery
Warning	Some parts of the route can become overgrown. One pond overflow has a 1m-deep gully to step over. Tenbury Wells does flood with severe rainfall: always exercise caution during periods of heavy rain.

Tenbury Wells is a fascinating ancient market town, tucked into Worcestershire border country. The Pump Rooms of 1862 hark back to the days of mineral water tourism, and there is the Round Market and several 16th-century and Georgian buildings to admire as you progress through the town centre.

The countryside has a large number of orchards, Hops and some vineyards. Part of the route takes you through a large-scale tree nursery. Among active agricultural activity, corners of ancient landscape are found, such as mill ponds, now unused and rarely visited. Oldwood Common is a large grassland area that once would have been critical to the survival of the local villagers, where animals could graze without charge.

Kyre Brook feeds into the River Teme at Tenbury Wells. Both waterways bring regular flooding to the town, and some of the flood defences can be seen during the walk.

Leave the car park heading south and bear right before the bridge to the sports centre. Follow the path in front of the distinctive blue-and-white Pump Rooms.

MINERAL SPRINGS

In 1839, a Tenbury resident sank a deeper well in the hope of finding a better source of drinking water. Instead, the water he found both smelt and tasted unpleasant, as it was rich in salt and iodine. Rather than being despondent about his find, Mr Godson saw an opportunity to benefit from the popularity of spas and water with healing properties. The market town of Tenbury became Tenbury Spa, and the Pump Rooms were built to house a new spa when the railway was opened.

During the world wars of the 20th century, the buildings were used for various purposes and the fabric started to deteriorate. Luckily for us, they were renovated at the end of the century, providing an architectural focal point for the town as well as a ceremonial space.

The Round Market in Tenbury Wells

At the main road, turn right and then immediately left onto Cross Street. Take a little detour to see the Round Market at the next junction, then continue along Cross Street. Turn right at Berrington Road.

Continue until the road starts going uphill. Pass Brierly House, and before Bednalls House, take the footpath on your right. Continue along the path behind the gardens and as you emerge into your first field, bear right. Continue with the wood on your right, shortly crossing a stile into the wood.

The woodland path gently descends, bearing right. The path leaves the bottom edge of the wood above the valley, where undergrowth can crowd the route for approximately 200m. The path then ascends back through the wood and makes a final descent down wooden steps to the lane.

Turn right and proceed uphill for a short distance over the road bridge. After 70m, cross the stile on your right and bear left up into the pasture, heading towards the trees. There is a stile to cross at the end of the small wood. From here, follow the tarmac track uphill.

Continue through the tree nursery (Frank P Matthews) at Berrington Court, turning left at the signpost, and head towards the farm buildings and shop. Turn right onto the lane, then take the first left downhill. Take the bridleway just to the right-hand edge of the house. Pass through two gates and then follow the path left. Take a diagonal left through the pasture, heading uphill to a gate in the fence line near to a stable block on the right.

Abandoned farmstead near Brick Barn

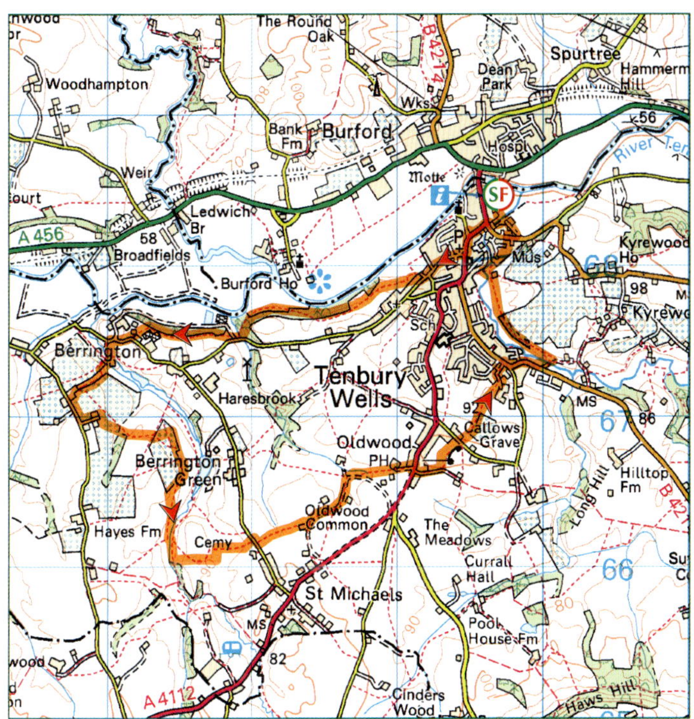

Go past the stable block and an old water pump; just before the exit at a metal gate, turn left onto the footpath and then into the orchard. The footpath goes through the orchard, which will make for very difficult walking, or you can also follow the right-hand boundary around it. Turn left at the far side of the orchard, skirting around the house boundary.

Worcestershire is famed for its **apples**, around 29 varieties of which originate from the county – although Herefordshire also claims some of them. In total, there have been over 6000 named varieties of apple, about one-third of which survive today. Because apples must cross-pollinate, a pip could be a mix of genes from any of the surrounding trees. Trees grown from discarded pips have been known to form new, much-loved varieties, such as Granny Smith, Keswick Codlin and Shaw's Pippin.

The orchard at Holmefields, south of Berrington

A field track skirts the house garden alongside a more recently planted orchard, and heads for a gap in a plantation of poplar trees on the right and a mixed wooded hedge line. Take the path through the gap to the edge of a large, dammed pond.

Continue round to the left of the pond. Step over the pond overflow. The path rises to a hedge line. Go over the stile and follow the tree line straight ahead, which directs the route to a partial metal gate into an orchard. Turn right. The footpath cuts diagonally through the orchard, or an easier route is to take the clear aisle between trees, on the left.

On reaching the field boundary, turn right and follow it, past a view of Cadmore Lodge at the edge of **Berrington Green** by the lake. Take the first footpath on the left. This brings the path into grassland. Turn right and make your way along the boundary to meet a wide cut path through the field, going uphill. Turn left at the top onto a narrow footpath which then drops to the stream below.

Ignore the path curving to the left and continue to the right above the gully. The path then drops down to the brook. Cross a footbridge on your left. The footpath bears right on a diagonal across the field. When the crop is growing, you may decide to follow the field boundary around this field and the next. At the end of the second field, turn left at the field boundary and then right at the stile. Cross the field, go through the gate and left up through the field past a small **cemetery** to meet a lane. Turn right.

After 30m on the lane, take the footpath on the left. Aim straight for the gate ahead next to the oak tree and straight across the next field to another gate. Turn right, joining the gravel track, which then turns left to skirt around **Oldwood Common**. As the gravel track turns left towards farm buildings, continue straight on the grass track following the hedge. Take a small footpath into trees, just before Spring Cottage.

Join the gravel track and follow it. At the track intersection 100m after the cottage, bear right. As the gravel track comes to the edge of the open common, take the narrow footpath on your left across a footbridge in the wood. On leaving the wood, turn left behind the houses. Join the driveway to the houses, taking the route straight ahead. On reaching the **A4112**, turn right and then first left down a track signposted as a bridleway – this is Spring Grove Lane.

As the lane bears right, take a footpath on your left and follow the left-hand field boundary to the gate. Take a right diagonal across this field to the stile, cross the road and the next stile, and continue across the next three fields with a boundary on the left. Bear slightly right in the last field where the houses of Tenbury are now visible.

Walk down to the residential road and then turn left. At the T-junction, turn right, then right again at the next junction. Continue past Terrills on the right, then past Mill Meadow on the left. Take the next lane on the left.

As you walk up the slope, a wide grass splay is on your left, leading to a footpath to the left. Follow the path with the field boundary on your right. Cross the first stile and turn right. Follow the field boundary as it bears left back down to the stream. Take the path left to view the Kyre Brook stepping stones and then retrace your steps to follow the path uphill bearing left.

Now entering **Tenbury Wells**, follow the gap and alleyways between residences. Cross the road, turn right and then take the left to Tenbury Community Pool. Pass the sports centre, cross the bridge and walk into the car park where the walk started.

WALK 2

Eardiston and the Teme Valley

Start/finish	Eardiston lay-by (SO 695 683)
Time	5hr 30min
Distance	18.6km (11.6 miles)
Ascent/descent	410m (1340ft)
Terrain	Undulating, with two climbs. Part of one of the climbs is steep and slippery. There may be obstacles such as fallen trees and a locked gate to navigate.
Refreshments	Eardiston Social Club (open to non-members); café at Stanford Bridge
Public transport	Infrequent buses 758 and 825 from Tenbury Wells
Parking	At start/finish
Warning	Some short sections can be overgrown – we recommend wearing boots and long trousers. One steep and slippery section would be easier to tackle with walking poles, and there are some fallen trees to navigate – only for people with good mobility. Footbridges have some holes and areas of rot.

This is a varied walk along complex paths, through agricultural valley fields and orchards, fantastic steep-sided woodland and beautiful rolling pastures with long-distance views.

Highlights include the elegant bridge at Stanford, Orleton Court orchards – an example of how to provide an excellent camping site, and the wonderful steep-sided woods of Wall Hills Wood and Pennel's Bank on Quarry Hill, with magnificent trees, rich understorey, many flowers, fungi, birds and mammals to spot. A hidden bridge across a lily lake is to be discovered; and then, to finish the walk, stupendous views from the summit of Linkhill across the River Teme Valley and surrounding woodlands.

From the small lay-by starting point, proceed along the A443 past the deregulation speed limit signs and take the footpath on the right, entering a woodland. Exit the woodland at the bottom right-hand corner over the brook. Climb over the gate and walk straight on for five paces, take the stile on your left and follow the field boundary alongside Dumbleton Brook. As you draw parallel with a triangular

Stanford Bridge

copse (which is a diamond shape on the map), look for and cross a footbridge in the field boundary to your left.

Turn right into the field and follow the boundary on your right-hand side. Cross the stile in the corner of the field and continue following the right-hand field boundary to the next stile. The **River Teme** is on your right. Follow the footpath as it crosses this next field on a diagonal, missing out a bend in the river. Aim for a stile in the hedge line, about one-third in from the river boundary on your right-hand side. Cross the stile and take the footpath straight ahead across the field, through a gap in the hedge line. Now maintain your route with the River Teme on your right. Take the gate at the next field boundary and cross over the footbridge.

Cross the stile, following the river boundary at first, and then bear left towards the post-and-rail fence in the far left-hand corner. As you progress, you will spot a gate to the right of the rails. Pass through onto the footbridge.

Turn right to cross the bridge over the River Teme at **Stanford Bridge**. Turn right onto the road, passing the garden centre. Choose your route along the road with regard to traffic, until you pass a timber yard. The footpath is on the right, 100m afterwards. Bear left through the first gap in the hedge line into a Hop field.

HOPS

This walk passes through one of the two main Hop-growing areas of the country. Most British Hops are grown either in Herefordshire/Worcestershire or in South East England. Here in the Teme Valley, Hops have historically been grown alongside orchard fruits. During the autumn picking season, the area would fill with travellers and those from the industrial areas of the Black Country and the Welsh Valleys.

The Hops were dried in layers over a fire, known as a Hop kiln, in a building known as an oast house. Many of the oast houses in this area have a pyramidal roof with a cowl on top to encourage air flow and allow the moisture to leave, whereas in the South East they are more likely to be conical. Hops were traditionally transported to the Hop market in Worcester.

Follow the right-hand boundary, upslope, turning left at the top. Through the gap in the hedge at the end of the Hop field, turn right and follow the track until you enter an orchard with **Round Hill** rising to your left. Turn right to follow the field boundary down. Turn left along a gravel track before the next field boundary, through a combined orchard and campsite with on-site brewery and tap room.

Take the track between pools and then turn left onto the drive of **Orleton Court**. At the lane, turn left. As the lane turns almost 90 degrees left, turn right

The lake at Orleton Court

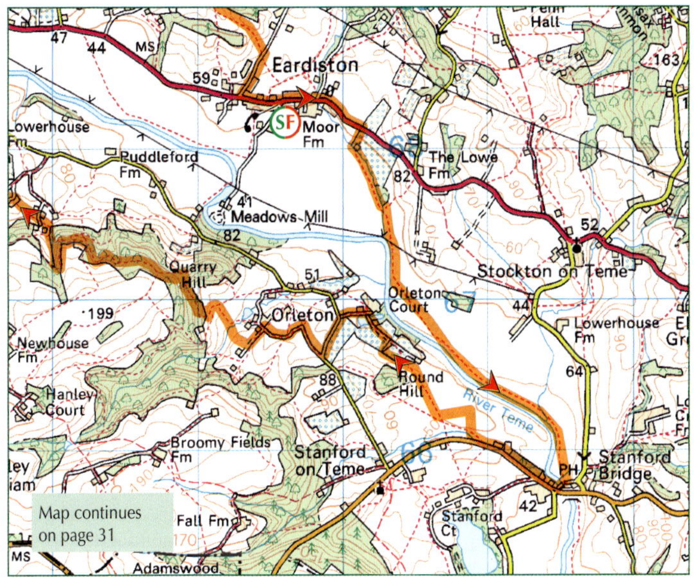

Map continues on page 31

down the track to Spring Valley Retreat. Follow the concrete road as it bears left and head towards the woodland on the hill. At the Upper House farm buildings, swing round to the left. There are two available routes: take the right of the two initially parallel paths, straight on up towards the woodland and Orleton Grange. Take the right onto the gravel track just before the house. The white building on the hill ahead is Ferny Hill House.

Continue on the gravel track as it descends into the valley, crossing a brook and then going uphill on the other side. Just before Ferny Hill House's gate is a footpath which winds its way up the hill. Follow the waymarked but at times indistinct route uphill to an intersection with a level footpath. Turn right. This is Wall Hills Wood on **Quarry Hill**, full of Wild Garlic in spring.

Keep gently ascending, heading north-west. Several fallen trees over the path require a bit of a scramble. Shortly after the fallen trees, at a path intersection, turn left and follow the steep and slippery path straight up the ridge. On reaching a contour track at the top, turn right. Keep along the top of the wood, following the path as it gently meanders and then descends along the valley side. This is now Pennel's Bank – a really lovely woodland of Hazel, Oak, Sycamore, Beech, Holly, Hawthorn and loads of Wild Garlic.

The barn at Walker's Cottage

On joining the access track to a smallholding, turn right. Continue following the track on a sharp right-hand bend to curve steeply downhill; continue downhill and skirt around a property on the left. Cross the drive to the property and take the footpath through a gate on top of the bank. Walk straight across this little field. Cross the stile into the next field and head just right of the large boulders towards a stile giving access into the caravan park.

Head for the only gap in the hedge to the right and turn left, joining the internal caravan park track. As the track curves around an earth dome, take a left down a narrow-flagged path and steps between caravans. Turn right and after passing a couple of caravans, turn left. Opposite the reception, take the footpath into the field on the left. Go through the gate into the fields and follow the post-and-rail fence.

Pass the old pond and go through the metal rail gate. Take a right diagonal to the break in the hedge line just above the larger fishpond. From the hedge line, head straight up the field to the iron-rail fence line of the house in front of you. Climb the gate onto the driveway, and turn right onto the access drive to **Eastham Grange**. Pass the grange and bear left downhill, passing beside Mill Cottage to a field gate. Cross the stream and go through the next field gate. Head for the field gate in the right-hand corner, into an orchard. Continue straight through to a gate onto the road. Turn left.

Go through the hamlet, passing Eastham Memorial Hall, and continue until you reach Walker's Cottage. Turn right down the track past its barn. Cross over the stream and start climbing uphill to the fork in the track. Take the left fork and then

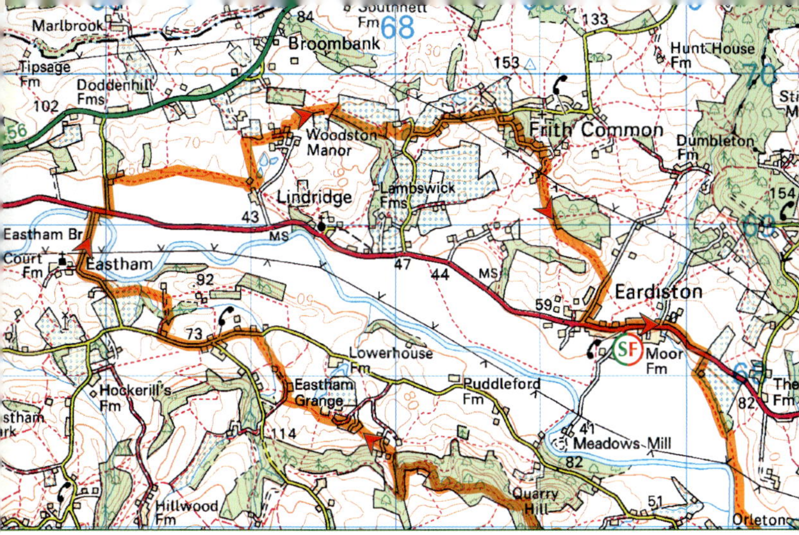

go left through the big metal field gate. Head for the lower left-hand corner of the field. Cross the stream and head up the steep bank. Bear right on a diagonal across the orchard, heading for a metal field gate and on to the lane. Turn right. Reaching the A443, cross **Eastham Bridge**, turn right and then take your first road on the left. Turn right just after Brickyard Cottages.

EASTHAM BRIDGE

When looking at Eastham Bridge today, we see a new construction that replaced the original Grade II listed bridge. The old bridge collapsed in May 2016 after one of its piers was a victim of scour. Scouring occurs due to fast-flowing water and can lead to the removal of sediment around bridge piers, leaving them unsupported.

The original bridge was built of red and blue brick with sandstone structural accents. Two circular flood outlets were added in each of the central spandrels. The new bridge is not as beautiful by any means, but it is still special, as 12,500 of the original historic bricks have been used to clad the modern steel beams and fixings.

Go through three field gates; at the third, with the intersection of paths, carry straight on. Exit the field in the far right-hand corner. Cross the footbridge, cross over the stile and walk straight along through the field to a yard. After the yard, turn right at the intersection of tracks and after 10m take the footpath up steps on your left.

Oast houses at Woodston Manor Farm

Climb over the stile into the field and turn left in front of the mill pond. Follow the path around the left and top field boundaries. Exit via a gate in the corner. Carry on past Woodstone House (at **Woodston Manor**), turning left into a stable block yard. Exit through the metal gate, turn right and then go through the gap in the fence line. Make your way up the slope, bearing right. Go through the gate and follow the fence line on your right. Curve around the field slightly left and then exit by the stile in the corner.

Enter the orchard and turn right, following the boundary round to the far side. Take the right-hand gate, with a view through to farm buildings. Head towards the metal railings that edge the property and follow down to cross a bridge across the lily pond.

On reaching a lane, turn right and after a few paces turn left. Follow the lane to the first drop down a hill and the drive leading to Oldfield Cider (600m). Turn right and follow this lane for 400m. Turn right at Holly Cottage, following the footpath through the parking area. Drop down the footpath, joining a field track, turn right and continue along the track, which proceeds to an isolated cottage. Just before the gates, take the footpath on the left. Follow this across the field downhill to cross the stream on the right-hand edge of the woodland in the valley.

Follow the woodland edge to a field gate and then through and up Linkhill. At the summit, follow the vehicle tracks to a gate in the far right-hand corner below. Turn right onto the lane and follow it downhill until it meets the road running through Eardiston. Turn left and walk along the pavement until spotting the red telephone box and the small lay-by in **Eardiston** where the walk started.

WALK 3

Abberley Circular

Start/finish	Abberley village hall car park (SO 747 679)
Time	2hr 30min
Distance	7.9km (4.9 miles)
Ascent/descent	325m (1060ft)
Terrain	Tarmac lanes, field paths, woodland paths; several stiles – not dog-friendly
Refreshments	Manor Arms Inn in Abberley Village
Public transport	Infrequent buses from Worcester to Clows Top Road, Abberley Common

This delightful, well-maintained and well-waymarked route starts at the village hall, as there are so few parking spaces in Abberley Village itself. It therefore begins and ends along a road, but there is little traffic. Abberley Village is small, but it has a pub that serves food and an unusual Norman church built on Saxon foundations.

The first section of the walk undulates across farmland before rising to Shavers End and again onto the ridge of Abberley Hill. From here, most of the walk is on a wide path through shady woodland, undulating along the ridge. At two key points, the route skirts the edge of the woods and offers a view first of the Malvern Hills, then of the Clock Tower and Abberley Hall before dropping back through the woods to the village.

From the car park, turn left onto the lane and follow this into Abberley Village. At the Manor Arms Inn, continue ahead. About 10 paces after the drive for Crocketts Farm, turn left over a stile to skirt the bottom edge of the field. Through a hand gate, aim for the far left-hand corner of the next field. Through a kissing gate, turn left along the drive and continue through the gate, then to the left of the house up some steps. These lead to another stile.

The path continues around the right-hand edge of the field until it reaches a hand gate. Pass through this and continue in the same direction, first with the hedge on your left, then diagonally right across the field. The route is clearly waymarked and leads over a rise and down to a gate. Turn left along the lane. After 200m, turn right onto a track signposted Worcestershire Way, along a garden hedge (Netherton House). This leads between fields, rising to a lane. Turn left to walk around **Shavers End**.

Abberley Clock Tower from Abberley Hill

Pass the entrance to the now-closed **quarry**, then take a footpath heading right, uphill, through woods. When the path bears right and crosses a meadow, look left for a view of the end of the Malvern Hills. The route steepens as it climbs **Abberley Hill** and passes the entrance to Ramscombe Coppice.

WILD GARLIC

When place names in England start with Rams-, it usually means that Wild Garlic, also known as Ramsons, grows there. The plant is distinctive, with its broad, glossy leaves that smell strongly of garlic. If Ramsons are growing in a wood, it can be a strong indication that it is an ancient woodland, which is the most complex terrestrial habitat in the UK.

If you are walking here in spring, you may be able to take home a tasty treat. The leaves can be added to salads or used in cooking to add some garlic flavour, and can also be used to create a very strong pesto sauce. The flowers have a similar flavour.

At the top of the slope, turn left following the waymarkers. The path now undulates along the ridgeline until it reaches a gate. Turn right in front of the gate, then left to continue along the ridge. When this path meets another, continue ahead. Now stay ahead on the ridge until a view over Abberley Clock Tower opens to the left and you pass a trig point (after almost 2km along the ridge).

> **Abberley Clock Tower** was built for Abberley Hall, and is now part of a school. It was probably built as a status symbol, to show off to other local landowners. Whatever it was built for, it is certainly impressive – and visible from miles around. The tower is almost 50m high and orginally housed a clock with 16 bells. During World War 2, it was used by the Home Guard to search the skies for enemy planes heading towards Birmingham.

The path soon starts to drop off the end of the ridge. Bear right at the fork and proceed down to the lane. Here, the route separates from the Worcestershire Way. Turn right along the lane. After 200m, turn left down some steps with a fence on your right. Through a gate, continue downhill along the edge of a hayfield, then between fields to reach a drive. Turn right to return to **Abberley Village**. Turn left, then left again to return to Abberley Common and the start.

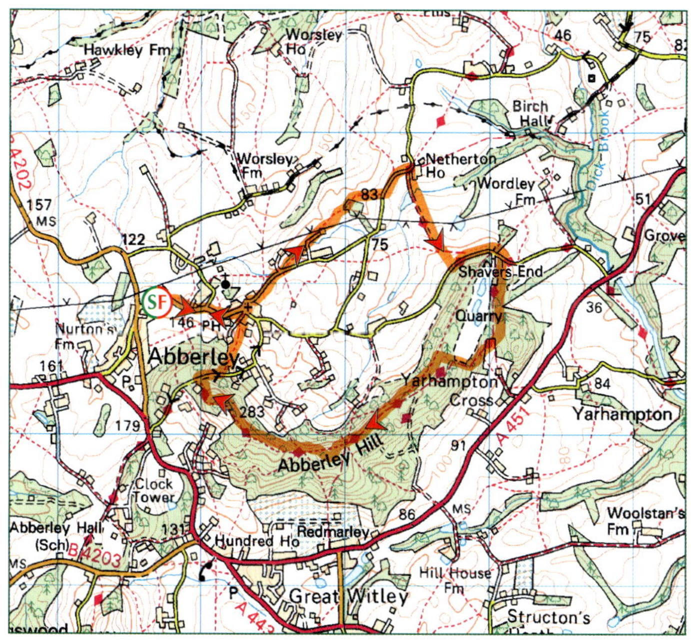

WALK 4

Martley Circular

Start/finish	St Peter's Church car park, Martley (SO 756 598)
Time	3hr
Distance	10.2km (6.3 miles)
Ascent/descent	240m (780ft)
Terrain	Field paths, tracks, woodland path, riverside paths – of variable quality; several stiles
Refreshments	Picnic benches in the Chantry Orchard near the start of the walk; the Crown café and pub in Martley, 300m from the end of the walk
Public transport	Bus from Worcester to Garage stop, Martley village centre
Parking	At start/finish

This walk provides a good sense of the western reaches of Worcestershire. It crosses fields and meadows that characterise this pastoral landscape, visits a community orchard and a larger commercial one, and climbs onto the hills that extend north from the Malverns. For a while, it follows the ridge of Rodge Hill with a view over Herefordshire to the west, and Pudford Hill within the embrace of woodland, before dropping to the winding River Teme and finally ascending gently back to Martley, where refreshments await at the popular pub and café.

Head past the left end of the church. Cross the road and continue ahead along a stone drive. At the end, continue ahead on a footpath past the Chantry Orchard. Alternatively, take the parallel path through the orchard, where there are picnic benches. The two routes join up again at the end of the orchard.

St Peter's Church has Norman origins, with most of the structure built from the 12th century onwards. Different architectural styles are exhibited, as additions and alterations were made over time, according to different fashions, to meet changes to the congregation's needs. As well as medieval stained-glass windows, the church has some wall paintings which date from before the Reformation, when it was a Catholic church. The tower has a peal of six bells, which are still rung today.

The Martley Circular is generally well signposted

When you reach the edge of an arable field, turn right, keeping the hedge on your right. After a short distance, the path passes through the hedge and skirts the edge of a **school sports field**. Fencing guides you to the gate on your left. Through this, head diagonally right across the field. If the path is not clear, head towards the mature oak tree.

Turn left along the lane and follow it to the right at the junction. On reaching a farm, turn left along a stone track, which leads to **Alden's Farm**. Continue in the same direction between barns and remain on the track to a stile on the right. Cross this and take the clear path towards a hedge and another oak tree on the left. This leads to another stile with the clear route continuing directly ahead afterwards.

At the lane, turn towards the junction and take the field gate directly ahead on the far side. Through this gate and then another, the path continues ahead with the remains of a hedge on the left. Through another gate, cross a small bridge and then turn right along the right-hand edge of the pasture.

Through another gate and across another bridge, turn left across the middle of the next field, aiming for a gated gap in the hedge. Continue ahead across the following field, then turn back on yourself to the right before you reach the gate. You are now aiming for the far left corner of the field, where the route continues through a gate and along the left edge of a field you have just crossed. This is a convoluted route because this is where the public rights of way run.

The relative position of the two gates indicates the onward direction of the route across the following field to an orchard. Once there, turn left and then right on a track through the trees. On the approach to the buildings of **Prickley Green Farm**, turn left between the apple trees and the barn. Follow the avenues of trees forward and then diagonally left through the rows of trees, following a clear waymarked route.

APPLE ORCHARDS

Worcestershire is known for its orchards. Apples are grown for eating, juicing and cider, and around 30 varieties originated in this county. Apples are often grafted because, if grown from a pip, the tree could be a cross with any of the surrounding trees. However, that lucky happenstance has resulted in several commercially grown varieties. For example, Granny Smiths first grew from a compost heap.

Apple trees are great for wildlife, especially in old orchards. Insects live in the bark, Bullfinches eat the buds, Thrushes love the fallen fruit, and Blackbirds will nest in them when they get bushy. This, of course, generates food for bats and a habitat for mosses and lichens to grow in. In spring, when the trees are in flower, the orchards are particularly charming.

Apples ripening in the orchard

After crossing the orchard, the route continues along the left side of a field. At the end of the hedge, continue ahead and then bear right between fields. At the next boundary, turn left to follow the hedge line on your right. This leads to a fast road.

Turn right along the road for a short distance, then left along the first driveway. At a junction, continue straight up the hill on the track ahead. At the next junction (by **Rodge Hill Farm**), continue uphill along the track. On reaching the ridge, now at the edge of a wood, turn left, still uphill. From here, the view begins to open up, making the climb worthwhile.

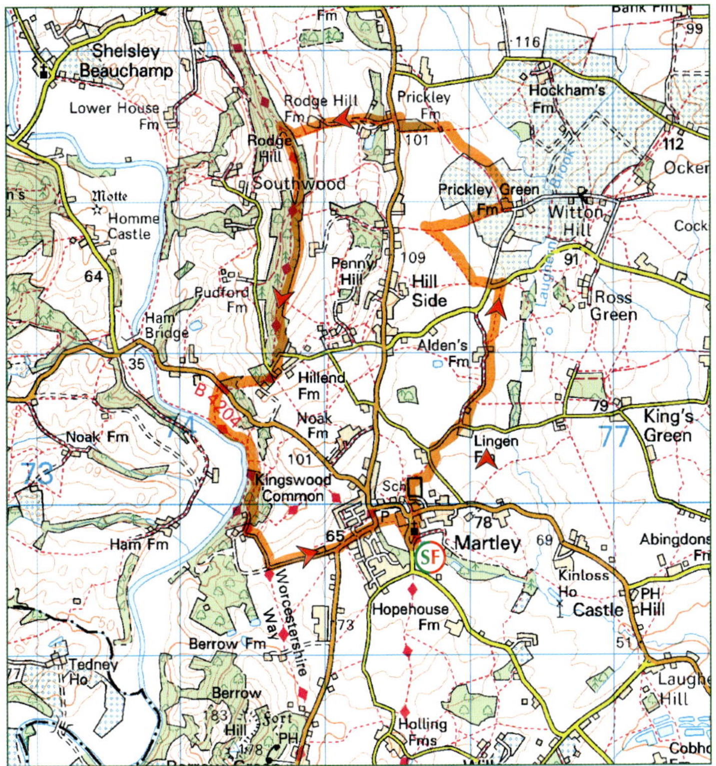

At a junction of paths, turn right, then left to continue in the same direction, following the waymarkers. This path continues along the ridge of first Rodge Hill, then Pudford Hill, through woods for some time. After dropping for a while, ignore the path to the left leading to the lane, and continue ahead along the ridge to join the lane a little further down.

Cross diagonally right and take the metal hand gate leading onto a footpath that continues to drop through the woods. Through the next gate, head diagonally right downhill. Pass a defunct stile and continue in the same direction to a road.

Turn right, then, after 20m, turn left down the side of one field and across the middle of the next to the **River Teme**. Turn left and follow the riverside path until you reach an open area with a bench overlooking the river. Bear left uphill past

The view to Berrow Hill on the final stretch of the walk

a mature Ash tree to a small bridge. Cross and continue ahead, taking the lower path at the fork. At a pair of gates, turn left uphill. This leads to a lane. Turn left uphill again.

Past the houses, take the public footpath on the right, waymarked for the Worcestershire Way. This runs parallel to the lane along the left edge of a field and has a terrific view south to Berrow Hill.

On reaching a junction, turn left along the lane. At the T-junction, turn left into **Martley**. Where the road bends to the left towards the Crown, continue ahead through a gate and over two stiles. Follow the clear route around the left edge of two fields, through a kissing gate to a lane. Turn right, and you will soon see the car park and St Peter's Church on your left.

WALK 5

Knapp and Papermill Nature Reserve

Start/finish	Entrance to Knapp and Papermill Nature Reserve (SO 751 521)
Time	3hr 15min
Distance	10.8km (6.7 miles)
Ascent/descent	230m (750ft)
Terrain	Mainly mown paths, stone paths and tarmac; one section (avoidable) across a hayfield; two stiles, not dog-friendly
Refreshments	Picnic area at start; community café at Alfrick (at 7.8km)
Toilets	Just inside the nature reserve, up the slope and to the right
Access	Accessible for all-terrain buggies as far as the mill cottage (1.5km). The mown path continues around the nature reserve where the route turns onto a narrower path.
Parking	A handful of parking spaces opposite the entrance to the reserve; one parking space for disabled people at the entrance
Warning	This route can flood and can get muddy in places. Keep dogs on short leads through the nature reserve.

The Knapp and Papermill Nature Reserve offers a diverse range of habitats for wildlife, including the stream, ponds, meadows and woodland, and the dominant sound for this part of the walk is birdsong. Shortly after leaving the Knapp and Papermill Reserve, the walk continues through two other nature reserves: Blackhouse and Ravenshill Woods here, the wildlife is perhaps a bit more shy, but sightings might include deer and flocks of tits.

The return leg is mainly on quiet lanes, along which it is quite likely you will see no vehicles. Passing through Alfrick, there is an opportunity to take a short detour to the community shop and café, and then the final stretch follows the course of an ancient sunken lane, shaded by trees.

Take a hand gate into the reserve. The stone path rises to a junction. Turn right for the toilets or left to continue into the reserve. As you pass the house, you can pick up more information about the reserve and make a donation towards its upkeep in the porch. Through another gate, the path drops back into the valley.

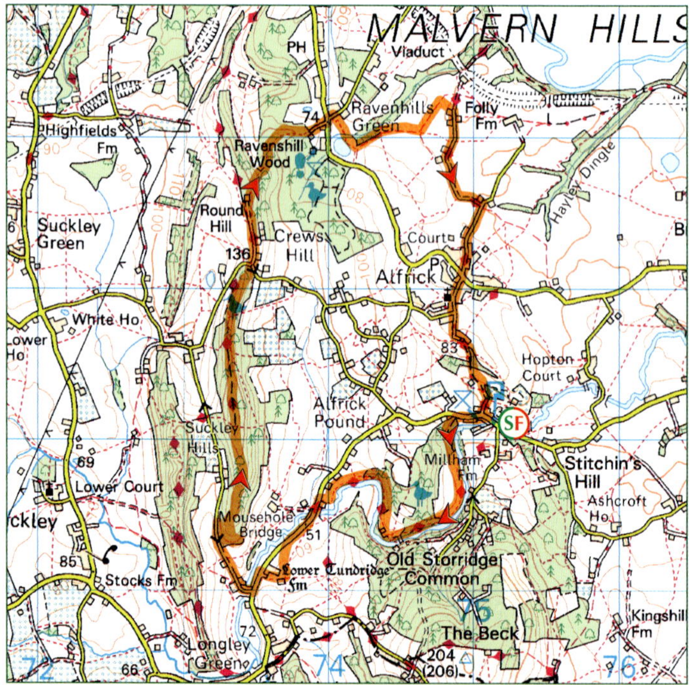

Continue ahead along the bottom of the valley, past an orchard, ponds and meadows, through woodland and along the stream.

> As you walk through the **orchard**, keep an eye out for Nuthatches, the only birds in Britain that climb down trees head first. You might also see Green Woodpeckers feeding on the ground. If they are close to the path and you disturb them, they are likely to make a looping flight into a tree and completely disappear, as their camouflage is very effective. In late summer and autumn, look on the ground to see birds and butterflies feeding on fallen fruit.

After passing Papermill Cottage, take the gate ahead where the mown path bends to the right. Papermill Cottage was once an industrial building. Now, it is closed to humans and home to a colony of bats that uses it as a summer maternity roost. The path leads to a delightful woodland path along a **stream**, Leigh Brook.

The ancient pollarded beech

Leigh Brook is home to lots of shy wildlife that you are unlikely to spot. Otters find shelter in the trees that line the water and in artificial holts built by volunteers in the nature reserve. Small fish and the metallic River Shingle Beetle live among the stones on the stream bed, and River Limpets cling to them. Please stay away from the water, to avoid disturbing them.

A farm gate marks your exit from the reserve. Continue ahead with the stream on your left. After crossing a stile, turn right to follow the path for a short, steep uphill section, then turn left after an ancient pollarded beech tree to skirt the edge of a paddock. This leads to a kissing gate.

Through the gate, turn left along the lane. Cross a bridge, then take the stile immediately past the drive for Tundridge Stables. From here, the route is not clear as it crosses the hayfield. To avoid walking across the hayfield and filling your shoes with seeds, continue along the lane. Aim slightly to the left of the house with picture windows, where a wide gate leads to a drive. Cross, and pass through another gate, then turn right in the next hayfield to follow the line of the drive back to the lane.

Turn left, then take the first lane on the right, which passes through the converted buildings of Upper Tundridge Farm. Continue along this lane to where a track joins from the right. Turn sharply right onto this; you are now in Worcestershire Wildlife Trust's Blackhouse Wood on the **Suckley Hills**. Almost immediately, the track narrows to a path. At a junction, turn left onto a path that rises along the ridge of the hill. On reaching a fork, stay high. After a bench on the right, continue ahead at the crosspaths. At the next junction, you can see a gate ahead, which will take you to a lane.

Cross and continue along the drive ahead, taking a moment to look right for a view to the end of the Malvern Hills. Immediately after a house called 'The Crest', fork left along a path between hedges. After 250m, look for a waymarker on the left and turn right through the hedge on a footpath under trees. This soon reaches a drive. Turn left, then right before the gates, through the woods. Stay on the path around the top of a meadow that is now planted with Ash trees, then ahead through **Ravenshill Wood**, until you reach a road.

COPPICING

Ravenshill Wood has been coppiced in the past. This process involves cutting down trees to ground level to encourage them to regrow with multiple straight stems. This sounds as though it would hurt the tree, but there is a Small-leaved Lime tree near Westonbirt Arboretum that is thought to be over 2000 years old, and its longevity is considered to be due to coppicing. One theory is that our broadleaved native trees adapted to be able to withstand damage from megafauna, such as Woolly Mammoths and Aurochs, that once roamed this land. Those that regrew from the ground are the ones that survived.

Cross onto the lane ahead, then turn right by the speed limit sign before the first drive. A mown path leads directly across the meadow to another gate. Through the gate, continue ahead around the end of the garden with the bank rising to your right. Just before a eucalyptus tree, turn left through a gate and over a small wooden bridge to follow the bridleway into the woods. On the far side of the woods, the path continues along a wide field margin with trees on the left. Where the boundary on the left turns, continue diagonally right on a clear path across an arable field.

At the far edge, a gate leads to a path along the right-hand edge of a hayfield. Where the hedge ends on the right, pass through a gate and along the right-hand edge of this field. Turn right onto the lane at the end and continue to the lane end. Turn right along the next lane into the centre of **Alfrick**. Turn right here for the community shop and café.

Cross the road through the village and continue ahead along the lane opposite. Pass the **church**, and where the lane bends to the right, continue ahead along a drive. As it passes Patches Farm, it becomes a stone track. At the end of the farm buildings, fork right down an old sunken lane. Stay ahead, and at the end, you will be able to see the entrance to the **Knapp and Papermill Nature Reserve** to the left.

A well-defined path across an arable field

WALK 6

Malvern Hills end to end

Start	South to north: small car park near Chase End Hill (SO 757 349); north to south: North Quarry car park (SO 771 469)
Finish	South to north: North Quarry car park (SO 771 469); north to south: small car park near Chase End Hill (SO 757 349)
Time	6hr 30min
Distance	15.7km (9.7 miles)
Ascent	South to north 980m (3220ft); north to south 890m (2930ft)
Descent	South to north 904m (2970ft); north to south 970m (3180ft)
Terrain	Often steep and exposed; mainly stone paths, some with loose stone
Refreshments	Hotel and kiosk at Wynds Point; café and hotel at Upper Wyche
Toilets	At Wynds Point and Upper Wyche
Public transport	Only to Great Malvern and Upper Wyche

The Malvern Hills rise from the Severn Plain like the back of a stegosaurus, and this is the iconic walk along them. On a clear day, the view extends to the Welsh mountains to the west, the Bristol Channel to the south, the Cotswolds to the east and Long Mynd to the north. Alternatively, the summits can be in cloud – or peeking out above the murk. Although the hills are not particularly high, they are exposed and steep, and this is a challenging walk with significant ascent and descent. This route climbs the peak of each hill; for a slightly less challenging walk, most of the northern hills have alternative routes to one side of the peaks.

The walk can be completed in either direction, each of which is described. However, if you cannot park a car at each end, it is advisable to start at the southern end and walk north towards Malvern, so you can grab a taxi back to your car. If you try it the other way, book your return transport while you have a phone signal, or you might find yourself stranded.

Malvern Hills end to end – south to north

There is no gentle lead-in to this walk; a wide stony track ascends straight from the car park, first through woodland then across grassland to the trig point on **Chase End Hill**. From here, there are views north-west to Eastnor Castle and Obelisk, and east to the Cotswold escarpment and Bredon Hill.

From the trig point, head downhill in the direction of the obelisk. This section of the path is steep and can be slippery underfoot, but it soon turns into a delightful route under the trees. Through the gate, continue downhill to the hamlet of **Whiteleaved Oak**.

THE WHITE-LEAVED OAK

The oak tree with mottled leaves, after which the hamlet of Whiteleaved Oak is named, was thought to be around 500 years old when it was destroyed by fire in July 2020. As this leaf colouration is so unusual in oak trees, they tend to be revered and have special spiritual significance attached to them, and this one was no exception. Some claim it was on a ley line, or where several cross. People from around the world visited the tree and left offerings, and one theory is that a lantern left by a devotee is what started the fire. What we do know is that there is no longer a white-leaved oak tree here to visit.

Pass Cider Mill Cottage on your right, then turn right onto the road. Pass the village noticeboard and stocks, following the road round to the right. After another few metres, bear left up the drive to Elsie's Cottage. Follow the track around to the left, then almost immediately bear left past a stone waymarker that says 'Ragged Stone'. Follow the narrow footpath as it climbs along a ridge. At a fork, bear right to stay on the main footpath.

When the footpath emerges from the trees, bear left onto the rocky ground, towards the obelisk, to reach the summit of Ragged Stone Hill. From here is the first view along the length of the Malvern Hills.

Construction of **Eastnor Castle**, in the valley to the left of the obelisk, began in 1812. It was designed to impress and to reflect the standing of the family, rather than act as a fortification. The Napoleonic Wars (1803–1815) were raging when the castle was being built, and the Earl's son died in the conflict. The obelisk was erected as a monument to celebrate his life. Although it appears to be solid, it is actually hollow. Even so, it must have taken some effort to transport the materials up onto the ridge.

Bluebells thrive on the western slopes of the Malvern Hills

Fork right just off the summit, heading directly towards Midsummer Hill, to the right of the obelisk. Follow this path as it drops steeply and ends at the **A438**. Turn right here and follow the road for 130m to a car park on the left. From the car park, head straight up the grassy slope. The path becomes stony, then continues to climb through the trees and eventually onto the summit of **Midsummer Hill**.

As you near the top, Eastnor Obelisk comes into view again on the left, now much closer. The distinctive ridged outline ahead is that of British Camp hill fort (Millennium Hill and Herefordshire Beacon). Continue in the same direction until you have passed through the north gate of Midsummer Hill's fort, which is now a gap in the mound around the hill. Follow the path down to the left until you reach a track.

Turn right, then 400m later, immediately before the cattle grid, turn right onto a gently rising track. After some distance, the track reaches another cattle grid. Turn right here on the footpath through the woods. This path exits the woodland and rises to the top of **Swinyard Hill**. Midsummer Hill and Eastnor Obelisk are now behind you. From the summit, continue north for a gentle descent, with British Camp now looming ahead.

At a junction of paths, turn left uphill. After about 50m, take a smaller path on the right, more steeply uphill. This path bends to the left to reach the long flat summit ridge of **Hangman's Hill**, with the Shire Ditch on the right. It then rises again before bearing left. British Camp hill fort is now dominating the view ahead and to the left.

At the round stone waymarker, continue straight up the steps and zigzags onto **Millennium Hill** and along the well-worn path to the top. Continue over onto **Herefordshire Beacon**, the other part of the hill fort. From here, you can see the rest of the hills marching north. Table Hill is the furthest you can see – End Hill is hidden behind it.

From the summit, head down the rough concrete path to and down a flight of steps. At the bottom of the steps, turn left at the junction of paths. Fork right downhill to take you to the British Camp car park at **Wynds Point**. Here, there are public toilets, a kiosk serving light refreshments and a hotel serving drinks and meals.

From Worcestershire Beacon, the view extends south beyond the end of the hills

Cross the road, walk down the side of the **Malvern Hills Hotel** and take the path straight up the hill immediately after the hotel car park. Pass some benches, then turn left at a junction of paths over a hill without a name. From here, continue along the line of hills, crossing each summit, for approximately 3km. There is an alternative route around the west side of most of these hills if you prefer a slightly less strenuous walk.

You know when you are nearing the end of this section, because you will see some houses directly ahead of you, and Malvern is now visible down to the right. The path descends to the left of the ridge and ultimately down some steps to the bus shelter at **Upper Wyche**.

> **Refreshments** are available at Café H_2O in the Innovation Centre, slightly downhill to the left, and the Wyche Inn, through the cutting on the right. On busy days, there is often an ice cream van here, too. The public toilets are behind the bus shelter.

Cross the road, then head uphill on Beacon Road. The residential street soon becomes a drive to a car park. Continue through the car park and up onto the hills, first summiting **Summer Hill** and then **Worcestershire Beacon**, the highest

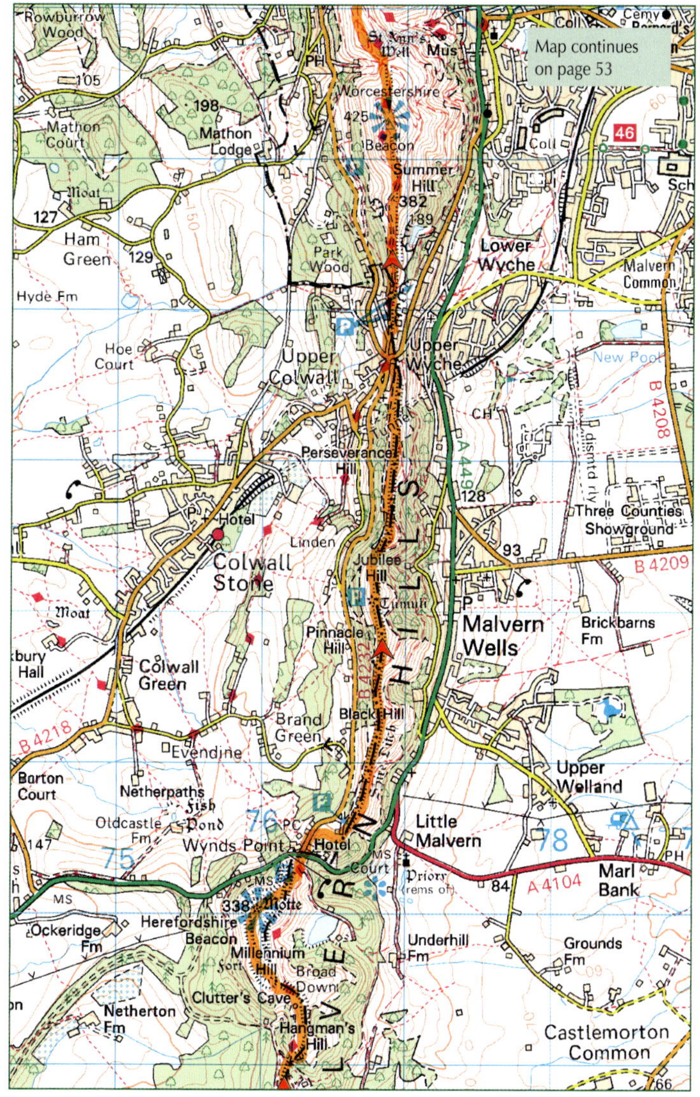
Map continues on page 53
Rowburrow Wood
105
198
Mathon Court
Mathon Lodge
Moat
127
Ham Green
129
Hyde Fm
Hoe Court
PH
Worcestershire
425
Beacon
Summer Hill
382
189
Park Wood
Mus
Coll
46
Sch
Lower Wyche
Malvern Common
Upper Colwall
Upper Wyche
New Pool
B 4208
CH
dismtd rly
A 449
128
Perseverance Hill
Hotel
Linden
Colwall Stone
Jubilee Hill
Tumuli
Three Counties Showground
93
B 4209
Moat
Hall
Colwall Green
Pinnacle Hill
B 4232
MALVERN HILLS
Malvern Wells
Brickbarns Fm
Black Hill
Brand Green
B 4218
Evendine
Barton Court
Netherpaths
Fish Pond
Oldcastle Fm
147
75
76
PC
Wynds Point
Hotel
Upper Welland
Little Malvern
78
Court
MS
Priory (rems of)
PH
Marl Bank
A 4104
84
338
Motte
Herefordshire Beacon
Ockeridge Fm
Millennium Hill
Fort
Broad Down
Underhill Fm
Grounds Fm
Clutter's Cave
Netherton Fm
Hangman's Hill
Castlemorton Common
66

For those not wanting to summit every hill, there is a lower option for most of them

point of the Malvern Hills. Check out the toposcope if you'd like to know what's in the 360-degree view.

Head north from the summit. You can almost see your destination now. Take the path down to a round stone waymarker in the dip between hills. From the waymarker, head diagonally left to the top of Sugarloaf Hill. Continue in the same direction down the hill to a junction of paths, then ahead up a track that bends to the right to the dip between Table Hill and **North Hill**. From here you can, of course, ascend both hills if you wish to complete all the summits.

End Hill is directly in front of you to the north. As you drop down, you will see it ahead and to your left. Fork left and descend to the gravel track. Cross the track and continue ahead to the summit.

Continue in the same direction, downhill for a while, then over another small bump and down the far side. At the end of the path, turn right, still heading downhill. The route descends into some woods and eventually reaches the road. Turn right and follow the road until you reach a clock tower and **North Quarry car park**, which marks the end of the walk.

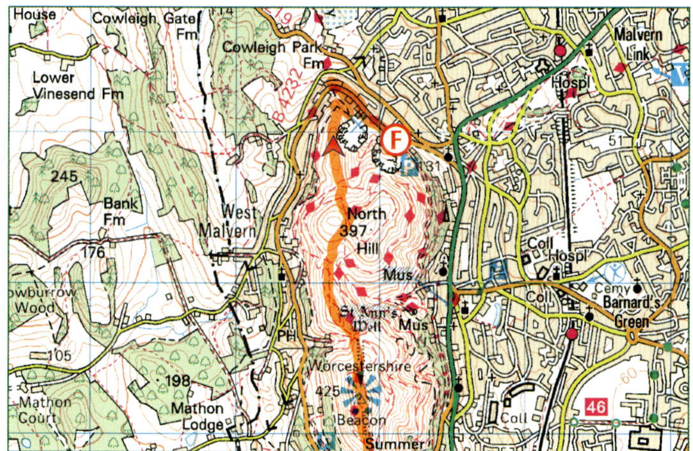

Malvern Hills end to end – north to south

From North Quarry car park, turn left along West Malvern Road. Opposite the railing on the left bend, take the footpath up into some woods. About 50m after exiting the woodland, turn left, steeply uphill, and continue in the same direction until you reach the top of End Hill.

Head south from the summit and aim for the dip between the two hills ahead. When you reach a track, take the narrow path ahead, rising between **North Hill** and Table Hill. If you wish to summit all the Malvern Hills, turn left here to the top of North Hill, and right to the top of Table Hill.

Then continue down the path, diagonally right. Cross the next junction of paths, and ascend Sugarloaf Hill. From the summit, continue in the same direction down to a round stone waymarker. From here, head straight uphill, until you reach the summit of **Worcestershire Beacon**, where a toposcope indicates what is in the view.

Descend to the south. At the col between hills, ascend **Summer Hill** ahead. To miss out this summit, take the tarmac track instead. From Summer Hill, take the steps down to the track, and continue ahead downhill until you pass through a car park to a road junction at **Upper Wyche**.

Refreshments are available at Café H_2O in the Innovation Centre, slightly downhill to the right, and the Wyche Inn, through the cutting on the left. On busy days, there is often an ice cream van here, too. The public toilets are behind the bus shelter.

From British Camp (Herefordshire Beacon), a view extends along the northern section of the Malvern Hills

Cross the road. Head up the steps to the left of the bus shelter and onto the ridge. Follow the line of hills over each summit for approximately 3km to **Black Hill**. There is an alternative route around the west side of most of the hills if you wish to have a slightly less strenuous walk.

BRITISH CAMP HILL FORT

As you near the end of the 3km section to Black Hill, the view of British Camp hill fort is fantastic. Imagine being one of the people cutting these ditches by hand! The ramparts were created by digging into the slope and piling up the debris on the outside edge, forming a steep ridge. This was initially done in two phases of construction in the Iron Age. Over a thousand years later, in medieval times, significant additional work was done on the ditches, forming the ringwork we see today. It is likely that the building that used to stand within the ringworks was a hunting lodge. British Camp extends across two hills: Herefordshire Beacon and Millennium Hill.

On descending Black Hill, keep left for one more ascent, over a hill with no name. At a junction of paths, turn right in front of a row of benches, and follow this path down to the Malvern Hills Hotel at **Wynds Point**. Turn left along the side of the hotel. Here, there are public toilets and a kiosk serving light refreshments, as well as the hotel.

Cross the road, then the car park opposite the hotel and take the gate halfway down. This path will lead you onto the hill. At a fork in the path, turn right uphill, then up a flight of steps. At the top of the steps, turn left onto a rough concrete path which leads to the summit of **Herefordshire Beacon**, also known as British Camp.

Take the stone sett path off the summit, heading south, down then up onto **Millennium Hill**. Follow the well-worn path down from the summit on the right-hand side of the hill, to some steps and a path that zigzags down the slope. At the round stone waymarker, continue ahead onto a path that shortly bears right along **Hangman's Hill**. Walk along the flat ridge and continue heading south to find the path off the hill. Where this path joins another, turn left downhill.

At a crossroads of paths after about 50m, turn right uphill and follow this route to the top of **Swinyard Hill**. From the summit, continue south towards Midsummer Hill. As the path starts to drop, look for a well-hidden round stone waymarker and turn right there, down through the woods. When this path reaches a stone track, turn left onto the track, which is gently descending.

At a junction of tracks, continue ahead uphill. Pass the gate for Midsummer Cottage on the left. After another 30m, where the track bends slightly to the right, take the path on the left heading gently uphill. Follow the path uphill, round to the right through the Iron Age defences, and continue to the summit of **Midsummer Hill**.

Midsummer Hill is also an Iron Age hill fort. It is highly unusual because it encloses two hills with a ravine between the two, housing a spring. There were 483 buildings here, which suggests a significant population.

Once you've reached the top, pass the shelter and information board on your left and head towards Ragged Stone Hill, which comes into view to the south. Turn right onto the **A438**, for about 130m, then turn left through a gate into the Eastnor Castle estate. From the gate, fork left to head up the wide track that turns into a wide grassy path rising steeply up Ragged Stone Hill.

From the summit, continue heading almost directly south onto a path that soon enters woodland. At the bottom of this path, turn right onto the track which passes a couple of houses and then reaches a road. Turn right and follow the road to the left at the village noticeboard and stocks. A few metres later, turn left down what looks like a private drive, past Cider Mill Cottage onto a footpath under trees. Through the gate, bear slightly left and continue uphill.

Continue straight ahead up a steep section of path to reach the trig point at the top of **Chase End Hill**. From here, take the wide path that gently drops down the ridge and then into the trees and finally to the car park at the end of the walk.

WALK 7

Great Malvern and Worcestershire Beacon

Start/finish	Great Malvern railway station (SO 783 457)
Time	3hr
Distance	8.1km (5 miles)
Ascent/descent	365m (1200ft)
Terrain	Steep ascent and descent, mainly on stone paths, tarmac and grass.
Refreshments	Café H_2O near the Wyche Cutting at 4.6km; the Morgan pub close to the end of the walk; many options in the town centre
Toilets	At the Wyche Cutting at 4.6km
Public transport	Train to Great Malvern; two buses an hour from Worcester to Great Malvern railway station stop
Parking	At start/finish

The Malvern Hills are popular with walkers for good reason, offering fabulous views after a relatively short walk on well-maintained footpaths. This walk starts at Great Malvern railway station and rises through the town past Malvern Priory onto the hills. The ascent is steep but glorious. Almost as soon as you leave the town, the soundscape changes into one dominated by birdsong and the rustle of leaves in the breeze. At the top of the first ascent, the views open up across the Severn Plain to the east. For a while, the route follows the contour, offering welcome relief for legs and lungs, before rising steeply again to the summit of Worcestershire Beacon. Here, though, there is a gentler alternative for the final push. The Malvern Hills rise above the surrounding landscape for a considerable distance, making the views from the top impressive in every direction.

The route then descends to the Wyche Cutting, where, on a good day, an ice cream van awaits. Through the cutting, it continues steeply down and traverses one of Malvern's commons on the way back to the station.

From the station, turn right along the length of Imperial Gardens to Avenue Road. Turn left and left again at the end to continue uphill on Church Street until you pass Malvern Priory.

Just before the top of this road, if you wish to fill your water bottle at the only one of Malvern's springs that is filtered, take a slight detour up the steps and left. This is **Malvhina**, created in 1998 by Rose Garrard, and fed from springs in Happy Valley, Rushey Valley and Ivy Scar Rock.

The sculpture represents the three sources of water that feed it, the three roads that join at Bellevue Island and the three most significant periods of Malvern's development: the arrival of the ancient Celts; the arrival of Christianity and the priory; and the significant growth of the town during the Victorian period due to the Water Cure. This is one of many springs that locals fill water containers from; however, it is the only one that is filtered.

At the top of Church Street, turn right, then left up the far side of the Unicorn. Where the road bends to the left, continue straight ahead, still uphill. You will soon pass a restored donkey shed on the right.

This is one of several **donkey sheds** that used to stand in Happy Valley. When Malvern was a Victorian spa town, visitors would head onto the hills to rise above the polluted air. As it was the air rather than the exercise that was considered healthy, donkeys were available for hire to carry people up the slopes, and the sheds provided shelter for the donkeys and the women who owned them.

Donkeys were available for hire until the middle of the 20th century, but these days we must rely on our legs and lungs to ascend the hills.

The route up Green Valley, one of the most peaceful places in the Malvern Hills

Lady Howard de Walden Drive leading towards Worcestershire Beacon

Where the tarmac path swings sharply left, continue ahead up the same valley (this section of which is known as Green Valley), now on a rough stone track. Over the brow of a rise, the path forks. Bear left along the stony path. This will take you to a junction above the trees. Turn left onto a track running along the contour, known as Lady Howard de Walden Drive. The first significant view over the Severn Plain, Bredon Hill and the Cotswolds soon appears on the left, and Worcestershire Beacon is visible in the distance ahead.

Continue in the same direction until you reach a round stone waymarker. If you prefer a gentle ascent from here, head diagonally left onto a track that sweeps up to the top in long, sinuous curves. Otherwise, choose any of the paths leading uphill, and continue in an upward direction until you reach the trig point and toposcope on the summit of **Worcestershire Beacon**.

To leave the summit, walk away from the toposcope past the trig point and continue in the same direction. After an initial downhill section, this path soon

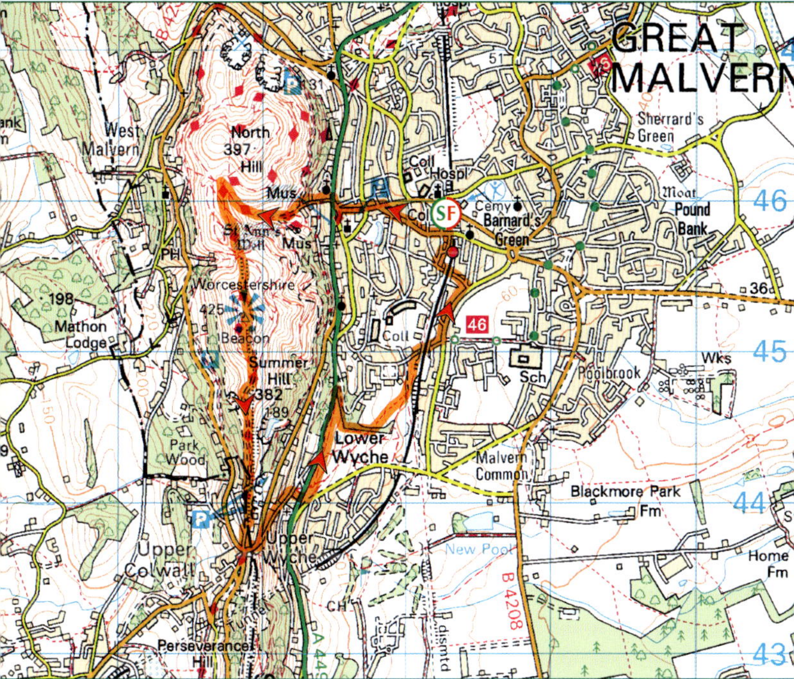

joins a track. Follow this for 1.6km, all the way down to a road junction at **Upper Wyche**. Turn left through the Wyche Cutting.

Head diagonally left down Old Wyche Road. After passing house number 40 on the left, take the steps downhill to the right, past a school, to the A449 at **Lower Wyche**. Cross and continue downhill to arrive at another road and a small parking area. Turn left onto a broad grassy track that runs above Malvern Common (known to locals as Peachfield Common).

Ultimately, this track reaches a stone wall on the right. Turn sharply right along another track with the wall now on your left. After a while, the path turns to the left, and the wall is replaced by railings. Turn left through a gap in the railings, past a large Sweet Chestnut tree (identifiable by the barber's pole pattern in the bark).

The path down towards the Wyche Cutting, with views across Herefordshire

This land is owned by **Malvern College**, one of several private schools in the town that attract pupils from across the region and world. Its establishment and success during the period of Victorian prosperity, along with good transport links, encouraged other schools to establish in the area. Some of the college's buildings are impressive and host events such as concerts for the wider community.

Head straight down the wide mown strip to a kissing gate by another Sweet Chestnut tree. Through the gate, head diagonally left across the meadow. This path leads to Thirlstane Road. Turn right along the road under the **railway bridge**, then left at the end. After 230m, turn left along Clarence Road. Take the first right after passing under the **railway bridge**, then turn right into Imperial Road to return to the **railway station**.

WALK 8

Little Malvern and St Wulstan's Nature Reserve

Start/finish	British Camp car park at Wynds Point (SO 763 404)
Alt start/finish	St Wulstan's Nature Reserve car park (SO 780 414)
Time	3hr
Distance	9.5km (5.9 miles)
Ascent/descent	285m (930ft)
Terrain	A combination of tarmac and concrete lanes, and stone, grass, woodland and field paths that are generally well made and easy to follow. One steep descent and ascent with gentle gradients in between. A handful of stiles.
Refreshments	The Malvern Hills Hotel and a kiosk at Wynds Point (start/finish); picnic tables at St Wulstan's (at 3.8km)
Toilets	At start/finish

This walk with fine views starts high on the Malvern Hills and drops steeply to visit Little Malvern Priory and then St Wulstan's Nature Reserve. The priory is a beautiful church that is usually open, and it contains a historically significant stained-glass window and medieval tiles. It also has links to the poet William Langland. The nature reserve was historically a hospital with gardens, so the range of trees and plants includes more exotics than you would expect, including an impressive Blue Atlas Cedar (easily identifiable from its colour). Climbing back onto the hills, a short detour will take you to the graves of Sir Edward Elgar and his family.

The alternative start/finish allows for the uphill section earlier in the walk, with everything downhill after refreshments at Wynds Point.

Exit the car park downhill, away from the road, to a **reservoir**. As you reach the reservoir, look behind you to your right for a view of the ringworks of British Camp hill fort. Continue downhill past the reservoir. Keep to this wide path as it drops below the tree line and passes underneath some power lines to a stone track. Turn left.

Follow the track as it leads back under the power lines to a gate. On the other side, continue on the track, now with a fabulous view across the Severn Plain, with Bredon Hill visible on the right and Old Hills directly ahead.

The track eventually passes **Underhill Farm**, with its black-and-white farmhouse, and becomes a concrete drive. Follow this for 700m to the **A4104**, passing

Looking back towards Little Malvern Priory and British Camp hill fort

the garden of Little Malvern Court, which features a topiary hedge with geometric shapes and peacocks guarding each of the gates.

> **Little Malvern Court** was the prior's hall and has remained in the same family since the Dissolution of the Monasteries in the 16th century. Its gardens are open for visitors several times a month from April to July. Check the website for details: littlemalverncourt.co.uk.

LITTLE MALVERN PRIORY

If you are interested in churches, it is worth visiting Little Malvern Priory. The stained-glass window behind the altar is considered significant because it is only one of three that remain in England depicting Edward V. The window shows Edward IV with his wife Elizabeth Woodville, along with their son, who would later become the king.

The priory also houses some medieval floor tiles, still in situ. These were created by stamping sun-dried clay with a carved woodblock. The prominent parts of the block created indentations in the clay, which were filled with slip – liquid clay. A lead glaze was added before firing, which turned the slip into a honey colour and brought out the red in the more solid clay. The result was tiles so durable that they have survived hundreds of years. The clay probably came from Hanley Castle, and the tiles were probably manufactured at Great Malvern Priory.

The larger church has a bigger collection of tiles, although there, they have been placed on the walls to protect them. Others from Little Malvern Priory have been placed in the British Museum for additional protection.

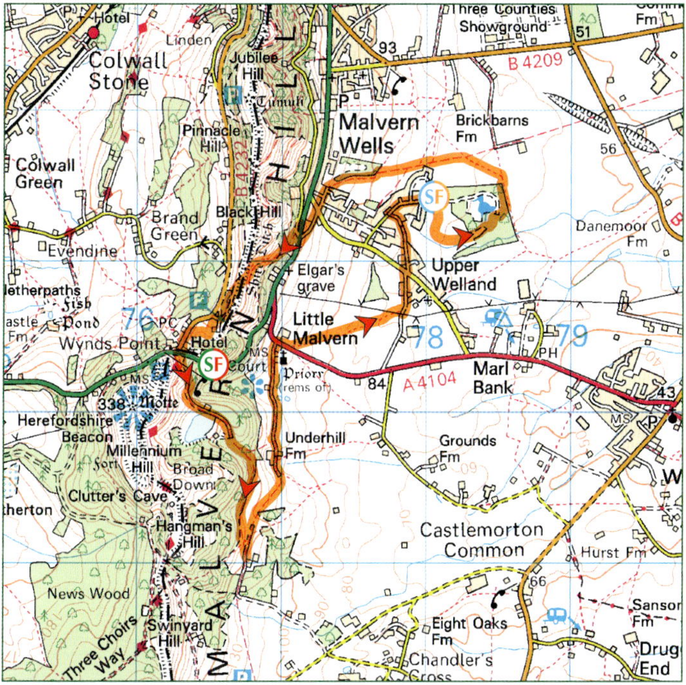

Topiary lines the garden of Little Malvern Court

Turn right down the road past the car park for **Little Malvern Priory**. After another 20 paces, turn left through a gate and then diagonally right on a clearly defined path across an arable field. Through the next gate, the route continues along a wide, strimmed path across scrubland. Turn right on the track at the end, then after a short distance, sharp left along a track that leads past houses to a road in **Upper Welland**.

Cross and take Chase Road ahead. At the end of the road, take the narrow footpath to the right of The Paddock's drive. At the next junction, turn right along St Wulstans Drive to the car park for **St Wulstan's Nature Reserve**. This is an alternative start/finish point for this walk.

On arrival at the car park, turn right through the gate to cross the meadow. After crossing a small bridge, continue ahead to circumnavigate the next meadow. When the path reaches the edge of the meadow, stay ahead through a wide gate onto a stone path. Follow this through another gate and to the left.

ST WULSTAN'S HOSPITAL

St Wulstan's Nature Reserve was part of Brickbarns Farm until World War 2. The land was requisitioned in 1943 to build a hospital to treat American servicemen in preparation for the D-Day landings. It was first used for shell shock and battle fatigue (now known as Post Traumatic Stress Disorder), then as a general hospital. After the war, it was a displaced person's camp before being used as a tuberculosis hospital, and then a psychiatric hospital.

During this whole period, there were several hundred people living on the site, so it had all the facilities of a small town. It's hard to imagine now, as the hospital was demolished in the early 1990s and the site was transformed into a Local Nature Reserve. Some of the ornamental trees and plants that grew in the gardens have been kept in recognition of the site's historical use.

After a while, the path runs close to the edge of the reserve, with a field on the right. When it reaches the corner of the reserve, turn right to cross a bridge, and then left along the edge of the field. This leads to a junction of paths in the corner of the field. Turn left over a stile, then diagonally right. This part of the route is unclear on the ground: aim towards the utility pole on the left and then the field gate to the right of it when it comes into view. Through the gate, turn left to continue along the left-hand edge of fields. You are now walking towards the Malvern Hills.

Stay ahead over a couple of junctions, keeping the ditch and hedgerow on your left. At the end of the field, a hand gate leads into woods. Now the path has a fence on the left and trees on the right, and starts to rise up onto the Malvern Hills. On reaching a drive, continue ahead along a residential street. At the T-junction and the crossroads, stay ahead on Kings Road, which ultimately rises to the **A449**.

To visit **Elgar's grave**, take a short detour left along the pavement to St Wulstan's Catholic Church. Take the drive down the side of the church, then turn right behind it. The grave is beyond the church on the right. After visiting, retrace your steps to rejoin the route.

If not visiting Elgar's grave, turn right along the pavement beside the A449 and then immediately left along Holywell Road. After 80m, turn sharply left onto a path that heads uphill through woods. At a crosspaths, continue ahead uphill towards Black Hill. At the next crosspaths, close to the summit, continue ahead, and at the junction a few paces later, turn left to gently descend to **Black Hill car park**. Turn right along the car park drive, then left along a path above the road, which will return you to British Camp car park at **Wynds Point** where you started the walk.

If you can face another climb, take the path from the car park up to **British Camp**. This is a spectacular Iron Age hill fort with equally spectacular views along the length of the Malvern Hills and over the surrounding region.

A Blue Atlas Cedar in St Wulstan's Nature Reserve

WALK 9

The southern hills

Start/finish	Hollybush car park (SO 759 369)
Time	2hr 45min
Distance	7.8km (4.8 miles) (northern loop 2.1km, southern loop 5.7km)
Ascent/descent	380m (1250ft)
Terrain	Two significant ascents and descents, one on each loop of the walk, with gently undulating paths elsewhere; mainly on well-maintained, easy-to-follow paths

This walk has a distinct character compared to others on the Malvern Hills. The southern hills are quieter, although still popular with those who prefer a more intimate landscape. With a good mixture of woodland and open vistas, the first part of the route takes you through trees to the summit of Midsummer Hill, from where there are terrific views over Herefordshire and Wales, and sunsets can be enjoyed in their full glory. The route passes through the Iron Age ramparts as it drops back down the hill and returns to the car park.

The southern loop is longer and takes in the two most southerly hills in the range, although it only ascends one. A woodland path circles the western edge of Ragged Stone Hill before dropping to the tiny hamlet of Whiteleaved Oak. From there, it skirts Chase End Hill before ascending a wide, grassy slope to the summit. There is an alternative route to the summit, but it is steep and covered with loose stones; ascending on that route is a bit of a scramble. The route drops back down before undulating along the east side of both hills on the return to Hollybush.

From the car park, head through a gate up the steep grassy slope towards and then through a woodland. The path becomes gravelly before the tree line – if you are still on a grassy path when you reach the trees, move further left. The path eventually flattens off and opens up. Continue uphill to the summit of **Midsummer Hill**. Look left for a view of Eastnor Obelisk and Castle. From the top of the hill, the line of the Malvern Hills can be seen running north.

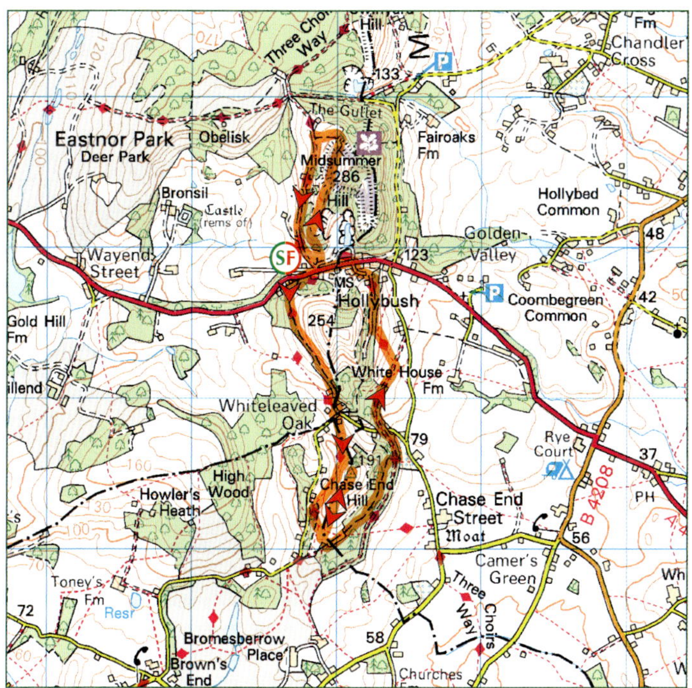

Midsummer Hill is an Iron Age hill fort that is highly unusual because it encloses two hills, separated by a ravine that houses a spring. There were 483 buildings here, indicating a substantial population.

From the summit, continue north, towards the hills and through the ramparts. Follow the gravel path as it heads downhill, bending to the left. At the bottom, turn left onto a stone track that becomes a tarmac lane, leading you around the hill and back down to the car park at **Hollybush**.

Turn right onto the **A438**. After 120m, take the gate on the left. Immediately after the gate, fork right. At a junction of paths, bear right, keeping the hill on your left. After some distance, the path gently descends and then forks. Take the right fork downhill, past a garden on the right, through a gate and down to a track. Turn left to the road, passing some stocks on your right.

The **stocks** are fully functional, if you want to give them a go! Stocks were used for over 1000 years as a form of punishment for people who perpetrated a crime that was not considered too serious, but they have not been used in the UK for over 150 years. Public shaming was quite normal as a punishment, but those in the stocks were not just laughed at. If they were disliked, they might be pelted with rotten produce, excrement or even stones. And they were sometimes left outside for days with no provisions, toilet breaks or shelter.

This is the hamlet of **Whiteleaved Oak**. Turn right along the road and take the first track on the left, past Cider Mill Cottage, then up between hedges. Pass through a gate and continue ahead. Where the path starts to become steep and splits around some bushes, turn right and follow it around the hill, across a more open area. There are fine views to the south-west from here. If you are feeling adventurous, continue straight up to the trig point on Chase End Hill instead of turning right.

At the end of the open area, turn left at a junction of paths, keeping the hill on your left. At the fork, stay left, then turn left up the wide ride to the trig point

Eastnor Obelisk and the view over Herefordshire

on the top of **Chase End Hill**. This path is braided, so don't worry which route you choose.

From the summit, retrace your steps down the hill. As you near the woods, fork left and follow the path to the left, keeping the hill on your left. Ignore the gate on the right. Over some distance, the route passes through two wide gates. Just before the next, narrower gate, switchback right, downhill. If you reach the road, you have gone too far.

Pass through another small gate and turn left onto the wide path a few metres ahead, which crosses the road on a bridge after 200m. This eventually leads to a field gate into a pasture. As you approach the second stand of trees in the pasture, turn diagonally left uphill past the dead tree and through the gate in the corner of the field. This short section of the route is not visible on the ground.

Pass another gate on your right, continue uphill for a short distance, then through the small gate ahead. Turn diagonally right to meet the track. Follow the track with the hill on your left for some distance until it reaches the road at **Hollybush**. Turn left to return to the car park.

WALK 10

Castlemorton Common

Start/finish	Swinyard car park (SO 766 381)
Time	2hr 45min
Distance	9.7km (6 miles)
Ascent/descent	165m (540ft)
Terrain	Gentle ascents and descents across common land
Warning	At the time of writing, one stile was dilapidated and another missing. A degree of mobility may therefore be needed to complete the walk.

The hills are alive with the sound of birdsong – particularly Skylarks in profusion, ascending, competing for territory and for a mate. The base of the Malvern Hills also provides habitat for massive Black Poplar trees.

If views make you soar, then this walk does not fall short. The Malvern Hills are close and welcoming, in places bare, and in other areas wooded. The views across the Severn Plain take in Bredon Hill and the Cotswolds. At night, you can see the glow of Birmingham.

As you walk, you sense history around you. The very commons where you start your walk evoke historic rights of access that have existed for centuries. The people of Malvern even rioted to maintain these rights. Many ancient tracks are walked en route. At Castlemorton, the motte and bailey earthworks are still very impressive, nearly a thousand years after construction, and the Norman church has an excellent carved arch to the doorway.

Cross from the car park to the green gate opposite its entrance. Follow the path which heads straight onto the common and after 10m starts to bear right. Continue across the common for 750m until you reach a gravel track. Continue north, bearing slightly left, and head uphill signposted Dales Hall.

Pass Dales Hall on your right, following the wide field track heading straight ahead. As the boundary hedge bears right, you also bear right with it onto Shadybank Common. Bear left downhill to the bottom left-hand corner of the field. Take the field gate on your left, turn right and follow the field boundary to the bottom right-hand corner of the field and step through the gate. Continue

The path across the common

along the greenway onto **Castlemorton Common**. Bear left to follow the track towards the left-hand field boundary which eventually joins Hancock's Lane. At the lane, cross the ford and turn right.

> In the 17th century, King Charles I sold a third of the **Malvern Chase**. The new owners began to enclose the area, blocking access for those with common rights over the land. The commoners rose in anger, until the situation was clarified legally and their rights were retained. The land is now owned by the Malvern Hills Trust, and some local property owners still have commoners' rights. The most widely used right is to graze livestock on the common.
>
> Please note that the sheep and cattle here have right of way on the roads, so take extra care when driving in this area.

When the lane reaches a fork, turn right over the small bridge. Continue following this lane as it bears to the left then, after 400m, sharply right. On reaching the **main road** (B4208), dogleg right then left onto a track.

The view over the Severn Plain from just after Dales Hall

The gravel track splits to the left and right, but ignore this and continue straight on to join a greenway below the dwelling. Go through the wooden gate, continuing downhill. Continue on this track as it bears sharply left. There are three paths leading off to the right from here. Take the third signposted path, on the right.

Across the field, you can see **Sansome Farm**. The path heads towards the left-hand side of the farm buildings. Follow the post-and-rail fence down to the bottom of the field. In the corner, you'll find a gate in the fence. Go through and cross the footbridge into the farm gardens. Join the farm drive and turn left to follow it to the road: **Drugger's End Lane**. Turn left onto the road and then immediately right over the stile and into the field.

If you ever hear something high above your head that sounds like a 1980s game of space invaders, then you are probably listening to a **Skylark**. The males rise from the ground almost vertically, to as high as 300m, where they sing for up to an hour before dropping back to earth.

Although Skylarks are usually heard singing high above, they are ground-nesting birds, and their nests are extremely difficult to spot. Please ensure you stick to paths when walking through areas where you can hear Skylarks during the summer months, to avoid accidentally stomping on their eggs, and keep dogs on short leads.

Head straight up the slight slope, keeping the field boundary on your right-hand side. Keep to the field boundary, following it right then left. In the field corner, turn left for 25m. Take the stile on your right. **Warning:** At the time of writing, this stile was dilapidated – please cross with care.

The footpath goes straight across the field. If the route is unclear when an arable crop is growing, you might choose to follow the field boundary around to the left, turn right at the hedge line and right again on reaching the far side. A footbridge is located about 40m along the boundary on your left. Cross the bridge and proceed along the right-hand edge of the field to a stile, cross and then take a diagonal left across the flower meadow to **Castlemorton**. Turn left to explore Castlemorton Church and old motte and bailey.

Turn right to continue the walk, keeping on the lane until you reach a junction of roads. Cross straight over to follow the track beside the farm buildings of Bannut Tree House. Continue on this lane and take the second footpath on your left (400m) into Hollybed Farm Meadows Nature Reserve. The path goes straight ahead with the field boundary on your right.

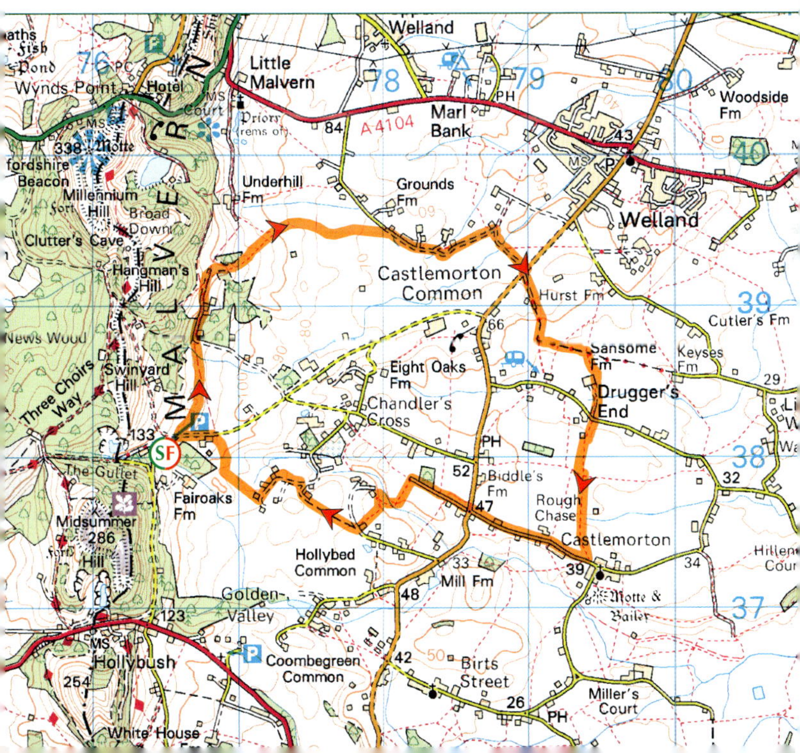

Hollybed Farm Meadows is Worcestershire Wildlife Trust's largest meadow nature reserve. After they acquired the site, hay from the most diverse meadow was strewn over the other meadows, increasing the diversity of plants across the site. This diversity and sheer abundance of plants attract insects, birds and mammals, including the elusive Hazel Dormouse, whose footprints have been seen in specially devised footprint traps.

As well as meadows, the reserve has a traditional pear orchard, into which the Wildlife Trust has planted some new perry trees. This is used to demonstrate traditional orchard management.

At the first gate, continue straight through with the boundary still on your right. Bear right and then turn left down into the valley. At the bottom, turn right, heading for a gate in the fence line. Cross the footbridge and look for the next footbridge and small gate, and then cross the field uphill to the metal gate. Bear left to the post-and-wire field boundary gate for the footpath. Head across the field to the large poplar and oak trees ahead of you. From here, aim for the right of the building that you can just see the roof of now, which is where your exit point is: at the time of walking, there was no stile in place here but a climbable rail fence. Once over the fence, go through three gates to meet with the gravel track.

Cross onto **Hollybed Common** and take the wide grass track heading diagonally right towards the Malvern Hills. Skirt round the two cottages on the common. As the path nears the gravel drive to the cottages, bear left to meet the next gravel track at an intersection. Turn left and take the right-hand fork uphill, and continue along the track to then bear left. Pass a large property on your right (Midsummer Farm). As the gravel track bears left, the greenway to follow is on the right.

Follow the wide greenway heading gently upslope towards the trees and the Malvern Hills. Bear right as the path curves upslope. As the path flattens, follow it to the left, and on reaching the lane, turn left uphill. The ponds on your right were dug around 2020 and quickly naturalised. The **Swinyard car park** where you started is directly ahead, just 100m further up the road.

WALK 11

Birts Street and Castlemorton

Start/finish	All Saints Church, Hollybush (SO 769 367)
Time	2hr 15min
Distance	8km (5 miles). Can be split into two circular walks: the western loop is 3.2km (2 miles) and has most of the descent and ascent; the eastern loop is 4.8km (3 miles) and flatter – park near the school in Castlemorton.
Ascent/descent	120m (385ft)
Terrain	Grassy paths, field paths, many paths across meadows – in summer, gaiters and/or long trousers may be beneficial. Multiple stiles – not dog-friendly.
Refreshments	Farmers' Arms, Birts Street (at 2.4km)
Parking	At start/finish; if the church car park is full, the lane to the right of the church leads to more spaces.

Starting with fabulous views along the Malvern Hills and across the Severn Plain, this route soon drops into the pretty landscape below. A quiet lane leads to the Farmers' Arms pub, from where the route heads across fields to the village of Castlemorton. As the name suggests, this was once the site of a castle, with the earthworks still prominent in the local landscape. Returning across more pasture and meadows, the route then sneaks between Coombegreen Common and Hollybed Common to pass the Mill Pond before rising back to the car park, with views over the southern Malvern Hills.

Facing the church from the car park, turn right past the church, then left onto a tarmac lane. The Malvern Hills rise on the left of the view from here, and the Severn Plain opens out to the right. Follow the lane around to the right and through the grassy parking area. Continue ahead, past a small collection of farm buildings below. Stay ahead at the first fork (a narrower path), then fork left at the next (path remains the same width). Follow this path across **Coombegreen Common** to the **B4208**.

> **Coombegreen Common** is home to many ants, which are the favourite food of Green Woodpeckers. This means that it's not unusual to see these birds flying from the ground up to neighbouring trees as you walk past. They are easily identified by the combination of their colour (moss green) and looping flight pattern.

Turn left, then take the first right towards and then through the hamlet of **Birts Street**. At the end of this stretch, where the road forks, you will find the Farmers' Arms, a popular pub with locals and visitors.

Take the left fork, then, between the junction and the car park entrance, look to the left for an archway in the hedge. Cross the stile and then the field to the opposite corner, where another arch has been cut into the hedge. Cross two stiles and a drainage ditch, and then head diagonally left over the next field. Through a gate and over another stile, turn right to keep the hedge on your right. After passing two field gates, you will come to a kissing gate.

Take this, then follow the path to the left to continue between the fences. Head diagonally right across the following field and through a gap in the hedge, with the smallholding buildings to your right. Another diagonal right will take you to a stile into the next field, and a third one will take you to the corner of that field, where a gate leads to a lane.

All Saints Church

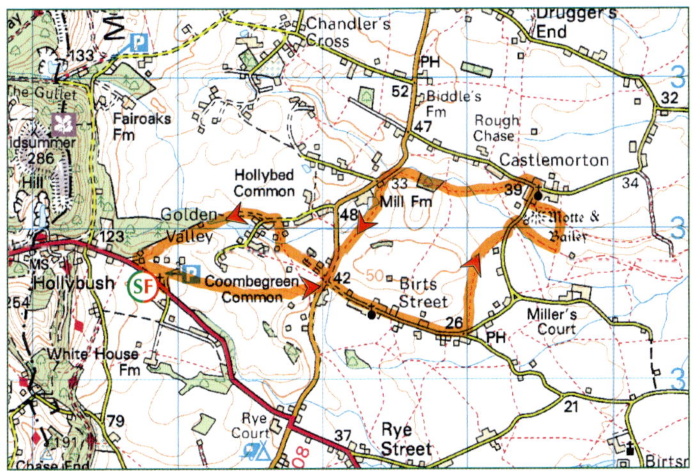

Turn left and follow the lane until you can see the Castlemorton village sign. At the bend in the road before the sign, turn right along a waymarked bridleway. After 300m, you will arrive at a crosspaths with a small bridge on the right. Turn left through the kissing gate and head straight up the hill with the hedge on your left. Continue ahead through two gates that are about 20m apart, then, after a few paces, turn left. At the end of the field, the path crosses a small wooden bridge to enter the remains of the old castle **motte and bailey**.

On the left, you can see **Castlemorton Tump**. This is the motte (artificial hill) on which a small wooden castle stood in the 12th century. It was built by the Folliotts, who were lords of the manor, and was more a show of wealth and status than a defendable fortress. When the castle and land were sold to the Abbot of Westminster in the following century, the castle's importance waned, so it was never rebuilt in stone.

Continue past the motte to an information board and a gate which leads to a lane that runs past the primary school into **Castlemorton**. Turn right, then left at the T-junction along Church Road. After 100m, turn left through a kissing gate, then diagonally right across the field. This part of the route is not clear on the ground. Aim halfway between the houses and the trees that mark the site of a spring. A clear path runs from the corner of the field through the hedge to a hand gate. Through this, cross a paddock to another hand gate visible ahead.

Summer Hill and Worcestershire Beacon from the route

This leads to a small bridge. Cross the stream and head diagonally right across the next field. Aim to cut across the first corner of the field, and you will soon see the next hand gate ahead. From here, head towards the field gate, but do not go through it. Instead, turn left up a faint path with the fence line on your right, through woodland that is carpeted with Ramsons (Wild Garlic) in spring. This section of the route can get muddy.

After a while, this path reaches a meadow. Stick to the right-hand edge and head through the wide wooden gate by the houses. Turn left immediately to keep the fence on your left until you reach a bridge. Cross the stream, then head diagonally left to a field gate. Turn left, with the **pond** on your right. After a short distance, at a junction of tracks, turn right, then immediately left over a stile. Strike out across the field towards the far corner, to the right of the gate that is immediately visible. Through the kissing gate, turn right to the **B428**, then left along the road into Coombe Green.

After a short distance, the route continues along the stone track on the right that follows the edge of **Coombegreen Common**. At the gate to The Hollands, it turns right along a mown path that leads to a tarmac lane. Turn left, then follow the stone drive through the car park to the **Mill Pond**. Continue on the stone path past the end of the car park, with the pond on your left. Stay ahead, in approximately the same direction, until you reach Bank Cottage.

> As the path rises, the hill directly ahead is **Ragged Stone Hill**, the second most southerly hill of the Malverns. In the 19th century, the hill featured in *The Shadow of the Raggedstone*, a novel by Charles F Grindrod. In it, a monk at Little Malvern Priory was cursed by a shadow he encountered on the hill. He caused a scandal by marrying despite his vows, and as a penance, he had to crawl daily, on his knees, up and down Ragged Stone Hill. Thankfully, this walk requires no such painful sacrifice.

All Saints Church, where the walk began, is in sight from here – follow the grassy path to the left to return to it.

The Mill Pond is a great place to fish, or simply to sit and enjoy

WALK 12

Upton upon Severn and Upper Ham Meadows

Start/finish	King's Head, Upton upon Severn (SO 852 407)
Time	2hr 30min
Distance	9.1km (5.7 miles)
Ascent/descent	55m (190ft)
Terrain	Mainly grassy paths, one gentle ascent; several stiles, not dog-friendly
Refreshments	Pubs and cafés in Upton
Toilets	On High Street, near start/finish
Public transport	Infrequent buses from Worcester to New Street stop
Parking	Hanley Road car park or free on-street parking on Tunnel Road
Note	Check for festivals in Upton before walking – roads and car parks will be busy during these periods. Dogs must be kept on leads across the meadows during spring and summer, as there are ground-nesting birds.

Upton upon Severn was once a thriving port, which explains the number of pubs you will find in the town. Since the river stopped being a transportation artery, Upton has reinvented itself as a centre for music festivals, helping to keep at least some of those pubs busy.

This walk starts by heading south out of the town between the river and the Upper Ham flood meadows. Turning inland, it climbs a gentle rise, giving far-reaching views across Worcestershire before dropping back across farmland and through a hamlet of wood-framed houses, typical of this area, to return to the town.

From the King's Head Inn, head south with the river on your left. Continue past the 'access only' sign. At the end of the drive, carry on along the footpath, with **Upper Ham Meadows** on your right.

UPPER HAM MEADOWS

Upper Ham Meadows are some of the oldest Lammas meadows in the country. These are meadows that are harvested in June or July and grazed from the Christian festival of Lammas (1 August) until early the following year. This management regime has resulted in a rich variety of grasses and wildflowers, providing a fabulous habitat for wildlife.

Ham was also used as a rifle range between the 1860s and 1925, and then again by the Home Guard during World War 2. Trenches were also dug across the meadow during World War 2 to make it impossible for enemy aircraft to land on what would otherwise have looked like ideal flat ground.

At the end of the meadows, continue ahead through a gate, keeping the river on your left. Eventually, you will reach a small angling association shed on the right. Turn right here to follow the access track away from the river, past a row of houses on the right, to a tarmac lane. Cross the lane and continue ahead along the left edge of a field.

As you climb, look back for a fabulous view over the Severn Plain and the church spire and **Pepperpot** in Upton. The Pepperpot is Upton's oldest surviving building, dating from the 14th century. It is the tower of the former parish church, which sported a spire until the 18th century, when it was replaced by the cupola with copper roof and lantern you see today. In 1937, the church was demolished, and the tower is now home to a heritage centre that tells the history of the town and its role in the British Civil Wars.

The spire of Upton Church across the meadow

Upton was once a busy port on the River Severn

When you reach a hedgerow and a junction of paths, continue ahead over a stile and along the left-hand edge of the next field, still gently rising. At the top of the hill, with a house in view directly ahead, strike out right, between the left edge of the copse and a solitary oak, to the far corner of the meadow. (There is no obvious path on this section of the walk.) The Malvern Hills are in the distance on your left, and Bredon Hill, an outlier of the Cotswolds, is on your right.

Through the metal gate or over the stile to one side, continue ahead with a fence on your left to another field gate. Pass through that and another to its left, then turn right over a pair of stiles and diagonally left across a field. Pass through a kissing gate and continue ahead along a faint path under the trees, then over a small wooden bridge to a track. Turn right onto the track and follow this to the lane.

Turn left and follow the lane past the black-and-white house (Holdfast Post) and for another 600m. On reaching a hamlet, follow the lane to the left, and then almost immediately turn right up a gravel track signposted 'The Close'. Past the houses, continue ahead over a stile to **Southend Farm** (with Upton steeple visible behind it).

Pass through two field gates and turn right onto the track through the farm. At a junction of tracks, cross to continue ahead, following a clear route that arcs across the pasture, initially towards the steeple.

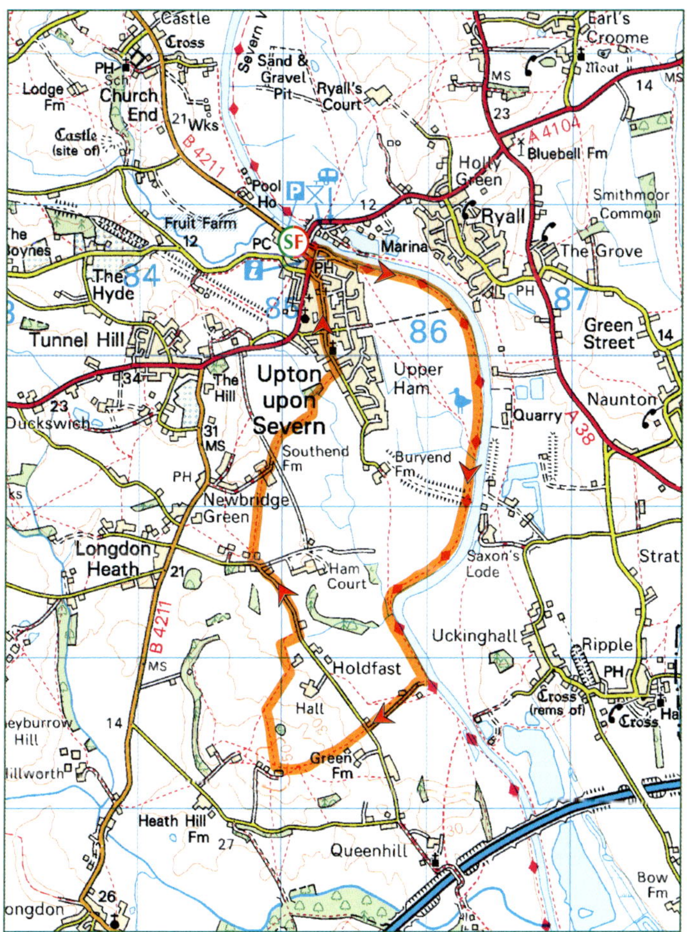

Another stile leads to a path between fences that continues to a kissing gate. Pass through the gate, cross the field and through the gate directly ahead to a residential street. Turn left, then continue ahead to return to the centre of **Upton upon Severn**.

WALK 13

River Severn and Croome Park

Start/finish	Hanley Road car park, Upton upon Severn (SO 850 408)
Time	5hr 15min
Distance	19.9km (12.3 miles)
Ascent/descent	145m (480ft)
Terrain	Flat river embankment with short grass. Agricultural, riverside and landscaped parkland. Slopes are mainly gentle. Stiles (no dog gates) in varied states of repair at field boundaries. Very quiet road sections.
Refreshments	Upton and Croome Court
Toilets	At start/finish and on High Street, Upton
Public transport	Infrequent buses 332 and 363 from Worcester
Note	Check for festivals in Upton before walking – roads and car parks will be busy during these periods.
Warning	There are two crossings of fast roads. Do not attempt this walk during periods of flooding.

The mighty River Severn brought huge trade wealth to this region, fertility to its soils, and flood devastation to its towns when disregarded and hemmed in by development. This walk starts with a stroll over the bridge at Upton upon Severn, a historic trading port, where 2000 sailors a night would throng the streets and its many pubs. Step down to follow the Severn upriver, letting yourself slow your pace to that of the gently sliding water and the peace of the rolling Worcestershire fields and woodlands.

Huge vistas open up to the Malvern Hills, if you remember to look back as you ascend Madge Hill. Shortly after, the route reaches the National Trust's Croome Park. The house and park are absolute gems, also providing the setting for St Mary Magdalene Church in Croome D'Abitot and the RAF Defford Museum. You even walk alongside service roads to the old World War 2 airstrip.

The land oozes abundance and history as you make your way through orchards, farms and sleepy villages back to the Severn, having a peep at some quality boats at Upton Marina before sampling a drink at one of the many fantastic pubs in town.

Upton upon Severn has long been challenged by **flooding**, a risk that is continuing to increase with the march of climate breakdown. Some of the roads in the area have been raised, although others still flood, and the town centre is protected by a bund, floodgate and flood wall along the river. This wall has glass panels along the top 45cm to allow a view of the river and has proved its value many times over.

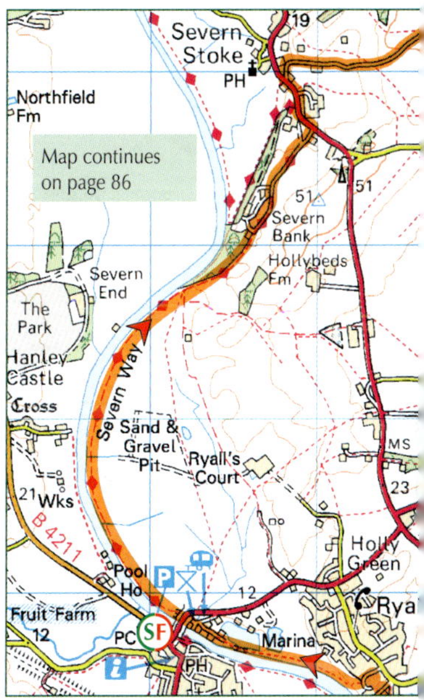

Map continues on page 86

From the car park, join the road alongside the River Severn. Cross the bridge on the left-hand side. As the road bends, take the steps down to the field on the left. Continue alongside the River Severn for just over 2km, heading upstream and following the diversion around the sand extraction operations.

Note a marvellous Black Poplar with several massive **Mistletoe balls**. Mistletoe is a semi-parasitic plant that grows on broadleaf trees, sending its roots into the tree for water and nutrients. It is entirely poisonous to humans, but not to birds. They eat its berries and wipe the goo off their beaks on bark, leaving the seeds behind in a perfect place to grow.

If you are lucky, you might catch sight of a Brown Hare

After 2km, at the intersection of a farm gravel track and the footpath, take the ascending track to the right of the small woodland. At the coach house, turn right onto the tarmac track, which leads to the **A38**. Turn left downhill for 230m towards **Severn Stoke**, to join Madge Hill Road on the right.

As you're ascending **Madge Hill**, look back to see almost the entire length of the Malvern Hills. Cubs Moor, topped by Croome Panorama Tower, is seen on the left as you ascend Madge Hill. Both are accessed via the Croome Estate.

At the top of Madge Hill, turn right at the road junction. Cross over the intersection, onto the dirt track heading east, with views of Bredon Hill and the radar dish near Defford Airfield.

The **Defford radio telescope** is one of seven in the UK in the e-MERLIN network, headed by the Jodrell Bank Observatory. They detect radio waves originating in space, from objects like stars, dust or even molecules of gas. As we can't see radio waves, the signals are converted into data that is then turned into visual images, which provides a far clearer picture of what is happening in space. They can even be used in the search for extra-terrestrial intelligence.

Follow this track down to the farm. From the left corner of the farmhouse wall, take a left diagonally across the field heading towards the **M5**. Follow the edge of the motorway for a short distance, exiting in the corner of the field over a stile. Turn right over the bridge and follow the road through to **High Green**. Pass the National Trust Croome estate office on your left. Depart at the curve of the road, picking up a footpath heading onto the **Croome Park Estate**.

This area is home to the **Brown Hare**. Introduced to the UK by the Romans, it can reach speeds of 72km/h (45mph). The field you cross on entering the estate is likely where the hares are breeding and raising their young.

The path is indistinct. Face directly into the field looking towards the copse, and pick a route that takes you on a diagonal between the copse and the woodland boundary on the right, aiming towards the church tower on the ridge. The path exits at the junction of a pond and a field hedge line.

Follow the woodland boundary, entering into the Croome Court main estate towards **St Mary Magdalene Church**. Take the path which exits from the side of the church into the graveyard. Beyond is an orchard and access to the Croome Court café and **RAF Defford Museum**.

The **RAF Defford Museum** is located at the Croome Court Visitor Centre, just off the route. The airstrip was built during World War 2 to test airborne radar, which was being developed in nearby Malvern. The work that was done here was crucial to the Allies' victory.

Continue following the path through the orchard until you reach the road. Turn right. On reaching the impressive entrance to Croome Court, on the road curve, take the footpath on the right.

CROOME COURT

Croome Court was the home of the Coventry family for centuries. However, the 10th Earl died during World War II and the estate's income was no longer enough to maintain the house. It was sold to a succession of others, and used as a Roman Catholic boarding school, the British headquarters of the International Society for Krishna Consciousness and a country club. Eventually, the Croome Heritage Trust bought it in 2007. Since 1996, the National Trust had owned much of the house's park, and now it also has a long lease on the house. This has enabled significant restoration work to be done on the house to secure its long-term future.

Croome Court from across the park

Upton Marina

You are now walking along the edge of **Defford Airfield**. Follow the track through parkland with open vistas to the lake, dropping to the right edge of the woodland ahead.

> **RAF Defford Airfield** was constructed as a training base for Wellington Bomber crews. The site soon became a base for testing radar, with a team from the Telecommunications Research Establishment in Malvern. Over 2200 staff and scientists were accommodated at the airfield. World leading radar technology was developed and the world's first automatic plane landing took place here.

From the side of the **lake**, take the path through the wood to a boundary wall and head left, up the hill, following the woodland boundary wall. A path emerges on your left from the wood; turn right here onto the track, heading due south through the field.

Cross the **minor road**, continue south along a drive and then join the bridleway. Your destination is the midpoint of the woodland at the far end of this narrow meadow. A fast road (**A414**) awaits at the end of the wood. Cross carefully and continue on the track south through a dilapidated farm complex.

After crossing the **M5**, turn left into the field. Take a right diagonal to a boundary junction and go through the gate. Carry along with the boundary hedge on your left, then into fields with a little kink around the woodland edge ahead of you. After that, start to bear right towards the 13th-century church at **Hill Croome**.

Descend right, alongside the church boundary, to a small gate into the churchyard. Drop down through the churchyard to the road and turn left. At the road island, turn left. Then turn right at a sign into Birch Tree Barn. Follow the path signs through the property and up the slope. At the third field boundary and a junction of paths, turn right to descend towards a line of oaks.

Ahead is a hedge through which a footbridge crosses a field drain. Follow the next field boundary on your right. A stile in the boundary hedge on your right then leads across the next field to another gate on a concrete bridge. Cross over and then continue on a right diagonal towards the white house.

Turn left onto the village lane. As it curves left into **Naunton**, turn right just before the telephone box library and follow the track off into the fields. The walkable route across these fields follows a sward edge in a dogleg, towards the

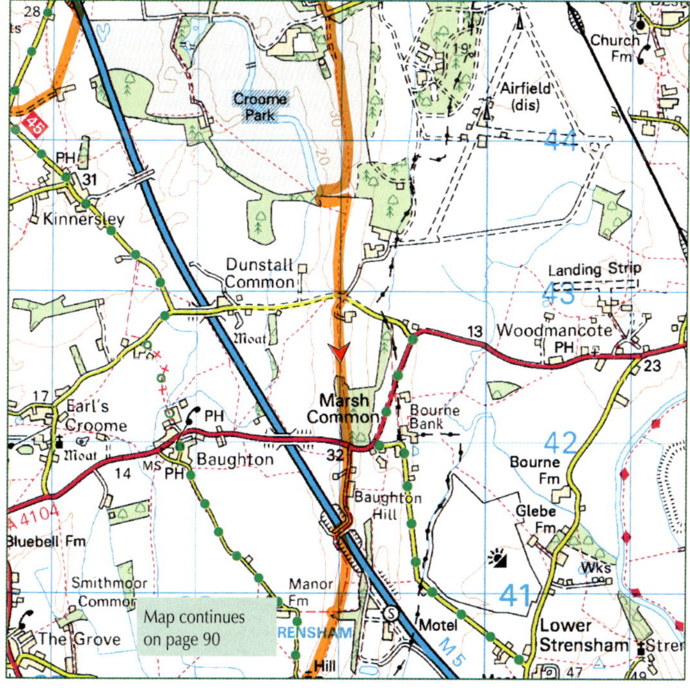

Map continues on page 90

An ancient oak tree is beginning to die

main road (**A38**). The official footpath goes across in a diagonal. Cross the road. **Warning:** This is another fast road – please be careful as you cross.

Walk alongside the access track to the sand pit, making your way towards the buildings. A gravel track intersects your route just before a security compound. Turn right along it.

A stile and gate after the warehouse need to be crossed. Another stile and gate follow and then there is a stile on your left in the hedge line. Climb over and walk through a small copse and into the vegetable garden of Ryall Cottage. On leaving the front garden, cross the road and take the alley into a residential crescent. Bear left to the end, where, on the right, a footpath leads off to the riverside and the final stretch past **Upton Marina**. Follow the narrow road to the bridge and return to **Upton upon Severn** town centre.

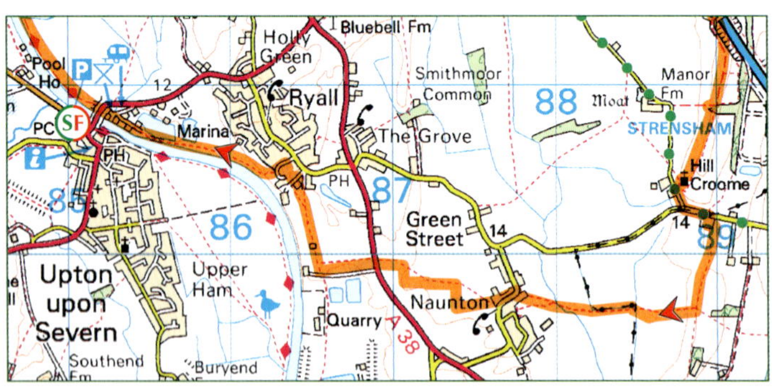

WALK 14

Old Hills

Start/finish	Upper Old Hills car park, Callow End (SO 829 487)
Time	1hr
Distance	3.6km (2.2 miles)
Ascent/descent	65m (220ft)
Terrain	Grassland, woodland, a track and quiet lanes; some paths can get muddy
Refreshments	Pubs and hotel in Callow End
Public transport	Infrequent bus from Worcester to Pixham Ferry Lane stop

The Old Hills are a popular destination for horse riders and Sunday strollers. A gentle climb takes you up a meadow to the top of the hill, where there are far-reaching views across Worcestershire from the trig point. The route then drops through a wood where horses are often tethered. After circling through the village, first along a track, then a lane, past houses and close to the pub, the route returns you to the car park via pasture. A short extension of 500m each way will take you to a picnic area by the River Severn.

The Old Hills rise from the pastoral undulations of the Severn Plain

The view of the Malvern Hills

From the entrance to the car park, take the track slightly downhill towards the row of houses. Follow the track to the left, keeping the houses on your right. Ignore the turning to the right. At the end of the track, continue uphill past a house called The Loose Moose at 110 Old Hills. At first, keep the open grass to your left and scrub to your right, then head for the white trig point ahead at the summit of **Old Hills**.

At the **Old Hills trig point**, turn around for far-reaching views across the gentle hills of the Severn Plain. Around 6500 trig points were constructed in the 1930s. On a clear day, each trig point could see at least two others, which enabled accurate mapping of the whole of the UK. Most trig points, like this one, are still at good viewpoints, although some have become surrounded by woodland in the intervening period.

Follow the path down a shallow valley away from the trig point. After a few metres, take the left fork (the right fork can become very muddy). From here, there are views across to the Malvern Hills ahead. Follow this path down to the gate visible at the bottom of the slope. Turn right along the wide green ride. There is a bench here, perfectly positioned to enjoy the view of the Malvern Hills.

Keeping the Malverns to your left, continue along the ride, ignoring side paths, until you reach the white house, 111 Old Hills. Turn right onto their gravel drive and follow it to the left over a rise and down towards a gate. Just before the gate, turn right in front of the hedge. Follow this path as it becomes a track (Bush Lane), enters the village of **Callow End** and meets the main road.

At the road, dogleg left and then right down Upper Ferry Lane. After around 220m, take the narrow gravel path just before number 20 (Priorsfield) and enter the field at the end. Keeping the hedge to your left, pass through two more gates. Head diagonally right to cross the drainage ditch and continue to the far right-hand corner of the field, and then Pixham Ferry Lane. Turn left here to reach the picnic area by the River Severn (500m along the lane).

Turn right back to the main road. Cross and turn left onto the footpath, past the postbox, to return to the **Upper Old Hills car park**.

In the past, the **Old Hills** were used by local people to graze livestock. The area is not fenced, so as the road got busier, keeping sheep here became less viable. As grazing declined, trees and scrub started to grow, impacting on some of the grassland species. These days, the Malvern Hills Trust uses a combination of mowing and grazing Highland cattle to maintain the grassland. Some locals still graze tethered horses on the hills, and it is a popular horse-riding area.

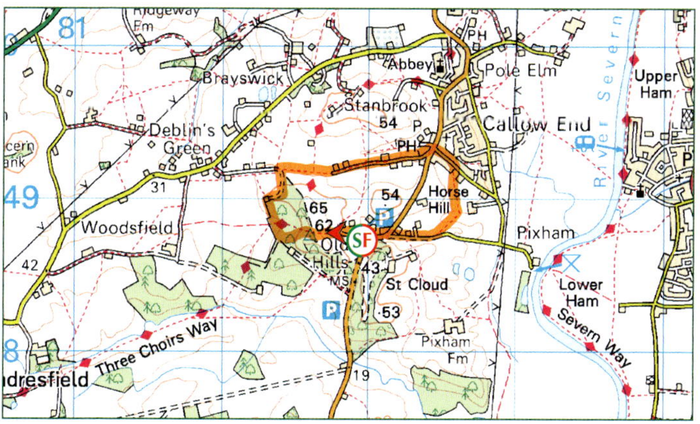

WALK 15

Worcester – rivers and battlefield

Start/finish	Worcester Foregate Street railway station (SO 850 552)
Time	3hr
Distance	10.8km (6.7 miles)
Ascent/descent	60m (200ft)
Terrain	Mainly flat riverside paths and streets, some slight slopes
Refreshments	Worcester, Diglis Locks
Toilets	At Asda superstore in Worcester, or at Worcester Foregate Street station for ticket holders
Warning	Do not attempt this walk in heavy rain or flood – Worcester is renowned for its flooding. Take care when crossing the golf course (flying balls) or standing close to the river (collapsing bank).

Worcester is a thriving city, busy with people and, at certain points, traffic. Yet it retains a rural feel – college children walking down the High Street in sports kit, local shopping brands, trees lining the River Severn, and a racecourse within a short walk of the city centre. Within 10 minutes' walk, you can be into countryside.

This city saw the first and last battles of the British Civil Wars of 1642–1651. Part of this walk enters a critical and very interesting battlefield where we can see the river crossings that challenged Cromwell and that his troops overcame. We can see how the tower of Worcester Cathedral gave an observation advantage to the Royalists. Yet the Parliamentarians were able to outmanoeuvre the Royalists with unexpected pontoon bridges put across the Teme and the Severn. The hedged landscape also delayed the redeployment of the Royalist troops over the fields that we walk through between the River Severn and Powick Bridge. Scenes of desperation, death, victory and demise are etched across our route.

At Powick, we also pass the world's first municipal hydroelectricity and steam plant, built in 1894. No longer operational, the buildings remain an impressive sight on the banks of the River Teme.

Whether or not you are interested in all that history, this is a lovely walk along the flat and peaceful river meadows that reach right into the centre of the city.

Powick Hydroelectric Power Station

From Foregate Street station exit, turn left. Continue along and cross the road, past the Slug and Lettuce, past Lloyds Bank, and then turn right down Broad Street. At the bottom of the street, take the pedestrian crossing opposite the church and, with the church on your left, head down Quay Street to the water fountains, then walk alongside the River Severn with the water on your right and **cathedral** elevated on your left. Continue your walk along the river until you reach **Diglis Locks** after about 1.5km.

Immediately past the cathedral, where steps lead down to the river, look out for the **flood markers** attached to the wall on the left. These show just how high the river level reaches. Worcester still floods frequently, but thanks to improvements in flood management, the damage is being minimised. In 1947, one of the highest markers, the city struggled to continue to supply its residents with water and electricity. The community garden on the landward side of the racecourse floods so frequently that they showcase building flood resilience into gardens, with floating greenhouses and beehives, planting that drains quickly when the waters recede, and an appropriate choice of plants.

Further along the river, you reach **Diglis Locks**. Before the locks were constructed, the river was only navigable to this point for just over half the year. In 1844, four locks and weirs were constructed, which increased the water level near the city during the drier months. Salmon are able to leap this weir, but other important migratory species cannot. A large fish ladder has been created to one side to make it easier for these species to reach their spawning grounds, with an underwater viewing window that is sometimes open to the public.

After the locks, turn right over the footbridge. Turn left down the steps from the bridge crossing, going through the first gate into fields, now with the River Severn on your left. Continue to follow the river downstream until meeting your first kissing gate. Note the view to the right, across the 1651 battlefield to the chimney of the hydroelectric power station at Powick Bridge. Continue to a viewpoint of the River Severn and River Teme confluence, about 1km further downriver.

The **River Severn and River Teme confluence** is thought to be where Oliver Cromwell bridged the two rivers in a daring and dangerous transfer of troops to outflank Royalist defensive positions at Powick Bridge. A fierce battle contested the beachhead for an hour before the Royalists retreated.

Powick Bridge

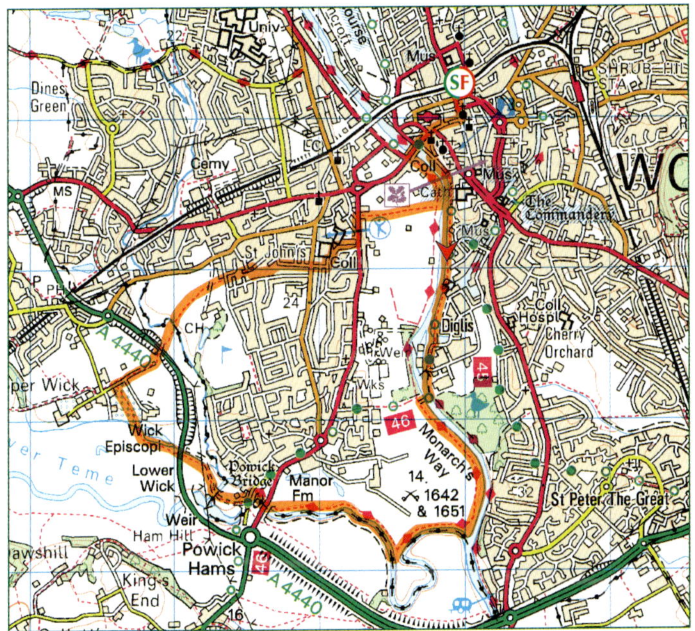

Warning: There are sheer drops to the river here. Take care on the approach and be aware of overhangs. Stand back from the edge at all times.

Follow the River Teme, the smaller of the rivers, upriver with the river on your left. Go through another kissing gate and continue following the path alongside the river. You reach a point where, on your left, there are gates to a large field; ignore that route and cross to your right to follow the banks of the River Teme once more. Go straight through the next kissing gate, retaining the river on your left, marked by the willows all along the bank. Go through the following kissing gate.

Through one more kissing gate, bear left and looking straight ahead, you'll see the tower of the power station at Powick as well as the more modern bridges. Aim for the red bridge directly ahead. Go through the gate and then take the tunnel under the road. Now head towards the base of the chimney.

Powick Mills were opened in 1894, and provided hydro- and steam-generated electricity to the city. The plant was owned by the Worcester Corporation, making it the world's first municipal hydroelectric power station, as well as being one of the largest in the country.

On reaching the lane, turn left and proceed over the old **Powick Bridge**. Follow the track around to the right; just before the first large gate across this track, take a small footpath, along which you can gain access to the River Teme and from which an excellent view of the old bridge is secured. Retrace your steps.

Continue following the track into the fields. Cross the bridge and then bear right following the wide track across the field, which leads to a tunnel under the **A4440**. Go under and through to fields on the other side. Continue straight ahead with the trees on your right-hand side. Go through the kissing gate at the far end of the field, then turn right, heading for the next gate with the post-and-wire fence on your left-hand side.

Walk through the remnants of a cherry orchard to join the road at a gate. Turn right. The lane ends at the cricket club and a private road. Continue straight ahead on the footpath and over the road bridge, crossing the **A4440**.

The cathedral from Worcester Bridge

Take great care as you then cross the **golf course** ahead – there are several places where golfers drive balls across the footpath. From the footbridge, carry on straight towards the trees and up the slope. Maintain your route straight ahead between tee 17 and the green on your right. Bear slightly right to a footbridge and carry on to the gateway across the next section of the golf course.

Leave the golf course at the kissing gate, going down an alleyway to join the road. Cross straight over Nursery Walk/Road and take the alleyway directly in front of you. Just before two bollards, take a right-hand alleyway. At the next junction in the alleyway, turn left. Carry on straight except for a small alleyway zigzag. Continue on down Pitmaston Road. Cross straight over Malvern Road into Vernon Park Road. Turn left on to Foley Road.

Turn right at the end of Foley Road beside the college grounds and follow the alleyway around the premises. At the end of the alleyway, turn left onto Bromwich Road. Cross the road when safe to do so and continue down the slope. At Slingpool Walk, turn right and follow the lane beside the cricket pitch, heading towards the cathedral. You soon reach the River Severn once more, this time opposite the cathedral. Turn left. Swans gather just a few metres along the riverbank, where they are fed.

THE RESURGENCE OF SWANS

In the 1980s, swans in the UK were struggling with lead poisoning from fishing weights and becoming ensnared in fishing lines. Numbers on the River Severn at Worcester plummeted, so the council and cathedral agreed to stop issuing fishing permits for the river where it flows through the city, thus establishing a swan sanctuary. The swans, who struggle to find enough food in the silt-laden river, are also fed from the steps near Worcester Bridge. Lead weights have now been banned, so swan populations have recovered across the country, and here in Worcester, where the fishing ban still holds, swans are now a commonplace feature of the river – and even the racecourse, when it floods.

At Worcester Bridge, turn right and cross the river. Carry on straight along Bridge Street. You soon see Quay Street once more. Cross the road at the pedestrian crossing to retrace your steps to the **railway station**. Alternatively, perhaps you've timed your return to allow for a multitude of food and drink stops through the city, probably one of the greenest cities in the UK.

WALK 16

Pershore, River Avon and Tiddesley Wood

Start/finish	Avon Meadow long-stay car park, Pershore (SO 951 461)
Time	2hr 45min
Distance	10km (6.2 miles) (shortened version 5.8km)
Ascent/descent	60m (190ft)
Terrain	Mainly riverside and wide forest rides; 500m of the route is along the verge of an A-road; one stile
Refreshments	Plentiful options in Pershore
Toilets	Abbey Park, Church Walk, Pershore
Public transport	Train to Pershore (2.4km from start); X50 bus from Worcester or Evesham

Pershore is famous for plums. Nowadays, Peregrine Falcons are also an important feature from May to July. A platform has been added to the Pershore Abbey tower, and Peregrine fledglings can be seen, their heads just visible, the adults diving in to deliver food. Inside the abbey is a unique bell-ringing platform and many other treasures.

The walk showcases a variety of habitats – human and wildlife. Walking along the thriving High Street, various shops and Georgian architecture create a bustling and enjoyable townscape. Over the River Avon, with its clear waters and many lilies, is the 15th-century bridge. The walk along the river is peaceful, the river clear and gently flowing. Tiddesley Wood contains a wide range of trees, flowers, butterflies, cider apple orchards and Pershore plums.

A brief return walk to the outskirts of Pershore brings you through the town to the Abbey Park, where you can admire the church and its nesting Peregrines. Back on the High Street, there is everything you could possibly need after a great walk.

From the car park, head towards the River Avon, turn right over a footbridge and continue along the Riverside Moorings. Turn right at the end of the sports field, then walk through the Asda car park. Turn left onto High Street and continue south to **Pershore Bridge** over the River Avon.

This area is characterised by chocolate-box thatched cottages

Just before the main bridge, take the flight of steps to your right and follow the path along the riverside for approximately 2km, as far as a footbridge over a small stream after a large arable field. Cross over the bridge and take a right diagonal route, heading towards the gate in the opposite corner of the field. Turn left along the **A4104** for 400m. Turn right along the road to omit Tiddesley Wood and shorten the walk.

At the 'Pershore Bridges Circular Walk' signpost, cross the road to enter **Tiddesley Wood**. Follow a gravel track through the wood, west for 250m and then north for 750m, to where it intersects with a wide woodland ride. Carry on straight over, keeping to the central gravel track for another 600m. Pass a Harry Green Reserve board and continue to Stocken Cider Apple Orchard.

Harry Green was a long-term supporter of Worcestershire Wildlife Trust, instrumental in growing the number of the trust's reserves from 20 to 80.

Turn left and follow the path between the wood and the orchard to a gate, after which the route turns left along the woodland boundary, with grassland, scrub, old plum orchards and Bow Brook on the right.

PERSHORE PLUMS

Pershore has been famous for plums since medieval times. After a lapse in production, the Pershore Yellow Egg Plum was discovered in Tiddesley Wood in the 19th century, growing wild. By 1870, 900 tons of Yellow Egg Plum were going to market each year. The original plum became the genetic source for a diversity of plum varieties that are now exhibited at the Pershore Plum Festival, held throughout August each year.

Pershore Abbey

Continue to a gate and turn left onto a wide forest ride. Follow to the wide gravel track you walked along earlier, cross and ascend a wide grass track to an exit point out onto meadows, to the east of the woodland. A horse sanctuary currently cares for 30 horses in the fields here.

Follow the fenced path between meadows and then bear right downhill towards a gate, beside which is a stunning black-and-white thatched home. Proceed downhill to return to the **A4104**; turn left. The shortened version of the route rejoins here. Follow the A4104 into the outskirts of **Pershore**.

Cross to the right-hand side of the road once you are past the town welcome signs. Step away from the main road into the parallel side road. The footpath is between numbers 59 and 57 on your right. Turn left at the end of

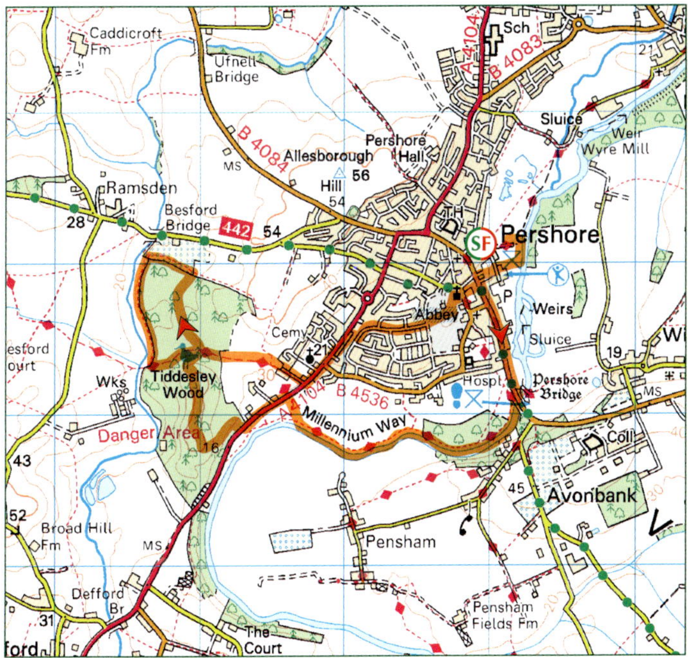

the short alley onto Farleigh Road. Stay on Farleigh Road until you face the Abbey Park. Cross over and join the path directly ahead, then head towards the tower of **Pershore Abbey** when it comes into view.

> In 2022, a pair of **Peregrine Falcons** nested on a waterspout on Pershore Abbey. All was well and good until it started to rain, and the nest was washed away. So, the powers that be decided to install a purpose-built platform to allow Peregrine Falcons to nest here safely. Every year, the birds return and raise a brood. A live webcam records their antics and you can, of course, watch from the ground, if you take a pair of binoculars.

Facing the abbey's main entrance, the route goes round to the right. Cross the road to pass **St Andrew's Church** and take the path through the garden and then onto the High Street. Cross the High Street, turn left to the Asda car park and retrace your steps back to the start.

WALK 17

Pershore to Broadway on the Wychavon Way

Start	Pershore Broad Street marketplace (SO 950 457)
Finish	Signpost by the memorial cross, Broadway (SP 095 375)
Time	8hr
Distance	27.4km (17 miles)
Ascent	465m (1530ft)
Descent	395m (1295ft)
Terrain	Mainly grassy paths and stone tracks with some on tarmac; several stiles; one significant ascent
Refreshments	Plenty of choice at start and finish; the Star Inn at Ashton under Hill
Toilets	Abbey Park, Church Walk, Pershore; Broadway car parks and town centre
Public transport	Train to Pershore or X50 bus from Worcester or Evesham to Royal Arcade for start; bus 1 to Moreton-in-Marsh (where there's a railway station) and several others from Lygon Arms (close to finish)
Parking	Several options at both ends
Warning	Do not attempt this walk when the River Avon is in flood – some of the route will not be passable.

This walk has a gentle start in the Avon Vale, visiting quaint, chocolate-box villages with timbered and thatched cottages, as well as walking along the river itself. The ascent of Bredon Hill is then split, with a section following a contour in between. From the top of the hill, there are views across most of Worcestershire, the Cotswolds and the entire length of the Malvern Hills. The gradual descent along the ridge gives plenty of time to appreciate the views.

More quaint villages and farmland on the flat area between Bredon Hill and the Cotswolds form the basis for the last leg of the walk, followed by a grand finale along Broadway's grand, honey-stone high street.

Most of the route is well waymarked as the Wychavon Way.

From the market square, turn along Bridge Street, away from the town centre. After a while, cross the old **Pershore Bridge**. There is a picnic area at the old bridge.

Pershore Bridge

Pershore's bridges were considered to be an important river crossing in World War 2, so the meadows around them had several anti-invasion measures constructed across them.

Back at the main road, turn left and almost immediately right along a minor road. Where this bends to the left, continue ahead on Pensham Hill. At the postbox, turn right along the drive for number 8A and through the gate at the end into a meadow. Follow the path around the edge to the far corner. Through the kissing gate, continue ahead on a wide track across fields. Bredon Hill with its tower is to your left, and the Malvern Hills are directly ahead.

When you reach a house, continue straight past the corner of the field. Turn left onto the lane through **Pensham** and continue to the end. From here, follow the waymarkers left along a track, right down to the valley bottom and round to the left.

Continue along the track with the river now sometimes visible on your right. Opposite greenhouses, bear right along a waymarked path. Cross a footbridge, dogleg right, then left to walk under trees next to the river. At a private fishing sign, ignore the waymarker pointing uphill and continue along the river. The paths here are braided. As long as the river is on your right, you are heading in the correct direction.

Poppies on Bredon Hill with the Cotswold Hills in the background

Through a metal gate, turn uphill. The track soon becomes a drive which, after a while, reaches a lane. Turn right into **Great Comberton**, then fork left along Church Street. After 200m, turn right to pass the church, under the boughs of an 800-year-old Yew.

Determining the age of a **Yew tree** can be challenging, as they tend to hollow out and have long periods with no growth, both of which make ring-counting unreliable. Almost every part of the Yew is poisonous to people, and that toxicity was used to great advantage in treating cancer. For many years, clippings were collected to have the relevant compound extracted, but now, it can be made artificially. Birds are able to eat the berries of Yew without dying because they do not ingest the seeds – they pass through their digestive systems unscathed.

Leave the churchyard on a grassy path between a series of Yew trees. This brings you to a road junction. Continue ahead, downhill. At the first bend in the road, take the footpath to the left, following the waymarked posts across the bottom of a pasture, eventually rising to a gate. Continue ascending with the hedge line on your left.

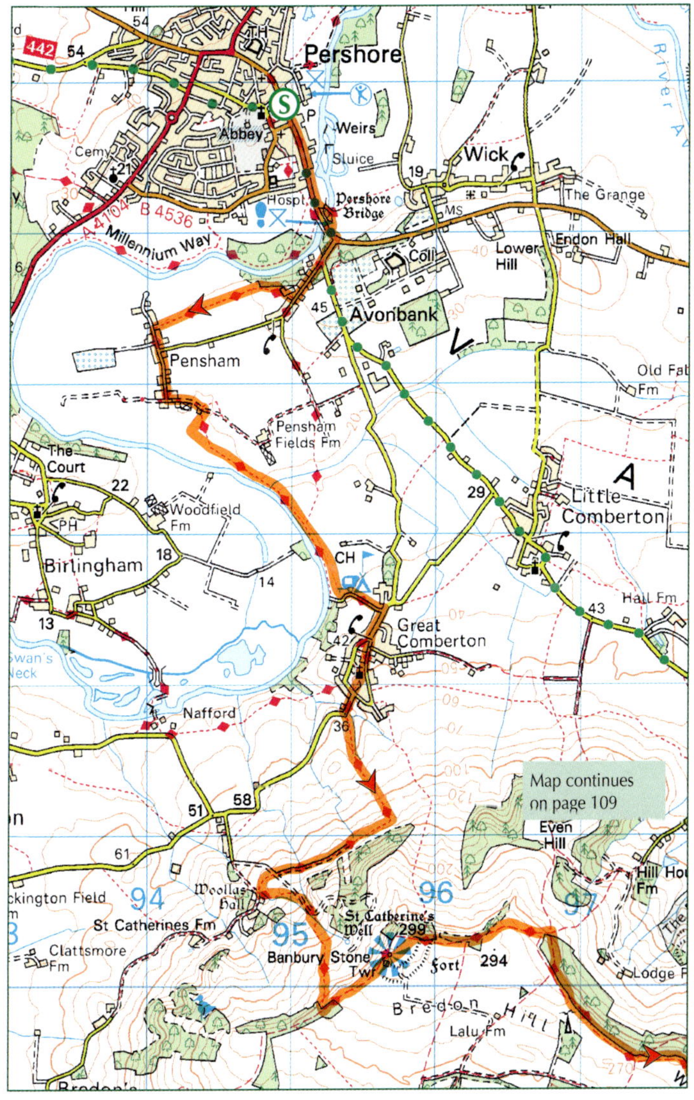

Map continues on page 109

At a crosspaths, turn right following the waymarker, along the slope. After crossing a track, continue to **Woollas Hall** with the fence on your left. Turn left over the stile about 20m before the cottage and follow the clear path as it winds up the hill. The tower at the top of Bredon Hill is now directly ahead.

At the track, continue along it uphill. At a junction of tracks, turn right and follow another clear path to the far corner of the field. From here, continue uphill on a track to a junction of paths in a wood. Turn left through the woods and then along the edge of a field to the tower which marks the summit of **Bredon Hill**. You are now in the middle of an Iron Age hill fort.

The tower is **Parsons Folly**, built in the 18th century as a summerhouse for the squire of Kemerton Court – whose name was John Parsons. The top of the tower reaches 1000ft above sea level, and some think it was his attempt to turn a hill into a mountain. It was clearly not designed to be aesthetically pleasing, and now houses several telephone antennae, which makes it appear even less attractive. You are, however, almost guaranteed a good mobile signal from here!

Approaching the church at Ashton under Hill

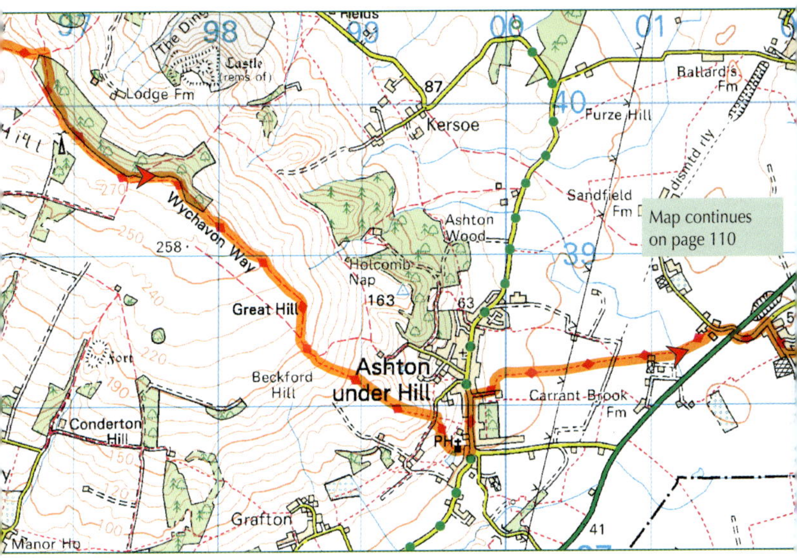

Continue past the tower to meet the wall that circles the hill, and then follow it to the right. At the end of the wall, the route continues along the top of the steep slope and then, at a waymark post, forks left to descend gently. Follow the waymarkers left down a stony path, then right through a gate to rise through woodland. Through another gate, turn left between fences to traverse the ridge.

After the path starts to descend, it turns to the right. Take the next path on the left through a field gate, heading down **Beckford Hill**. At a crosspaths, continue downhill through another gate, then diagonally downhill to the left. Continue in approximately the same direction, following the waymarkers, until you reach a stone track. Cross the stile and turn right along the track. As the route starts to drop, take steps to the left, downhill. Cross the stile and head diagonally right to the right-hand edge of the churchyard, then through it to a road.

Turn left through **Ashton under Hill**. Immediately after Larkspur (a house), turn right and continue ahead through a gate just before the playground. Turn left in front of the cricket nets to cross the field and turn right past some willows to a waymarked gate. The route then runs along the right-hand edge of an arable field. At the end of the field, cross the track and continue ahead in a similar direction all the way to and through a farm to Springfield Lane. Turn right, and continue to the **A46**.

The sign marking the end of the route

Take great care when crossing the road and continue along the minor road ahead. Turn right into **Sedgeberrow** on Main Street. Immediately after the school, turn left between fences. At the end of the field, turn right with a garden on your right.

Turn left at the road. At the T-junction, take the tarmac lane directly ahead and then the footpath on the right opposite The Mill. Fork left over a footbridge, then cross a field to a kissing gate and the following field to another kissing gate.

Through this, continue along the bottom edge of fields until the path reaches a bridge over a stream. Cross and bear left on a grassy ride, which eventually leads to another bridge. Cross and then head diagonally right across a field to a gate in the fence ahead, and then to the far right-hand corner of the next field. Turn right onto the cinder track and continue ahead to the road through **Aston Somerville**.

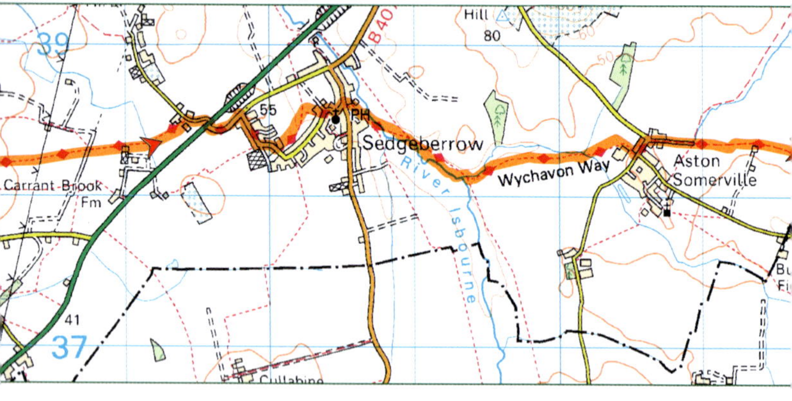

Where the road bends left, turn right along Glebe Road past the houses and on to a stony path. Broadway Tower is now visible on the ridge ahead, with Broadway church tower down and to its left.

> To the left of **Broadway Tower** along the same ridge is a nuclear bunker, designed to measure the concentration and extent of the nuclear fallout if Birmingham was ever attacked. The people inside had to climb out to take measurements, and breathed untreated air brought in from above. To find out about tours, check out the Broadway Tower website (broadwaytower.co.uk).

At a junction of paths, continue ahead. The clear route meanders along field boundaries, passing a bench and then, eventually, Slade Barn. Continue along the drive. At the road junction, stay ahead on the lane.

Pass the old cross (now with an urn on its column) and continue ahead past **Childswickham Church**. Cross a small wooden bridge, then turn right to first cross a meadow and then a holiday park. Continue ahead until you reach a field.

Go along the left edge of the field and straight over the crosspaths at the end, heading in the same direction until you reach a road. Under the **railway bridge**, turn immediately right onto a footpath that crosses a stream and then turns left along the edge of a field, continuing under trees with a stream to the left.

At the road, turn left, and at the T-junction, turn right, signposted 'Village Centre'. Walk into the village of **Broadway**, past the Broadway Hotel, to the signpost near the entrance to Cotswold Court and the memorial cross that marks the end of the route.

WALK 18

River Avon and Bredon Hill

Start/finish	Eckington village centre (SO 922 412)
Time	5hr
Distance	16.7km (10.4 miles) (river loop only: 5.6km; without river loop: 13.3km)
Ascent/descent	345m (1130ft) (river loop only: 18m; without river loop: 346m)
Terrain	Mainly grassy fields with some road walking. One steep ascent. This walk has several stiles, many of which are not dog-friendly.
Refreshments	Pubs in Eckington
Parking	On street on Station Road, Eckington – either side of the train line. (If you park on the west side of the tracks, start by walking away from the footbridge.)
Warning	If attempting this walk in the opposite direction, be aware that the first section of the descent of Bredon Hill is steep.

This walk showcases both major natural features in this area: the River Avon and Bredon Hill. The route heads down to the river and follows it around a wide loop before turning away from the water and heading uphill. There are excellent views of boats and river life, and across the river meadows to Bredon Hill and the Malvern Hills, but the views from the top of Bredon Hill are even better, encompassing most of Worcestershire to the north, the entire length of the Malvern Hills to the west and the Cotswolds to the south.

If you don't fancy walking the whole distance, the route can easily be split into two: one low-level around the river and the other up Bredon Hill.

At the Bell Inn, turn down Station Road. Cross the **railway** and continue ahead past two junctions onto Mill Lane to reach the **River Avon**. Turn right along the riverside path and follow it to the old red sandstone **Eckington Bridge** (3.4km). Turn right here to complete the river loop and return to Eckington.

'Avon' in Old English means 'river', which means there are several River Avons around the UK. This is the one that rises in Northamptonshire and

Eckington Bridge

wends its way to Tewkesbury, where it joins the River Severn. It is also the river that passes through Stratford-upon-Avon.

Cross the river and turn right to continue walking along the bank, now with the river on your right. After a left-hand bend, look for a gate on the right. Turn right through the gate and along a path that soon becomes a track. After a short distance, follow the track round to the left away from the river. At the T-junction of tracks, turn right and pass some houses on the edge of **Birlingham** to reach a road.

Turn right, then almost immediately left through a kissing gate along the side of a building. Another kissing gate leads to a path across the top of a field, over a stile and between gardens to a road. Go straight along the lane ahead, which becomes a compacted stone drive as it heads towards the river. Bredon Hill and its tower are visible ahead.

Stay on the track as it passes through two gates on its way to the river. Turn right across the weir at **Nafford** and continue ahead to the bridges over the lock and sluice gates, and then uphill away from the river. There are benches overlooking the river by the weir and the lock.

WEIRS

Weirs are usually constructed across a river to create a head of water to power mills, create some slow-moving water around the piers of a bridge to reduce erosion, make landscapes look prettier or increase the navigable length of a river. These barriers have the effect of stopping fish from migrating upstream, creating deeper lake-like conditions and allowing sediment to settle, all of which have a significant impact on the ecosystem. A fish ladder up a weir will resolve the issue of fish migration for some species, but the other issues remain. Where navigation is not a factor, many weirs are now being removed.

At the junction of paths, continue uphill. Turn left along the road and continue ahead on a footpath across meadows at the first bend. In the second meadow, the path becomes indistinct. Keep the fence on your right and aim for the far right-hand corner.

Continue across the bridge and up the right-hand side of the next field. At the end of the field, take the hand gate in the top right-hand corner and carry on in the same direction. Where the fence turns a corner, the path drops to a ledge lower down the field. Towards the end of the field, fork left towards a wooden field gate and a clear route up the far side of the valley that will take you to **Great Comberton**.

Turn right onto the lane through the village. Where the road bends to the right by the Old School House, continue ahead along Back Lane. At the next junction, continue ahead along a roughly surfaced drive to and then through Manor Farm. After the buildings, continue ahead over a stile and along a gently rising grassy track.

Turn left at the end to follow a path between a fence and an old hedge line. At the top, follow the waymarker right, still between a fence and an old hedge with a small stream running below it. Climb steadily until you reach a field gate. Through the gate, take the next field gate on the right and walk uphill along the fence line. Shortly before a tree that has seen better days, a waymarker indicates where the path strikes off diagonally to the right.

Before long, a wooden field gate comes into view. This is a red herring! Look to the left of it for a gate in the fence at the top of the field. Follow the waymarkers

Defford
Defford Br
Landing Strip
Woodmancote
PH
B 4080
The Court
Birlingham
Woodfield Fm
Pensham Fields Fm
Little Comberton
Great Comberton
CH
Hall Fm
Bourne Bank
Baughton Hill
Bourne Fm
Glebe Fm
Wks
Eckington Bridge
Swan's Neck
Cemy
Nafford
Eckington
Lower Strensham
Strensham
Motel
M5
Moat Fm
Castle (site of)
Weirs
STRENSHAM
Water Works
Upper Strensham
Bredon Field Fm
River
Eckington Field Fm
St Catherines Fm
Clattsmore Fm
Woollas Hall
St Catherine's Well
Banbury Stone
Twr
Fort
Even Hill
Hill Fm
Lodge
Bredon Hill
Lalu Fm
Bredon's Norton
Norton Park
Park Fm
Stones

The route rises steeply onto the top of Bredon Hill

through two gates to continue uphill with the fence on your right. At the end of the fence, continue to another field gate with a waymarker.

Continue uphill, now with a fence on your left. The final push is up a short but very steep section of path to a wall. Turn right and then climb over the stone stile and make your way to the square tower, which is now visible ahead at the top of **Bredon Hill**. The banks and ditches on your left are the remains of an Iron Age hill fort.

From a distance, the **tower on Bredon Hill** looks impressive, like a castle's keep. As you near it, you will see that it is, in fact, a rather uninspiring block, bristling with communications antennae.

Drop down from the tower to continue with the wall on your right. Follow the path as it passes through the gate and then a small woodland. Just before the end of the woods, turn right downhill on a clear path. Leaving the trees, the path continues to wind its way down the hill. Through a kissing gate, the route remains clear as it crosses to the far corner of a pasture.

The large satellite dish on the plain ahead is **Defford radio telescope**, part of the Jodrell Bank e-MERLIN. The seven radio telescopes in the network act together to form a 217km span across the country, providing information about deep space.

From here, follow the stone track downhill. Immediately beyond the cattle grid, bear diagonally left across the field, following the waymarked posts down towards **Woollas Hall**. Take the drive downhill. Pass the business park, then turn left along a tarmac lane. A few metres beyond the deer park sign, turn right through a high kissing gate and follow the footpath downhill, first along the right-hand edge of the deer park and then through the vineyard.

In **vineyards**, roses are grown at the end of rows of vines for several practical reasons: they act as an early warning for conditions that might lead to mildew on the grapes; they are more attractive to some pests, thereby alerting vineyard managers to potential issues; and because they are attractive to those pests, they also attract predators, which helps with pest control on the vines. They are, of course, also a beautiful addition.

At the lane, turn left and follow it for around 1.5km to a T-junction. Turn right and, taking great care of traffic, follow the road back into **Eckington**.

Rose bushes mark the end of rows in the vineyard

WALK 19

Elmley Castle and Bredon Hill

Start/finish	Queen Elizabeth Inn, Elmley Castle (SO 982 411)
Time	4hr 30min
Distance	13.5km (8.4 miles)
Ascent/descent	475m (1560ft)
Terrain	Moderate, many waymarked sections, wide tracks; some small sections of road; huge views. One stile.
Refreshments	Pub at Elmley Castle
Toilets	Pub at Elmley Castle
Parking	Village roadside and a small car park near the cricket ground

Did somebody mention that Queen Elizabeth I visited Elmley Castle? The remaining village pub, community-run, is named in her honour. In 2025, the Big 450 Bess-tival celebrated the 450th year since the queen visited!

Further outstanding history is recorded in the Norman church, housing striking alabaster monuments, a 13th-century font and (in the graveyard) 16th-century sundials. Your walk leaves the graveyard and heads uphill past monumental dead elms, passing close to the remains of Elmley Castle itself. The castle, an early Norman fortification set within the embankments of an Iron Age fort, became the county administrative centre and seat of power for the Beauchamp family.

The first ascent of the Bredon Ridge brings views to the Cotswolds. The historic track down beside woodland to Overbury is a real pleasure, as are the buildings and church of the village. As you rise back onto the ridge, the unique King and Queen standing stones are set on a precipitous slope; look out for gaps in the hedge that allow viewing from the path.

Reaching the brutalist folly on the summit of Bredon Hill, there are tremendous views all around. The walk continues across the banks and ditches of the Iron Age fort, before descending to meet once more with the queen.

Just after starting the walk, as you approach the main entrance of the **Norman church**, you pass a stone pillar in the graveyard on your left, with several sundials set at different angles. The church has exterior walling with 11th-century herringbone masonry, an intriguing 13th-century font, some of the best alabaster tombs in the country, dating from the 17th century, and an 18th-century memorial to the Earl of Coventry.

Walk 20m south from the Queen Elizabeth Inn and enter the churchyard through the gate. The footpath exits the churchyard left of the church underneath a Yew. After the first stile, cross the field to the far boundary to reach a footbridge. Cross over and head for the left boundary corner, keeping a magnificent dead elm on your right. Cross the second footbridge and turn right, then follow the path straight uphill to the third footbridge. Cross over and bear right. After passing the woods, bear right to the fourth footbridge, cross over and head towards a field gate. As you approach the field gate, your path bears left, straight uphill.

ELMLEY CASTLE

The route passes near to the earth embankments and low-level stonework remnants of Elmley Castle. The castle builders used the remains of an Iron Age fort for its defences. From the site, there is a clear view of the Malvern Hills. Imagine Simon de Montfort and his army pouring through the Wyche Cutting on the far west horizon, hoping to join with his son's army making its way from Kenilworth. The future King Edward I had captured the banners of Simon the Younger during battle and used these to lure his father towards Evesham. Too late, Simon de Montfort realised that the army facing him was not his son's but his foe's. He and his army were trapped at Evesham and annihilated.

Elmley Castle earthworks

As you ascend into woods, there is a gate on the right with 'Private no public' marked on it. Just after this notice, turn right uphill on the narrower track. On the ridge, take a moment to enjoy the view, then bear slightly right from the seat to take the gated track across the fields towards the pine trees and the Cotswolds. At the stone track, turn right along an avenue of pines.

At the end of the wood on your left, turn left. You are on a historic trail that soon follows the edge of Overbury Wood all the way down to the village of **Overbury**. The name Overbury refers to an 'upper burh', or fortified settlement.

Descend through the charming village, reaching Whitcombe House near the end of the houses. Take the road on the right. Pass the **church** and turn right at the road junction. After 400m, take the footpath on your right that cuts across the field to the village of **Kemerton**. On reaching a lane, cross and take the lane alongside the house 'Kings Lea'. At the end, turn right and start your ascent back up Bredon Hill.

After passing Daffurn's Orchard on your left, where the road bends to the right, take the track straight ahead going up the hill. The rare Joeby Crab cider apple and Worcester Pearmain are two special varieties that grow in Daffurn's Orchard. At the second field boundary, turn left at the junction of paths.

You are on **John Clarke Walk** and in the centre of a nature conservation effort. The immediate fields are test fields for arable plants and flowers.

The John Clarke Walk poppy fields

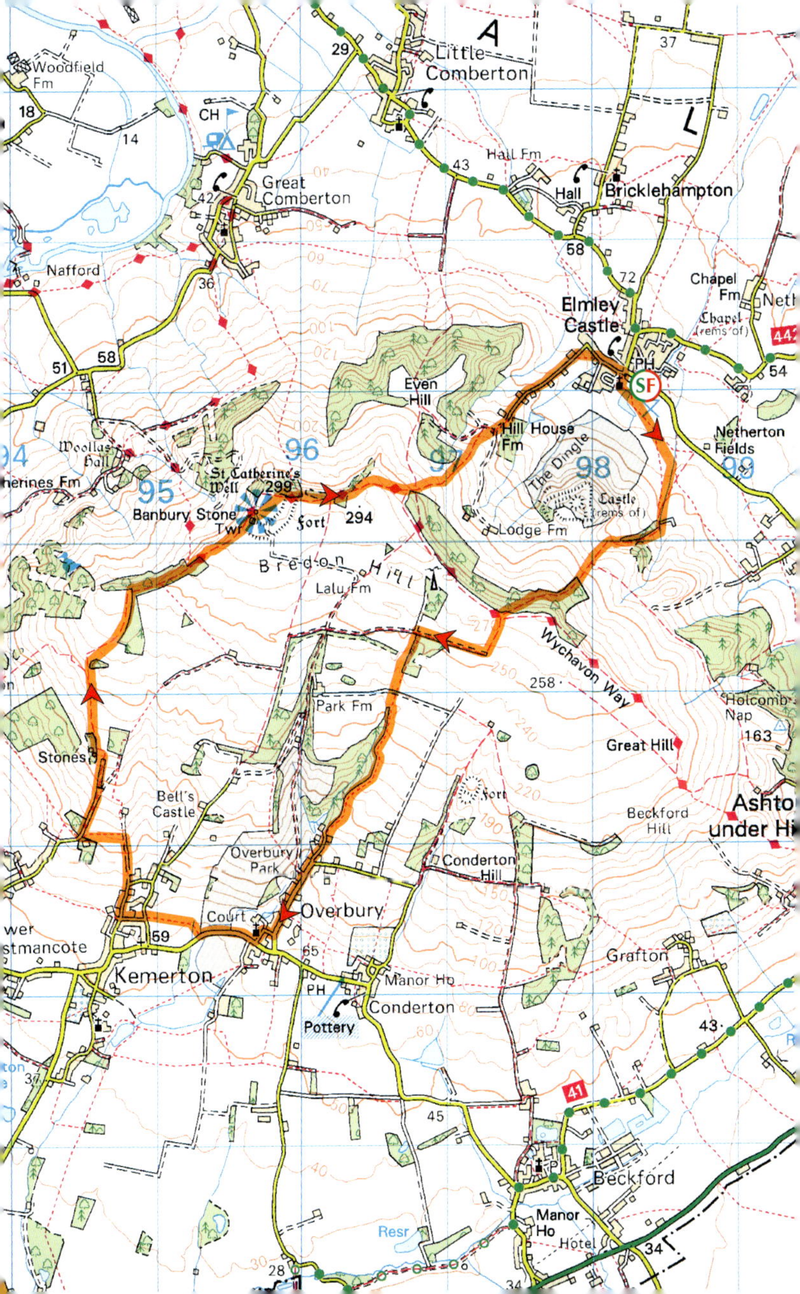

Little Comberton
Woodfield Fm
Great Comberton
Nafford
Hall Fm
Hall
Bricklehampton
Chapel Fm
Elmley Castle
PH
SF
Even Hill
Hill House Fm
The Dingle
Castle (rems of)
Netherton Fields
Woollas Hall
St Catherine's Well
Banbury Stone Twr
Fort
Bredon Hill
Lodge Fm
Lalu Fm
Wychavon Way
Park Fm
Great Hill
Holcomb Nap
Stones
Bell's Castle
Fort
Beckford Hill
Ashton under Hill
Overbury Park
Conderton Hill
Court
Overbury
Kemerton
Manor Ho
PH
Conderton
Pottery
Grafton
Beckford
Manor Ho
Hotel
Resr

Parsons Folly on the summit of Bredon Hill

Emerging onto the end of a tarmac lane, turn right to ascend the stone gravel track. At the road barrier, take the left fork uphill. Go through a gate, then shortly after the right-hand curve, the **King and Queen standing stones** are on your left on a steep slope, visible through the hedge. Maintain your ascent with a field boundary on your right. At the top of the escarpment, turn right and follow the woodland path along the ridge to the top of **Bredon Hill**. There are tremendous views from here to the Malvern Hills (west) and the Cotswolds (south-east).

Passing in front (west) of the tower, take a track that directs you to the end of the fort embankment and then turns right along the escarpment. Stay on this side of the boundary wall. Continue straight ahead and then take the gated path beside the Hazel coppice woodland, bearing left downslope shortly after passing this small coppice.

Continue now straight on the main track downhill to a metal gate and straight on through the next field, bearing right for the bottom corner. Turn right onto a gravel track that joins Hill Road, then left towards **Hill House Farm**. Now it's a 600m walk downhill to two thatched cottages on the left. Opposite the cottages is a footpath. Go through the hedge and take a left diagonal across the field, rejoin the road and turn right into **Elmley Castle**. The Queen Elizabeth Inn is moments away!

WALK 20

Broadway Tower and village

Start/finish	Broadway long-stay car park on Childswickham Road (SP 090 377)
Time	3hr 15min
Distance	10.1km (6.3 miles)
Ascent/descent	335m (1100ft)
Terrain	Moderate ascent and descent; good paths, gates and stiles
Refreshments	Several options in Broadway; Broadway Tower Country Park (6.5km)
Toilets	At start/finish: car park and Broadway town centre; at Broadway Tower Country Park
Public transport	Infrequent buses to local stop and village centre, including bus 1 to Moreton-in-Marsh, where there is a railway station

Shortly after starting the walk, you are sure to be enchanted by the fairy homes that Nick Knight and his family have built at the bottom of their garden, just beside the path!

Just round the corner, preparation for the flood defences led to the excavation of a late Bronze Age/early Iron Age roundhouse settlement with signs of storage platforms and plough furrows. Further finds provide evidence of human habitation over 8000 years. The settlement probably relied on Burhill Fort, about 1km distant, for defence. After the flood defences, a gradual climb affords great views of Broadway and the surrounding valleys.

Welcome shade and total peace prevail in Buckland Wood as a descent brings the route into Broadway Court. From here an ancient trackway, Coneygree Lane, leads up and out onto open fields with tremendous views all the way to Wales.

Broadway Tower Country Park makes a superb pit stop and gives access to its namesake, built in 1798. A rather newer structure, a Cold War nuclear bunker, can also be visited. The walk back down to Broadway is straight and fast, probably in part because of the delights of food and drink that await your stroll along the High Street to complete the walk.

Looking west from the track rising from Coneygree Lane

From the car park on Childswickham Road, turn left, and at the T-junction turn right along Cheltenham Road. Just before the 30mph speed limit marked on the road, take the alleyway on your left. The path runs through the bottom of the gardens where Nick Knight has built fairy homes for walkers' delight. Follow the fenced path around the flood defence across a double-gated entrance to the next gate. Information boards alongside the walk present evidence of human habitation in these fields for over 8000 years.

At the end of the enclosed footpath, turn right across the road and follow the path uphill towards and through Broadway Coppice. Leaving the coppice, bear left through a gate and head straight along the field boundary. A small dogleg through farm gates brings you onto a wide gravel track. Keep along this for 700m until a gate just before a green corrugated shed. Take the left path just in front of the shed.

Follow the boundary of **Buckland Wood** until you come down to an open field and turn left along the fence boundary. Turn right at the next field boundary and head down the next field towards two stiles in the corner. After crossing the stiles, head up the field to a third stile which brings you onto the road, where you turn left. Just before the white gates at the entrance to Broadway Court hamlet, opposite the church, turn right onto Coneygree Lane. At the top of the lane at a junction of tracks, take the right turn.

'Coneygree' means land set aside for a rabbit warren, indicating that the lane led to a rabbit warren, when rabbits were commonly farmed for their meat and fur. The depth of the lane, hedged boundaries and the route it takes between farms suggest it was also probably used later as an important transport route, possibly by drovers.

Ascend through this field, enjoying extensive views. At a junction of paths in front of two sturdy stone gateposts, turn left through the metal gate and uphill. Carry on up the hill passing Rookery Farm. About 50m after the farm, take the footpath on the left.

On entering a picnic area, take the right alongside the barn. Refreshments are available here. Further along, passing another small picnic area on your left with deer willow sculptures, turn left to **Broadway Tower**.

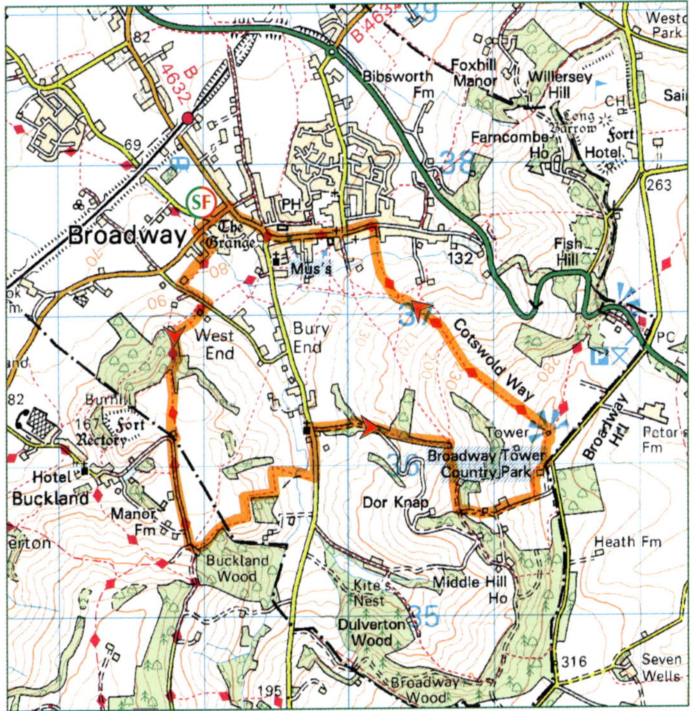

Broadway Tower was built at the end of the 18th century for Lady Coventry. She reputedly said that she wanted to be able to see the beacon on the tower from her other residence, Croome Court (Walk 13), which is 35km (22 miles) away. Over time, the tower has been used for other purposes, such as housing a printing press and as an artist's retreat.

Broadway Tower

Go past the tower and through the black metal fenced gate of the estate; turn left. The wide mown path proceeds straight downhill, back towards Broadway. Keep following the Cotswold Way signs pretty well straight down the hill. The Cotswold Way is a National Trail that runs for 164km (102 miles) from Chipping Campden to Bath.

On reaching the outskirts of **Broadway**, continue through the concrete-surfaced farmyard, down the lane between the houses and turn left towards the High Street. Continue on past lovely buildings, food shops, bars, pubs and hotels, the memorial cross and the green. After the Swan Inn on your right, cross Springfield Lane; you are now leaving the main part of the village. Turn left along Cheltenham Road, then right along Childswickham Road to complete the walk.

WALK 21

Evesham and the River Avon

Start/finish	Evesham railway station (SO 037 444)
Time	2hr 30min
Distance	9.2km (5.7 miles)
Ascent/descent	70m (230ft)
Terrain	A low-level walk that is mainly flat with two minor ascents and descents. A mixture of tarmac, compacted stone path and field paths. No stiles.
Refreshments	Plenty of choice in Evesham; Raphael's Restaurant by the Hampton Ferry
Toilets	In Abbey Park (at 1.3km) and just after the A4184 on the river path (at 2km)
Public transport	Train to Evesham; frequent buses to railway station
Access	Accessible to all-terrain buggies as far as Hampton Ferry (the first 2.9km)
Parking	At start/finish and several other car parks in Evesham

Evesham is built in a loop of the River Avon. The town grew around the monastery, which was founded at the turn of the 8th century and generated significant prosperity. In the 13th century, rebel barons were trying to make the monarchy more accountable, but they were defeated at the Battle of Evesham and their cause was lost. In the 16th century, the monastery was dissolved, and the town's wealth abated.

It was the introduction of the railway in the 19th century that reinvigorated Evesham, as the local farms could now grow perishable crops. As the river was no longer needed for transportation, the locks and weirs were left to deteriorate. However, in the 20th century, volunteers made the river navigable again, boosting tourism.

This walk makes the most of these four facets of the town, visiting the river, religious sites and the battlefield, and starting and finishing at the railway station. First, the route passes through the town and the monastic sites. Coming to the river, it then follows the waterside path all the way around the loop to the north side of the town and the battlefield, before returning to the river for the final leg.

Turn left along the station approach road, and then right onto the main road into Evesham town centre. At the pedestrian crossing after the Royal Oak pub, cross the road and turn right, then left onto the drive through the churchyard, then between the churches and under the bell tower to the river. Turn right to follow the riverside path for just under 3km, passing the **Hampton Ferry** along the way.

Evesham Bell Tower and the Almonry (the building from which alms were distributed) are all that remains of the abbey, which was demolished and the stone reused after the Dissolution of the Monasteries.

Hampton Ferry has been operating across the river since medieval times. The monks who lived in Evesham had vineyards on the slopes of the hill opposite and used the ferry to travel between the two. It is now hand-pulled, using a chain that is lifted above the height of the river at crossing time.

Still following the river, you will pass underneath the **railway viaduct**, then a little later, to the side of a brick shed. After that, follow the permissive path to the right towards an industrial unit. At the **B4624**, dogleg left and then right in front of Ivy Cottage to pass between a meadow and more industrial units. Stay on the path as it turns left between fields.

The path along the river is popular with strollers

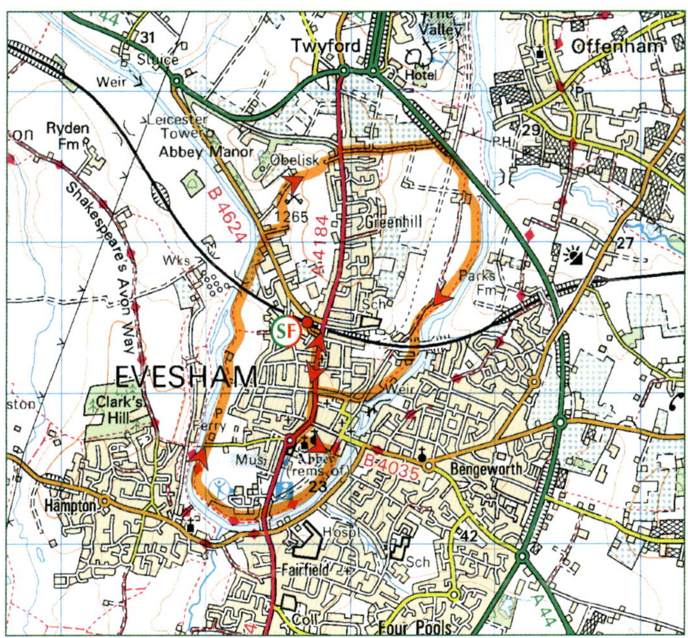

After a while, the path leads to an interpretation board. Continue ahead through the gate and along the clearly defined path up the slope of Greenhill to the far corner of the field, where there is another interpretation board.

THE BATTLE OF EVESHAM

Simon de Montfort, the Earl of Leicester, beat and captured King Henry III and his son Prince Edward at the Battle of Lewes in 1264. De Montfort and his allies ruled England in the king's name. Edward escaped in May 1265 and civil war resumed. The Battle of Evesham was fought on Greenhill on 4 August 1265. It was disastrous for de Montfort and his men. Woefully outnumbered by Prince Edward's army, the battle quickly became a massacre. As a storm raged overhead, blood flowed, and the bodies piled up. Today, the event is commemorated with a beautiful meadow that offers a view across the valley to Bredon Hill.

Evesham battleground was not always this peaceful

Exit through a kissing gate and carry on to the **A4184**. Dogleg left then right along Blayneys Lane and continue in the same direction, first on the lane, then on a footpath, to a junction with another lane. Blayneys Lane was the main road between Oxford and Worcester at the time of the Battle of Evesham.

Cross the lane onto a path that runs parallel to the **A46** along the edge of a field for a short distance before turning right towards Oxstalls Farm. Follow the permissive footpath waymarker left along the drive. Take the first kissing gate on the left into Oxstalls Meadows and fork right to the river. Follow the riverside path, which will eventually pass under the **railway**, over a slipway and past a **weir** and lock.

At the end of the path, turn right up a drive and right again up a residential street. At the T-junction, turn left, still rising. At the brow of the rise, continue ahead to the traffic lights on the main road, where a right turn will complete the route to the **railway station** and car park.

WALK 22

Inkberrow and Abbots Morton

Start/finish	Inkberrow village hall car park (SP 015 578)
Time	2hr 45min
Distance	9.8km (6.1 miles)
Ascent/descent	100m (330ft)
Terrain	Flat to rolling farmland and woods; several farm tracks; several stiles
Refreshments	Several options in Inkberrow
Public transport	Infrequent bus 149 from Worcester
Warning	Cows and bulls graze in these fields at certain times. Parts of the route flood in winter. At the time of writing, the stiles were not all well maintained.

You may find it difficult to leave Inkberrow – the Bull's Head and the Old Bull are opposite each other on the town green, and both are very welcoming. Maybe visit one on the way out and the other on your return?

Moats are dotted through this landscape. Mainly built for defence, some in this area may also have been built as landscape features. You will walk right by the moat at Abbots Morton and another as you return to Inkberrow.

Your journey is through primarily arable fields with some woodland and pasture, enjoying views all the way to the Malvern Hills in the west.

Leaving the village hall car park, turn right onto the road and then turn right onto the main road into Inkberrow. Pass (or drop into) the village store and take the left at the village green opposite the Bull's Head Inn and towards the Old Bull.

The **Bull's Head** was founded in the 1500s, and the **Old Bull** dates back to the 1600s. The latter is thought to have been the stop-off point for William Shakespeare as he was travelling to Worcester to collect his marriage licence to Anne Hathaway.

Turn right down the footpath through the graveyard of **St Peter's Church**, just after the Old Bull. Continue past the steps up to the church and down another 10m, then take the next footbridge on the right. At the next footpath junction, continue straight on.

The Old Bull at Inkberrow, one of two pubs in the village with 'bull' in the name

Descend the steps joining Pepper Street and walk past Ramble Close on the left. The road gently descends, bends right and comes to a T-junction. Turn left. Walk past the deregulation speed limit sign and your footpath is on the corner; take the right-hand path. After the gate, bear left to a gate in the hedge. Through this, keep the hedge on your left, then at the next field boundary turn right and go up the hill, still with a hedge on your left.

Continue through the field boundary straight across the crop field. On intersecting the corner of the hedge, continue with it on your right-hand side, straight on to the next gap. Take a very short left, then right through the main gap in the hedge. The next section of footpath heads off across the fields just slightly left of a small oak. Exit the field at the boundary with a gate into the next field and continue with the hedge on your left.

Turn right at the end of this short field for 10m and then turn left, climbing over the stile into the small woodland. At a junction of small paths, bear right and down to a footbridge over the **Piddle Brook**.

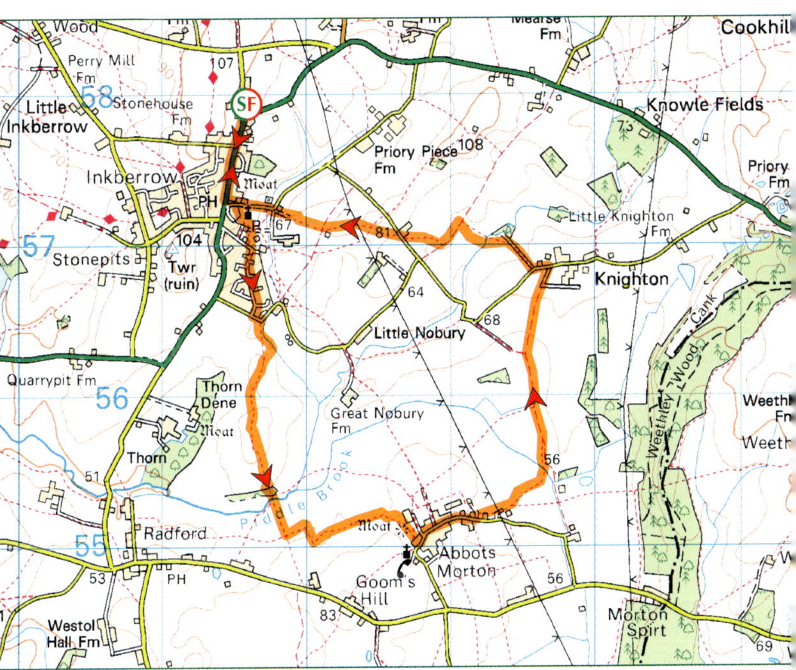

You are now entering **Long Meadow Nature Reserve**, which floods in winter. It is managed with a hay cut in July and grazing through the autumn months. Flowers include Green Burnet, Adder's-tongue Fern and Green-winged Orchid, and the meadow is also home to the Brown Hairstreak butterfly.

The footpath continues straight across the field in the direction of the large farmhouse. As you see the stile straight ahead, turn left to the left-hand corner of the field, to cross the stile in the hedge line. Once over, bear slightly left following the hedge, and as the hedge line turns right continue following it.

At the first post-and-wire fence with partial hedge boundary, go through the gap and turn left. Head for the first large oak tree in the next field, pass it and continue to the hedge, to cross the small footbridge and bear slightly left across the next field.

After crossing the stile, follow the farm track bearing off to the right and towards the buildings; keep to the field boundaries if cows with calves are in the field. The route passes a **moat**, the earthworks of which can still be seen. This moat once surrounded the country retreat for the Abbots of Evesham Abbey. After exiting the field near the church, turn left and walk through the village of **Abbots Morton**.

Walk past the 30mph sign, then the red postbox, then take the footpath on the left. Climb the stile and turn diagonally right to the corner of the hedge. From there, follow the hedge to the gate in the fence line. Continue along the field boundary on your right-hand side to the next field gate. Through this, turn left and follow the field boundary. Cross the footbridge and stile. Cross directly ahead to the field boundary and then turn left and continue with the hedge on your right.

Through the gate in the hedge on your right, turn left onto the farm track. Go through the gate and bear right, following the hedge boundary. A stunning 200 to 300-year-old oak projects over the path. Follow the field boundary to a gap in the right-hand corner, pass through and turn left. After a short distance, join a gravel track at Knighton Farm on the edge of **Knighton**. Turn left, then left along the lane. After 30m, take the public footpath on the right, along a wide farm track.

You might see **Alpacas** in this field. These curious animals originate from the Altiplano plateau in South America, which sits at almost 4000m above sea level. Until the conquistadors arrived, they were farmed for their fleeces, but the Spanish had other ideas and replaced many with sheep. During the next 450 years, Alpacas were only farmed as subsistence livestock for indigenous people. However, the Victorian industrialist, Sir Titus Salt, devised a process that turned their fleece into a luxurious fibre. This is one of the reasons Alpacas are so popular for smallholdings now. Another is the calm aura they exude.

Where the track bears right, your path bears left across the field. Head for the gate left of the telegraph poles, cross the ford and then walk along the field, with the hedge on your left. At the intersection of paths with a broad grass sward in front of you and arable field ahead, turn left. Go through the next field boundary onto a track with hedges on both sides. After 30m, turn right through a narrow gap in the hedge to find a path cutting across the arable field, heading diagonally left towards the farm buildings in the distance.

Step over the stile, walk straight across the road and step over the next stile. The path crosses this field diagonally right. Aim to pass right of the second pylon in view by about 30m. As you draw in line with the pylon, you'll see the gate in the middle of the hedge, directly ahead. Cross the two stiles and then note the stile directly across the field ahead. Cross two further stiles here. Then bear slightly left towards the summit of this field. From this viewpoint, you can see

Perry Field Farm and the church on the edge of Inkberrow. The Malvern Hills are in the far distance.

Descend the hill, crossing a bridleway, and continue to the metal gate in the lower corner. Turn right and follow the field track upslope and then downslope to join a minor road. Turn right, then a quick left. After crossing the small stream, look out for the **moat** on the right, part of the Inkberrow Millennium Green.

The **moat** is estimated to be about 800 years old and perhaps formed a landscape feature in a manorial farming complex, rather than having been built for defence. The site also has ridges and furrows that were created when oxen were used to plough the fields in strips in medieval times.

Continue uphill into **Inkberrow**, walking past the church, past (or into) the Old Bull and then retracing your steps to the right up the High Street and left at Sands Road to the village hall car park.

The moat at Abbots Morton

WALK 23

Grafton Flyford Hairstreak Butterfly Trail

Start/finish	St John the Baptist Church, Grafton Flyford (SO 962 557)
Time	3hr
Distance	11km (6.9 miles)
Ascent/descent	100m (320ft)
Terrain	Gentle slopes, woodland and field paths. Some quiet lanes. Some parts of the path are overgrown in summer but passable.
Parking	At start/finish. This car park belongs to the church – please consider leaving a donation to cover its upkeep.

Peace and quiet with acres of Worcestershire fields and woodland. This is where butterflies flutter by in goodly number, where birdsong is the loudest sound. This is also an area of long history as evidenced by some of the ancient tracks on this route, such as Black Pit Lane.

The first village the route visits is Himbleton, home of a 12th-century church, which is reached by crossing the line of a past stream bed. The church houses a wall painting of the coat of arms of Elizabeth I, one of only two examples in the country.

Next, Earl's Common and a jaunt across more butterfly country. Excellent specimens of pollarded willows can be admired just before joining ancient tracks on part of the Grafton Wood perimeter and then plunging into the haven of the wood itself, a nature reserve hosting the rare butterfly after which this walk is named – the Brown Hairstreak. For a chance to see a Brown Hairstreak butterfly, this walk is best done in July or early October.

The car park runs along the west side of the church. The 14th-century tower has an embattled parapet, within which is an unusual short stone spire. Exit the car park at the north end (opposite the entrance) and turn right along the farm track. A short distance later, take the footpath over the stile on the left, just after the little pond.

After the second stile, head diagonally right across the field and downhill. At the end of the field turn left over a footbridge among the trees, just before a remnant red brick wall. Turn right onto the road. Pass **Rectory Farm**, then, after a

Seasonal stream course on approach to Himbleton Church

THE LIVING FOSSIL

A Ginkgo Biloba tree is growing beside the first stile of this route, just after the little pond. It is an unusual tree and is sometimes referred to as a 'living fossil' because recognisable forms of it date back to the Permian period – some 270 million years ago. The tree grows well in ground that is both well watered and well drained, and it is relatively shade intolerant. It can grow to a height of 20–35m and is often deeply rooted. It is also said to have many health benefits – rich in antioxidants, it may help reduce inflammation and benefit heart, brain, and eye health – but can also make you very ill.

further 350m, turn left at the first road junction. Continue on this lane for 1km, through a right, gentle left and then a right-hand curve. Take the bridlepath on your right. Follow the path straight ahead all the way to New House Farm. This section is an old sunken track called Black Pit Lane. It can be rather overgrown in summer, although still accessible.

Black Pit Lane after the B-road near Huddington Hill Farm

Join the road at New House Farm and continue straight on to **Neight Hill**. At the T-junction, turn left. After a dozen paces, take the footpath through the gate on your right. Continue beside house gardens for a short length and turn right on meeting the road. At a junction of footpaths with the road, go left over the footbridge to **Himbleton Church**. Take the footpath diagonally left across the meadow.

Return to the road by the same route, crossing straight over. Take a diagonal route across the field, to a gate about two-thirds of the way along the boundary. On joining the road, turn right and continue through the small hamlet of **Earl's Common** to a T-junction opposite a parish council noticeboard; turn right. At a sign to the house 'Brackenfield', turn right onto the house drive.

Follow the drive and take the footpath on the right, just before the gates. After the second gate around the house, turn left, following the left-hand field boundary to the first stile. Over this, head towards the metal gate straight on. Next is a kissing gate; go through and then cross the field on a diagonal to the far right corner junction of the field boundaries. At the gate, go through and follow the left-hand boundary alongside the beautifully managed oak woodland.

In this **woodland**, the mature trees are growing straight and tall. This indicates a dense planting in early years with subsequent thinning (removal of weaker trees over time). As thinning takes place, an understorey, mainly of Hazel, is encouraged. Some deadwood is left in situ for biodiversity gains.

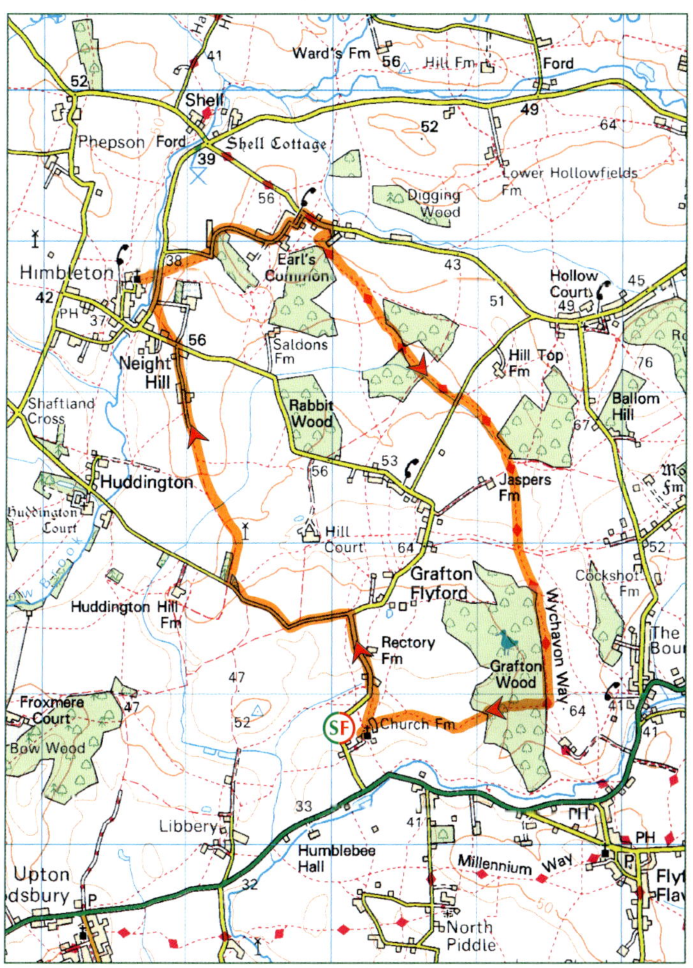

Go through the gap between the woodlands and turn right, following the right-hand boundary to the next boundary hedge. Pass through the kissing gate, then follow the path across the field. Cross over the country lane and onto the path slightly left of your entry point to the lane. Continue straight on across the next field, close to the field boundary. Go through the gate, noting to your right a seasonal stream route marked by willows. Head to the diagonal left-hand edge of the line of pollarded willows.

Pollarding is a pruning system involving the removal of the upper branches of a tree, which promotes the growth of a dense head of foliage and branches. This process provides wood and material for animal fodder. Willow was used for animal ailments and is the source for aspirin. Young growth can be easily planted to increase shelterbelts and future wood provision as well as being used to weave baskets and mats. More mature trees can be used to make cricket bats.

Cross the footbridge, pass through the gap in the hedge line, and you'll see a marker diagonally across the next small field. Cross another footbridge, go through the gate and follow closely the right-hand field boundary with its magnificent, mature oaks.

Go through the gap in the fence line into a large meadow. You're looking to traverse this meadow on a diagonal, heading for the dead elm in the far distance. At the gate with the dead elm in close proximity, go diagonally across the field to the left of the elm.

The path through Grafton Wood

The landmark dead elm

On reaching the corner of **Grafton Wood**, proceed into the next field with the wood boundary on your right-hand side. Go over the next two stiles on the edge of the woodland. The path enters a thick hedge line and then emerges into a field of thistle, oak, scrub and Dog Rose. Bearing right, you will find the remnants of a post-and-wire fence line, just inside the main wood. Follow this boundary until you find a gate in the fence line. Go through the gate, turn left to continue on your southerly bearing to follow the path along the edge of the main wood.

At a junction of tracks, on the right is the Worcestershire Wildlife Trust welcome sign to Grafton Wood Nature Reserve. Take this path into the wood and follow it straight through the wood on a gentle descent.

Grafton Wood is managed to retain a healthy population of Brown Hairstreak butterflies. This butterfly spends most of its time high up in the trees and particularly favours Ash. Females can be seen in July and early October, laying eggs on Blackthorn. Volunteers have been clearing areas to permit more sunlight to reach the woodland floor, and have planted many new Ash and Blackthorn.

Leave the wood on the western edge by the Grafton Wood Nature Reserve sign and information board. Cross a wooden footbridge and then find your path, bearing left, across the field. You can just see the gap in the hedge. On reaching this gap you can now see the church where you started. Follow the boundary and paths to the **farm** and then the car park at the **church**. There is a seat in the graveyard, just right for a last snack before moving on.

WALK 24

Droitwich Spa and Hanbury Hall

Start/finish	Droitwich Spa Lido long-stay car park (SO 901 632)
Time	4hr 15min
Distance	16.2km (10 miles)
Ascent/descent	120m (395ft)
Terrain	Varied – tarmac, stone track, meadow, field and woodland paths, towpath, mown paths. Can be overgrown in places. Several stiles – not dog-friendly.
Refreshments	Café at lido at start/finish; Barley Mow on re-entering Droitwich; plenty of other options in the town
Toilets	At start/finish: open 8am–6pm in summer and until 4pm in winter
Public transport	Train to Droitwich Spa (about 1km from start); frequent buses to Queen Street

A gentle walk around the pastoral landscape to the east of Droitwich Spa. This walk starts in a city park, crosses pasture, meadows, arable fields and formal parkland, dives into woodland, and follows the canal. There are no big hills or grand views, but there are plenty of opportunities to enjoy the varied habitats and wildlife of this part of Worcestershire. Look out for dragonflies, butterflies and birds along the canal and a wide variety of insect life in the meadows. And, as the route passes the National Trust's Hanbury Hall, it would be easy to combine a visit if you are so inclined.

From the car park, head into the park, with the lido and then the tennis courts on your left. Stay on the tarmac path as it crosses the park.

Look left as you walk through the park and you will see the edge of **St Peter's Fields**, a pine and conifer arboretum that offers an extension to the park. As the name suggests, it used to be a series of agricultural fields. They were sold to the town in 1951 for a mere 10 shillings.

When the path reaches a lane, continue ahead, passing St Peter's Manor on your right. At the end of the lane, the path curves to the left, and then the route continues on the far side of the road along a tarmac footpath.

This leads to a housing estate. Continue straight ahead to cross two streets diagonally and turn into Cherry Close. At the end, turn left on a path between houses that crosses another street and continues in the same direction, soon turning to the right behind gardens. Just before reaching a road, take the path to the left, then turn left under the **M5**.

On the far side, stay on the bridlepath, heading diagonally right. The path remains clearly defined as it crosses a **golf course**. With the roof of the clubhouse in view, the path deviates from the track by forking left and soon crosses the course. Beware golfers teeing off on your right. Continue to the right of some houses. Through a kissing gate, continue ahead past a wide metal gate. Stay to the left around more of the golf course. Past the sign for hole 7, turn right, this time on a woodland path along the edge of the course. Follow it as it swings left at hole 8. Past the tee at hole 9, cross the bridge and turn left, passing to the left of the wind turbine.

Turn right at the lane, and as it bends to the right, turn left. Stay ahead to walk around the painted cottage, soon turning right between hedges and across two hayfields, each with the next gate visible when you enter. After the second, continue ahead on a drive, with a **canal** on your left. At the end, turn left to cross the canal and then turn left under the bridge to continue with the canal on your right.

Flowers on the golf course

The combination of water and canalside vegetation makes this a vibrant habitat for butterflies, dragonflies and birds.

You will soon reach a fence with a sluice. Turn left here over a stile into a field. Head diagonally right, towards steps leading up to the **railway line**. At the base of the steps, turn left, then right under the bridge. After that, head diagonally right to the narrow gate, which is several metres to the right of the field gate. For the next 700m, the narrow (and in places, overgrown) path follows a thin strip of scrubby woodland.

When you reach a footbridge, turn left without crossing. You will shortly reach another gate. Continue to the right in front of the gate. This path leads to a stile. Cross this and rise to a pair of large ponds. Turn right, cross the land between the ponds and take the metal gate. Walk around the left side of the second pond.

This is **Goosehill Lane Fishery**. Look out for Grey Herons dodging the need for a ticket! Although they do mainly eat fish, Grey Herons sometimes prey on other animals, too, for example frogs and ducklings. If you see one in a harvested field, it could be hunting for mice.

Pass through the next wide metal gate, and now keep the woodland on your left until you reach a road. Cross and squeeze through the kissing gate on the far side. The route heads diagonally left across the meadow to another kissing gate, just to the left of the first oak tree in the hedge line.

In the next field, take a diagonal left to a field gate. Turn right onto the farm track and follow this for 400m. Look for a metal hand gate on the left to continue through a narrow strip of trees. Turn right past a house, then through a band of trees. Just before the second house, cross the pasture diagonally left to a field gate visible through the trees. Through this, head to and through the next gate, which is between the oak tree and the house. From there, it is a diagonal left to the end of the house's drive and lane.

Turn right along the lane. After some time, you will reach a T-junction with another lane. Head left along this until it meets the **B4090** (Salt Way) at **Mere Green**. Cross and continue ahead on another minor lane.

A few metres before the bend warning sign, take a left up some steps and over a stile. Turn right to follow the hedge around the edge of the field until the clearly defined path strikes out across the field to a waymark post on the far side. Cross the stile and then head towards the black-and-white house.

Turn left along the lane in front of the house, and then right immediately past its drive. Cross the bridge and take the clearly defined path across the middle of the arable field, approximately following the power lines. Continue to follow the

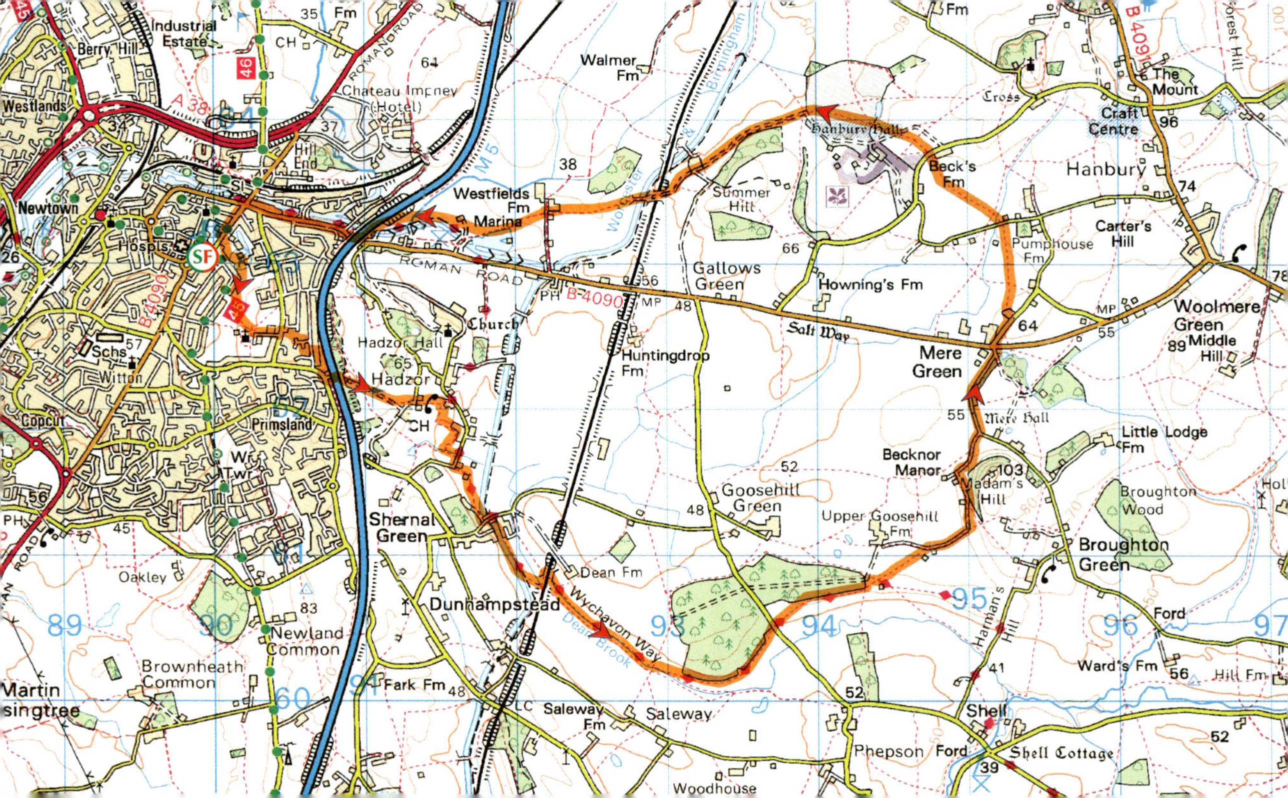

Industrial Estate
Berry Hill
Westlands
Newtown
Hospl
Schs
Witton
Copcut
Primsland
Chateau Impney (Hotel)
Hill End
A 38
M5
ROMAN ROAD
Walmer Fm
Westfields Fm
Marina
Summer Hill
Hanbury Hall
Beck's Fm
Cross
The Mount
Craft Centre
Hanbury
B 4091
Forest Hill
Carter's Hill
Pumphouse Fm
Gallows Green
Howning's Fm
Woolmere Green
Middle Hill
Salt Way
Mere Green
Mere Hall
Little Lodge Fm
B 4090
Church
Hadzor Hall
Hadzor
Huntingdrop Fm
Becknor Manor
Adam's Hill
Broughton Wood
Broughton Green
Goosehill Green
Upper Goosehill Fm
Shernal Green
Dean Fm
Wychavon Way
Dean Brook
Dunhampstead
Harman's Hill
Ford
Ward's Fm
Hill Fm
Oakley
Newland Common
Brownheath Common
Martin
singtree
Park Fm
Saleway Fm
Saleway
Woodhouse
Phepson
Shell
Shell Cottage
Birmingham
Worcester
SF

Hanbury Hall from the route

power lines across the next field. Over the next stile, the route turns right along the fence and to the left of the buildings of **Beck's Farm** to a road.

Cross and continue ahead through a narrow strip of woodland, over a stile and onto National Trust land. The route continues ahead, passing **Hanbury Hall** on the left and crossing several avenues of trees.

> **Hanbury Hall**, built in 1701, was the country retreat of the Vernon family. In 1705, formal gardens were added. As fashions changed, they were removed but have now been faithfully restored by the National Trust. Both the house and gardens are open to visitors.

After a while, the path leads to a kissing gate. Immediately beyond this, take the left fork, then continue on a mown path in approximately the same direction. Eventually, this leads to a stile. Cross and continue straight ahead, along the side of a field and then skirting Summerhill Wood. The path turns into a track, which will lead you to the left side of Summerhill Farm.

Past the farm, continue ahead through a gate. Keep the field boundary on your left until reaching another field gate. Through the gate, turn right along the edge of the field and then over the **railway bridge**. Continue in the same direction over the **canal**, and on to pass Westfields Farm on your right and a house on your left.

Through a gate, cross the farm drive and into the field ahead. The route of the path is clear, crossing the field diagonally to the left. Keep the water on your left as you pass the **marina**, then continue ahead over an access road to the **canal** itself. Turn right and follow the canal down a series of locks with the water on your left.

From Roman times, water from this area's briny natural springs was drawn into salt pans and left to evaporate, leaving the salt behind. The Victorians built the **Droitwich Canal** to transport the salt to the River Severn at Gloucester. When the motorway was built, the canal was filled in, then was reopened in 2011, this time for recreational purposes.

Nearing the M5, the towpath rises and crosses the canal. Turn right when it reaches the road and walk under the **motorway bridge**. At the mini roundabout, continue ahead. Before too long, you'll see the **canal** on your right. Rejoin the towpath and continue along the canal. After passing the Barley Mow pub on your left, the towpath passes underneath a low road bridge. Immediately afterwards, turn left up to street level and continue ahead to return to the car park at **Droitwich Lido**, where you began.

A flight of locks on the Droitwich Canal

WALK 25

Bordesley Abbey Meadows and Arrow Lake

Start/finish	Forge Mill Needle Museum (SP 045 686)
Alt start/finish	Arrow Valley Visitor Centre (SP 062 677)
Time	1hr 45min (Abbey Walk 1hr, Lake Walk 45min)
Distance	7km (4.3 miles) (Abbey Walk 3.5km, Lake Walk 2.5km)
Ascent/descent	15m (50ft)
Terrain	Mainly stone paths, mown grass paths and tarmac; some woodland paths
Refreshments	Kiosk with indoor and outdoor seating at Forge Mill Needle Museum; café and kiosk at Arrow Lake Visitor Centre
Toilets	At Forge Mill Needle Museum and Arrow Valley Visitor Centre when they are open
Public transport	Infrequent buses from Redditch to Abbey Stadium stop
Access	The whole walk is accessible for all-terrain buggies. The Lake Walk is wheelchair accessible.
Parking	At both start/finish options

A wedge of green space splits Redditch clean in two. This green lung offers a lush and wildlife-rich setting for a walk. The route starts by passing the remains of Bordesley Abbey and crossing the surrounding meadows, before heading south along a stream that once powered a paper mill, to circumnavigate Arrow Valley Lake. Although there is a background hum of traffic, in most places it is birdsong that dominates the soundscape. The meadows put on a good show of wildflowers, which provide food for insects and birds, and the streams and lake provide the perfect habitat for different species.

As a figure-of-eight walk, this route can easily be split into two, referred to in the description as the Abbey Walk and the Lake Walk.

Walk down the length of the car park towards the Forge Mill Needle Museum and turn left immediately in front of the main gates. This will take you over a bridge and into Bordesley Abbey Meadows.

Needles have been manufactured in Redditch since the 16th century. In the 17th century, watermills such as Forge Mill started to be used to polish the needles, and by the end of the 18th century, thousands of people were employed in the industry in this area. By the 19th century, Redditch was the global centre of needle-making, producing 90% of the world's needles. You can learn more about the history and process, and sometimes even see the waterwheel in action, at Forge Mill Needle Museum.

Continue ahead, ascending gently, to the abbey gate, where the stone path ends. The abbey is free to visit and accessible via a kissing gate on this section of the walk.

An **abbey** stood on this spot for 400 years. When the land was granted to the Cistercian order in 1138, the monks had to drain the surrounding land and divert the River Arrow before they could build. It was a grand church, funded by the income from 20 farms. In 1538, the abbey was demolished as part of the Dissolution of the Monasteries.

Continue on a mown grass path, with the abbey fence on your right. At a gate, turn left to pass the pond on your right. This is one of the medieval fishponds that were used to provide the monks with fresh protein.

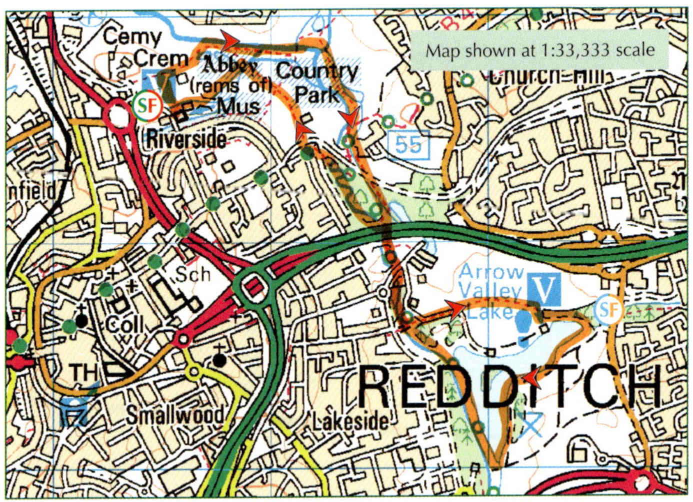

The monks' fishpond

At a junction of mown paths a few paces later, stay ahead with the embankment on your right, and then head along the left edge of the meadow. Once you reach the stone path, take the kissing gate, then cross a bridge to head left around the edge of another meadow.

At the end of the meadow, follow the path to the left and over three small bridges. Just before the path bends to the left under power lines, turn right over another bridge. This section of the path runs between a lake on the left and a stream on the right.

The **lake** once provided a head of water to power the paper mill on this site. It is likely that the water was also used in the process of papermaking.

At a junction with a cycle track, stay ahead on what is now a tarmac path. Turn left just before a road bridge. At the road, turn left and then, after 100m, turn right between metal bollards to a meadow. Turn left on a mown path under trees along its edge. On meeting a tarmac path, follow it under the **A4023 road bridge**. To shorten the route to just the Abbey Walk, turn right on the tarmac path.

At a minor road, cross and continue ahead. You have a choice between the tarmac path and a woodland path that runs parallel to it; both meet again at a crosspaths. Turn left for a short distance to meet Proctors Barn Lane. Turn right onto the lane until it bends to the right. Take the narrow woodland path to the left of the car park entrance. This emerges at the **Arrow Valley Visitor Centre**. This is where the Lake Walk starts.

During the **Covid-19 pandemic**, one of the local residents started to leave rocks painted with encouraging messages along her street. Others noticed and added to the line until it was 7000 stones long. A thousand of these were placed into a rainbow shape and protected with Perspex in a sculpture near the visitor centre, to remind us of the pain of the pandemic, the bravery of key workers and the way the community supported each other, even when they were unable to meet in person.

Turn left in front of the visitor centre gates on a tarmac path and follow it around **Arrow Valley Lake**, keeping the water on your right, for just over 1km to the junction of paths at the far end. Turn right to continue around the lake to another junction of paths. To complete the Lake Walk, turn right and follow the tarmac path back to the visitor centre.

To complete the full walk, continue ahead, leaving the lakeside. Another woodland path to the left runs parallel to the tarmac path. Follow either to a junction of paths and continue ahead, again taking the woodland path option if you prefer. At the lane, cross and continue on the tarmac path to pass back underneath the **A4023**. You are now back on the Abbey Walk.

Stay on the tarmac path along the side of a meadow. At the next junction, stay left, first with a stream on your left and then over a bridge. Keep the gardens on your left, and you will soon reach Seymour Drive. Turn right, cross Park Way and follow the path between hedges, which returns you to Bordesley Abbey Meadows.

Pass through two kissing gates and take the path diagonally across the meadow to a brick bridge. After crossing, turn left onto a stone path. Follow the same path until it passes the remains of **Bordesley Abbey** and **Forge Mill Needle Museum** and reaches the bridge back to the car park.

The remains of Bordesley Abbey

WALK 26

Lickey Hills and Worcester and Birmingham Canal

Start/finish	Barnt Green railway station (SP 006 737)
Time	4hr 30min
Distance	15.3km (9.5 miles)
Ascent/descent	290m (960ft)
Terrain	Varied paths through field and woodland, tracks, canal towpath and small sections of road
Refreshments	Several options in Barnt Green; Westmead Hotel (5.7km); Hopwood House pub (7.8km)
Toilets	Lickey Hills Visitor Centre during opening hours (2.1km)
Public transport	Trains to Barnt Green; infrequent bus 145 from Droitwich
Parking	At start/finish
Warning	The route crosses two main roads. The path after the Lickey Hills emerges straight onto a fast road with trees obscuring the view.

The trees of Lickey Hills Country Park are exceptional. Huge oaks, some easily 300 years old, coppiced chestnuts left to then grow to maturity, tall and massive beeches – the list goes on. Further surprises emerge at the visitor centre itself, including a robbery hoard and a World War 1 howitzer testing range with munition rounds from the 1830s. Drag yourself away for a walk across agricultural fields with views of the Upper Bittell Reservoir (a water supply for the canal), and then along the canal itself.

A very tall road bridge leads over the Worcester and Birmingham Canal to the entry to the waterway beside the Wast Hill Tunnel, along which the canal travels for over 2km, on its way into the very centre of Birmingham. The canalside stretch of the route is in a cutting, mystical and quiet, perfect for a relaxing and enjoyable walk.

Leave the railway station on the north-west side. Cross the road and head straight up into Lickey Hills Country Park, directly ahead of you, soon finding yourself among magnificent straight and tall oaks.

As you progress, note the mature multi-stem **Sweet Chestnuts**, coppiced over 100 years ago but then left to grow. Coppicing is the low-level cutting of a

The entrance to Lickey Hills Country Park

tree to encourage multi-stem new growth, which produces straight rods for uses such as house frames, fencing material and gateposts.

Maintain direction on the widest footpath heading north-west until the first right-hand curve going downhill. Follow this, then after a while the path flattens and crosses a stream. After the stream, turn left uphill. As the path flattens out again, merge with a track from the right. Now continue straight on the main path, going towards the **visitor centre**.

If you have time, enjoy the displays and stories in the **visitor centre**. Exhibits include a shell from the nearby Bilberry Hill Gun Proof Range, where field guns were tested after being refurbished in World War 1, and a bag of plunder found hidden underneath a Rhododendron bush!

Drop down from the visitor centre. Opposite the path to the play area, take a path going uphill beside a magnificent oak and the third bench down from the visitor centre. On reaching the path just before the car park, turn right. Take the path leaving the bottom of the lower car park area as it turns into the woodland underneath a beech. Descend the path for a short distance and as it flattens, note the log steps descending on your left towards the **B4120**. Take this path. **Warning:** The path emerges to fast traffic on a road corner with poor visibility. Please take care.

Fork right just before the road, and cross the road to the footpath directly opposite. Follow this path along the back of housing on the edge of **Cofton Hackett**, alongside fields. Maintain your course to a gate. Cross the small track into the field opposite and head downslope, turning right at the woodland boundary.

On reaching Cofton Church Lane, turn left and pass under the **railway line**. At the road junction, continue straight ahead to **Cofton Richards Farm**. Just before the Cofton security sign at the farm, take a path heading off to the right with security fencing alongside it. Keep the field boundary on the left as you enter the arable crop field.

There are views of the **Upper Bittell Reservoir** below. Both the Upper and Lower Bittell Reservoirs were constructed to store water for the canal system, rather than for drinking water. Although the canals don't flow in the traditional sense, they lose water every time a boat passes through a lock and therefore need to be topped up. The reservoirs are also now used for fishing and sailing.

After passing under the second set of overhead lines, take the footpath that turns right towards the end of Upper Bittell Reservoir. After the gate, turn right along the field boundary, following the wood fringe boundary to the **reservoir**, emerging through a gate into pasture. Follow the right-hand boundary and then head for the gate in the left-hand corner of the field.

Follow the gravel track past the house, caravan and farm to the **A441**. Turn right and cross the road (when safe to do so) into Lea End Lane adjacent to **Westmead Hotel**. Follow the lane to the canal. Cross the tall canal bridge and turn left along the road, then turn left downhill to the Wast Hill Tunnel entrance.

Walk along the canal with the water on your right, passing under bridge 67 and then past **Hopwood House pub** on the **A441**, continuing for just over 1km to bridge 66. Leave the canal here, crossing the bridge over the canal and walking uphill into **Bittell Farm**. Turn right on the gravel track midway between the farm buildings. The footpath has been diverted to the right here. Turn left up the slope

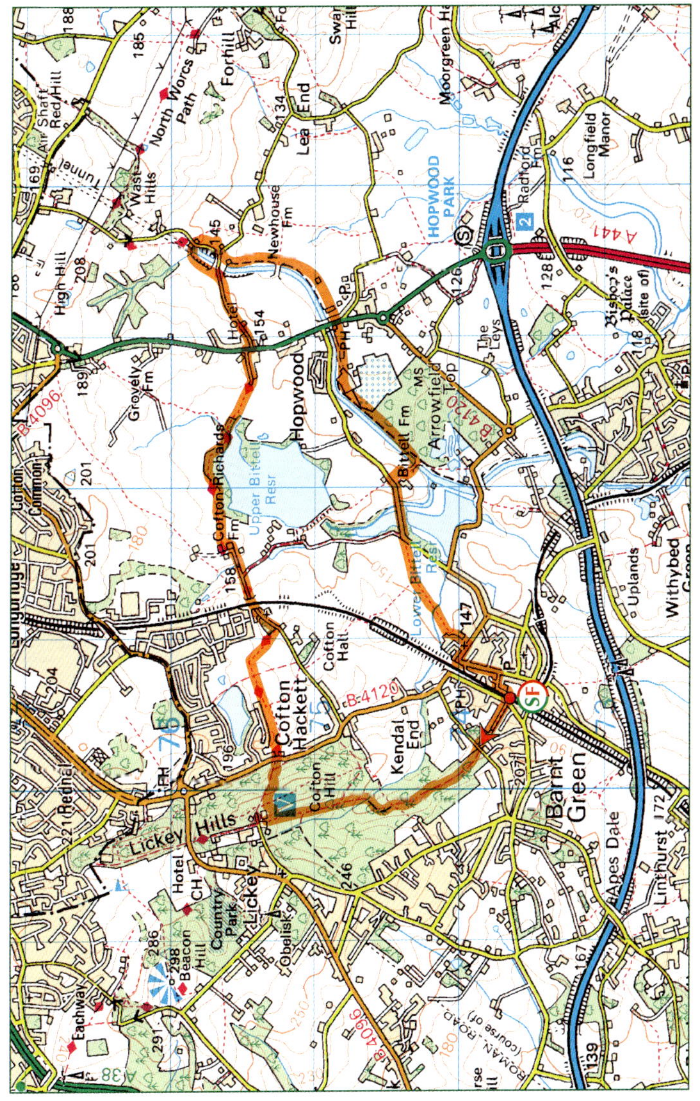

Forhill
North Worcs Path
Lea End
Moorgreen Hall
Longfield Manor
Radford Fm
Wast Hills
Tunnel
Air Shaft
Red Hill
High Hill
Newhouse Fm
HOPWOOD PARK
A441
Hopwood
Grovely Fm
Bittell Fm
Arrowfield Top
The Leys
Bishop's Palace (site of)
B4120
B4096
Cofton Common
Longbridge
Cofton Richards Fm
Upper Bittell Resr
Lower Bittell Resr
Uplands
Withybed Green
Cofton Hall
Cofton Hackett
Kendal End
Rednal
Cofton Hill
Lickey Hills
Barnt Green
Apes Dale
Linthurst
Hotel
Country Park
Lickey
Obelisk
Beacon Hill
Eachway
A38
ROMAN ROAD (course of)

A bridge on the Worcester and Birmingham Canal

in between rows of vehicles and caravans. Cross the stile to meet the road. Turn left and follow the left-hand side of the road down the hill to cross an embankment that splits **Upper and Lower Bittell Reservoirs**.

After crossing the embankment, the road bends to the left and the route continues straight ahead. Go through the gate, then head diagonally left across the field with a small copse and pond on your right.

Go through the first gate, keeping the field boundary on your right-hand side. Take the gate at the end of the field across the footbridge and carry straight on through the wood. On entering the sports field, keep to the right-hand side. Leaving the sports field, turn right in front of the **Baptist church** and take your next left-hand turn onto Hewell Road, signposted to Barnt Green Station. The **railway station** where you began is at the end of Station Approach. The local shops are just a short distance past the station.

WALK 27

Clent Hills

Start/finish	Car park on Adam's Hill, Clent (SO 926 798)
Time	3hr 15min
Distance	9.7km (6 miles)
Ascent/descent	310m (1020ft)
Terrain	Initial moderate climb, followed by varied paths and short sections of road
Refreshments	Café at start/finish and Nimmings Wood (2.5km); Vine Inn on Vine Lane (8.9km)
Toilets	Nimmings Wood car park (2.5km)

This is a walk of quiet woodland, nice climbs, great views. There are welcome places along the route for drinks and food. You will visit Clent Hills Country Park, enter under the carved arch, decide how old the oldest tree in the woods is and meet with the Four Stones on the summit. Is this a Stone Age monument or a more recent addition?

You also have Walton Hill to summit, and on the descent you can see all the way to Birmingham – a view from a quiet hill to the second largest city in the UK! After country lanes, there is a chance to drop by the Vine Inn, which started business as a pub in 1836. Prior to this it was a watermill.

The unusual, secretive hamlets of Walton Pool and Dark Pool hint at times past and changing circumstance – from active manufacturing to quiet village life. And on your return, well, the café is still open!

At the starting car park, you have the Four Stones café for coffee and brunch nice start! From the car park, head straight up the hill through the gates and turn left after the old pub (now closed). Go past the old toilet block (also now closed), following the main path to the right and uphill. At a junction of paths with a bench seat on your right, drop down on the path on your left. Follow this contour path through varied woodland.

You will come to a sharp curve to the right in the footpath by a grove of beech trees. Turn right. After 25m turn left. As you approach the lower path, with deer-fencing ahead of you, turn right. At the junction with the track to Clent Hills Lodge on the edge of the woods, join the track bearing right.

ROE DEER

Sometimes seen in the woodland of Clent Hills, Roe Deer is the most common species native to the UK, although rare in the Midlands. It is mainly brown, with short antlers, no tail and a buff rump. In summer, they tend to be solitary, although they form loose-knit groups in winter. The males start growing their antlers, which tend to have three points, in November. By spring, they are ready to shed the velvet, and mating (rutting) happens in the summer. Although mating occurs in summer the fertilised egg does not implant and grow until the new year, so that their young are not born until the weather has warmed up. Meanwhile, the males drop their antlers in autumn, ready to regrow them over winter for the following mating season.

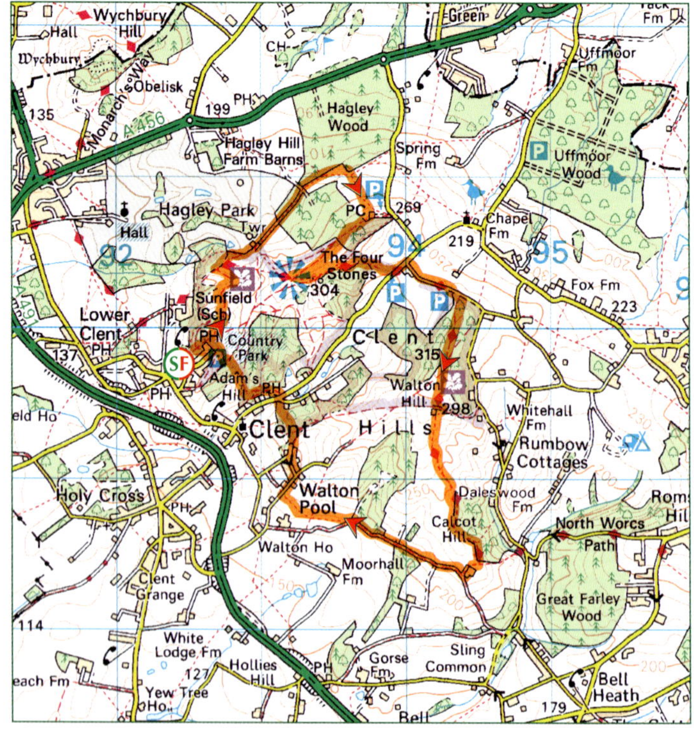

The route passes through several woods that flank the hills

At Clent Hills Lodge you can see the tower of **Hagley Park's folly castle**, built in the 18th century. The Gothic Revival castle is rectangular with a round tower at each corner and was built to look like a ruin.

Continue along the flat track until it goes left downhill. Keep on straight ahead, crossing the stile into pasture with the woodland boundary on your left. Cross the next stile, go through the gate and take the path directly up the hill towards another woodland. Go through the two gates either side of the small woodland (Stu's Spinney) across the field into the **car park**, where there is a toilet block and café. This is Nimmings Wood National Trust car park.

Take the path going out of the picnic area and zigzagging slightly above. Head right into the woodland. Then, after a few metres, pass under the welcome arch to the Clent Hills Country Park. Continue along the widest track up to an information board about the oldest trees on the Clent Hills, estimated to be 250 years of age. Carry on up to the panorama display, then turn left uphill to the **four standing stones**.

Unusually, the **Four Stones** are on the very summit of the hill, and they have been in situ for only 300 years. From here, you can see the obelisk and the castle tower we passed earlier. The Hagley Obelisk (also known as the Wychbury Obelisk and locally as Wychbury Monument) stands close to the summit of Wychbury Hill in Hagley. It was built in the 18th century by order of Sir Richard Lyttleton.

With the Four Stones on your right, take the track heading downhill (north-east). After approximately 25m, take the first fork in the track to the right, descending through the woods, until you emerge at a gate beside a small **car park**. Turn left onto the road, then right at the signpost for Walton Hill. At the large **car park area**, take the right-hand path into the woods, followed immediately by a left through the gate into Walton Hill Wood (National Trust).

On reaching the triangulation pillar on **Walton Hill**, take the left footpath downhill. At the junction of paths in front of the white building (Waltonhill Farm), turn left. Take the path on the right to go around the farm and keep along this track, following the wire fence boundary heading down the side of the spur. Cross the stile marked North Worcestershire Path (Walk 30) and continue down.

Exit the beautiful woodland through the gate into a field, with wide views ahead. Then turn right underneath the superb Ash tree and go through the next gate. Walk around Calcothill Farm, keeping the buildings on your left. On reaching the junction of tracks, turn right on the farm gravel track.

After 900m, you will pass a double-length galvanised metal gate to a large clearing on the edge of a wood. Take the path on the right through a small gate

The Four Stones

The skyscrapers of Birmingham city centre are visible from Walton Hill

into the field. Turn left and then note the beaten track across the field towards the stile in the field boundary. Head straight over the next field to Walton Farm and, at the next field boundary, take a right diagonally across the field. Exit over a stile onto the lane and turn right.

At the fork on the edge of the small hamlet of **Walton Pool**, go left downhill with the very narrow building, Canadian Cottage, on your right. Continue until a short climb brings you alongside Sunshine Cottage; turn right up the hill past Mona Cottage. Mona Cottage seems an appropriate name for a house adjacent to a short but steep climb!

A short distance into the wood, turn left downhill and within 10m take the path on your right beneath a gnarly oak. Follow this path as it descends through the wood, joining the road at the bottom in the hamlet of Dark Pool. Turn right and then immediately left on the far side of the road up a signposted bridleway. The Vine Inn is a short detour left downhill at this point.

As the metal railings give way to post-and-wire on your left-hand side and the path forks, take the right-hand fork uphill. The path goes to the top of the slope and a junction of paths, where you carry on straight ahead. At a crossroads of paths with a gate and a wooden fence to your left, take the path straight across, going up the hill. Exit the wood at the top of the hill and turn left, intersecting a large track. Turn left downhill and in less than 10m take the path on the right. You will soon recognise **Adam's Hill car park** where you started the walk, and another decision is required – left to the car, or right to the café?

WALK 28

Wyre Forest

Start/finish	Wyre Forest Visitor Centre car park (SO 751 740)
Time	2hr 30min
Distance	8.6km (5.3 miles)
Ascent/descent	180m (590ft)
Terrain	Mainly gently graded, well-surfaced forest tracks; some woodland paths with mud, tree roots and ruts
Refreshments	Café at start/finish
Toilets	At start/finish
Public transport	Bus from Ludlow or Tenbury Wells to Wyre Forest Visitor Centre stop
Access	The first 3km of the walk are accessible by all-terrain mobility scooter and all-terrain buggy. If you use wheels and would prefer a circular route, ask at the visitor centre and they will be able to suggest suitable trails. It is possible to rent an all-terrain mobility scooter at the visitor centre.
Note	Most of this route is on tracks shared with cyclists.

Despite the popularity of the Wyre Forest and the quality of its tracks, it does not take long to move away from the crowds near the visitor centre into relative solitude, only occasionally seeing other walkers and cyclists. This is a wonderful woodland walk. Although it is through commercially managed conifer woods, there are plenty of broadleaf trees lining the paths to let in light. The final stretch of the walk passes through commercially managed oak woodland, with oak standards and some oak coppice underneath.

The route mainly follows wide, well-surfaced tracks through the forest. However, the final third, which is not Forestry England land, has paths that are muddy and rutted in places. One section that has a narrower path is a delightful amble along the meandering Dowles Brook.

From the visitor centre, head downhill and then away from the play area. As you pass Go Ape, continue downhill on the widest route. Stay on the main track as it drops into a valley and up the other side, and continue ahead to a T-junction of paths. Turn right and stay on the main track as it gently descends. After 2km, you will reach a five-way junction with a fingerpost waymarker (Dowles House). Continue ahead.

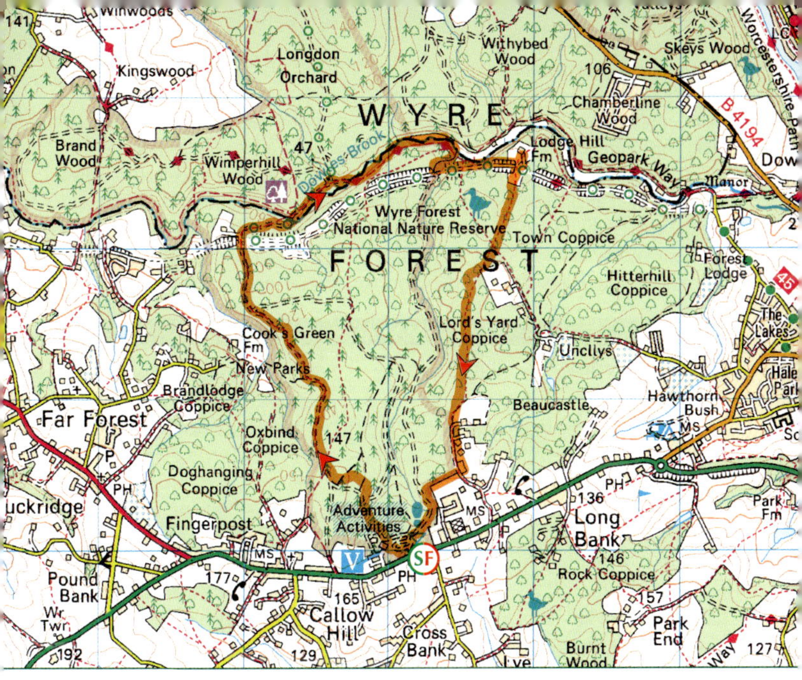

THE WYRE FOREST

The Wyre Forest is part of the largest woodland National Nature Reserve in the country. This area has been woodland for over 1100 years, and the mosaic of habitats attracts a wide range of plant and animal life. In spring, birds compete in the soundscape, and in summer, butterflies and moths take centre stage. Autumn brings a fabulous array of fungi, especially after rain, and towards the end of the year, overwintering birds arrive, changing the wildlife scene once again.

Autumn also brings the rutting season, when male Fallow Deer (bucks) compete for the right to mate with the females. This is an impressive sight – and also dangerous, as the bucks only have one thing on their mind! Some parts of the forest might be closed from mid September to the end of October – please observe any 'keep out' signs you see.

At the next junction of multiple paths, cross the stream then turn right in front of a small rock face. After 100m, fork right over a footbridge, then follow the path with **Dowles Brook** on your left for around 900m. Fork right, away from the stream, and follow this path around to the left until it meets a wide stone **cycle track**. This is an abandoned branch of the old Severn Valley railway line.

Turn left to follow the cycle track. A few paces after passing underneath a railway bridge, turn left then sharp left at the house, to cross the same bridge. Through a gate, take the clear path up the left side of the orchard. Through another kissing gate, the path soon meets another. Turn left and then after about 15 paces, fork right. Follow this path in more or less the same direction, past several junctions, for 2.5km.

FOREST MANAGEMENT

During the later stages of the walk, the route passes through oak forestry. Each tree is planted close to the next to encourage tall, straight growth. After a few years, they are thinned, and as they grow taller, the side branches are removed. This results in the tall, straight oak trees you see here, which contrasts with the spreading form that oaks adopt when they have space.

You might spot deer-fencing around some areas where many of the oak trees have been felled (with others left to grow to maturity). This is to protect the fresh, tasty shoots that grow back from the stumps. These will extend into straight lengths that are harvested every 15–20 years in a process known as coppicing. In this area, the coppiced timber was historically used to provide charcoal for the furnaces of the local ironworks.

When you reach an orchard, stay ahead past a series of houses on your left. Pass Birch Cottage and one more house, then turn right along the footpath following a fence. At a T-junction, turn left and turn left again at the next one. You are now on a wide well-made track that will return you to the **visitor centre car park**.

Some of the route is accessible for those using wheels

MULTI-DAY WALKS

A waymarker indicates the end of the North Worcestershire Path (Walk 30, Stage 2) and the start of the Worcestershire Way (Walk 31, Stage 1)

WALK 29

Worcester to Birmingham along the canal

Start	Worcester
Finish	Birmingham
Time	4 days
Distance	60.4km (37.4 miles)
Terrain	Mainly flat canal towpaths

The Worcester and Birmingham Canal was built in the early 19th century to transport goods between the River Severn (which could be reached from the sea) and Birmingham. One precious cargo was chocolate crumb, destined for the Cadbury factory at Bournville. As this route follows the line of the canal, it is mainly flat and easy to follow, although it does have 58 locks, 30 of which are in the Tardebigge Flight – the longest in the country.

Each stage of the walk starts and finishes at a railway station, which makes it easy to split into day walks. These stations are also in towns with accommodation if you wish to tackle the route as a multi-day walk.

The route is split into four days. However, if you prefer to walk further each day, it could be completed in two; for more information, please see the 'Distance' details in the route information boxes for Stages 2 and 4.

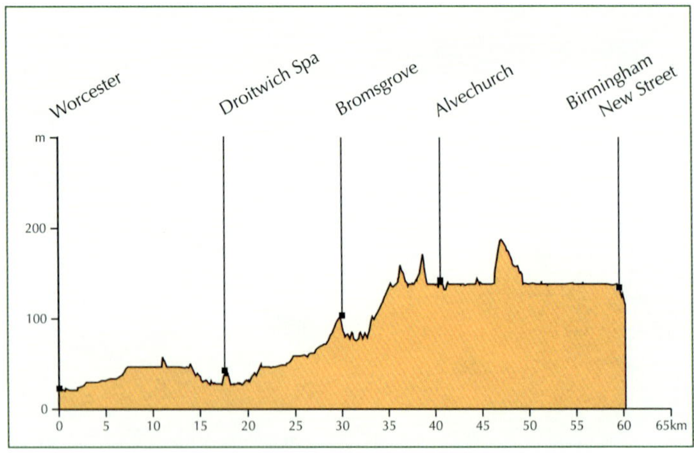

The canal early on Stage 4

STAGE 1

Worcester to Droitwich Spa

Start	Worcester Foregate Street railway station (SO 850 552)
Finish	Droitwich Spa railway station (SO 893 634)
Time	4hr 30min
Distance	17.8km (11 miles) including 3.6km from canal into Droitwich
Ascent	40m (140ft)
Descent	25m (90ft)
Terrain	Mainly flat canal towpath with uphill slopes at locks. A short section of track overland where the canal enters a tunnel, and another section across fields between the canal and Droitwich Spa.
Refreshments	Several pubs in each town and along the route; café at Dunhampstead (bridge 30), with a small shop
Toilets	Priory Lane in Droitwich; Asda superstore in Worcester; Worcester Foregate Street railway station for ticket holders
Parking	Several options in Worcester city centre; Droitwich Spa railway station
Accommodation	Several options close to start and finish

The canals represent a burst of economic activity that linked the country, allowing the transport of large quantities of goods at efficient prices and faster than relying on the roads. Now, the canals are a fantastic natural space for recreation and nature, extending right into the middle of towns and cities.

The scale of construction of the locks is impressive. Those at Droitwich Junction hold 227,000 litres (50,000 gallons) and have side basins to conserve water.

This stage links Worcester and Droitwich. Once away from the urban centres, the route is likely to be uncrowded. In the summer months, there are always fish, insects, birds and dragonflies aplenty. And at times, complete peace.

The pubs linked to the canal have many stories to tell of rowdy nights and merchants' deals. Then at Droitwich, there are historical accounts of the long-standing trade in salt, probably extending back before the Romans arrived. Chateaux were built, including Chateau Impney, which was built in 1873–75 for local industrialist and saltworks magnate John Corbett.

Leave the railway station and turn left. Take the next left onto Sansome Street. Take the next left, then the first right onto Sansome Place. Continue straight down to Lion Court. At the end, take the footpath on the right-hand side of the apartments. At the steps, turn left to join the canal towpath and pass under the **railway bridge** with an unusual circular aperture.

At the first lock, take the ramp with the raised brick inlay up onto the bridge over the canal. Turn left and continue along the towpath. From here, for a considerable distance, stay on this right-hand side of the canal.

ROACH

Roach can sometimes be seen in the canal. Their bodies have a bluish-silvery colour and become white at the belly, and their fins are red. The Common Roach is very adaptable and can be found in any freshwater ecosystem, ranging from small ponds to the largest rivers and lakes. It feeds at any depth, although its preferred food sources tend to be in shallower water. It tolerates organic pollution and is one of the last species to disappear in polluted waters.

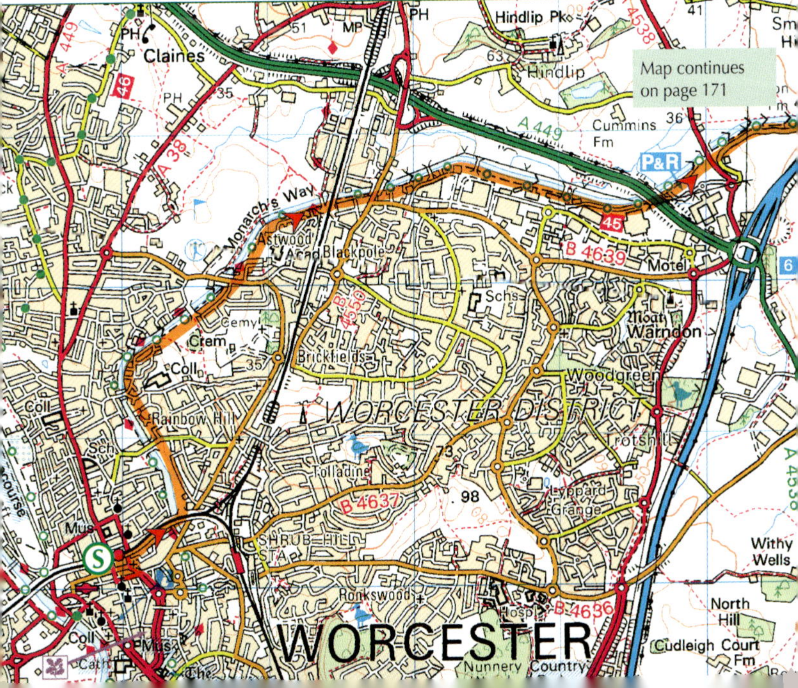

Map continues on page 171

The towpath is easy to follow

After a small marina at **Dunhampstead**, the path starts to ascend as the canal heads for the tunnel. The path joins a wide gravel track. Continue downslope on the track as signposted. Turn left at the tarmac drive and face the access drive to the farmhouse. Take the gravel track to the right of the farmhouse; follow this to a series of wooden steps and ramps around a landslide back onto the towpath.

On reaching the small Hanbury marina, take a right up into the car park of the Eagle and Sun pub. Cross straight over the **B4090** then turn left to walk over the canal bridge. At the first right turn to Westfields Farm, take the path that returns to the water. This is the junction of the Worcester and Birmingham Canal, which you have been following, and the Droitwich Canal.

Pass three locks in succession with side basins. Side basins are designed to be partially filled when a lock empties and then reused as a lock is refilled. Continue past the locks and keep alongside the canal. Take the wooden steps up, cross over an access road and turn right to cross the canal bridge. Turn left down the wooden steps to rejoin the towpath.

The path crosses a footbridge over the canal just before the canal disappears under the M5. Carry on under trees for a short while. Emerging onto the road, turn right and head for the tunnel under the **M5**. Continue straight over at the roundabout, crossing roads with care. Rejoin the canal just 50m along from the roundabout.

Westlands
Newtown
Great Pool
Hospls
Schs
Witton
Copcut
Primsland
Wr Twr
Hadzor Hall
Hadzor
Church
Westfields Fm
Marina
ROMAN ROAD
B 4090
Huntingdon Fm
Shernal Green
Dean Fm
Dunhampstead
Wychavon Way
Dean Brook
Oakley
Newland Common
Brownheath Common
Martin Hussingtree
Park Fm
Saleway Fm
Oddingley
Church Fm
Trench Wood
Netherwood Fm
Smite Fms
Smite Hill
Hotel
Sandyway
Hindlip
Offerton Fm
Cummins Fm
Evelench Fm
Tibberton
Motel
A 38
A 4538
A 449
B 4639
M 5
Copcut

Herons can sometimes be seen on the canal

Pass the Barley Mow pub on the left as you approach Droitwich town centre. Entering Vines Park, take the footbridge over the first lock, turn left and follow the main path towards the sculptures and historic features in the centre of the park.

The aluminium **Salt Worker sculpture** commemorates the people who once worked in Droitwich's salt industry. Briny springs arise in the area, and salt has been traded from here since the Iron Age. It was harvested by placing the water in shallow pans to evaporate, leaving the salt behind. This section of canal was dug to transport the salt to the junction with the Worcester and Birmingham Canal and on to markets. After a hiatus of about a century, salt is again being produced in Droitwich, at Churchfields Farm.

Continue along the canal to Netherwich Basin. From the basin, head towards the river and take the path leading out of the park to your left. Pass the Railway Inn on your left. Cross straight over to rejoin the canal going through a tunnel under the **railway line**.

Pass by the machine tools factory on your right, go under the next bridge, then turn right, ascend the steps and go right again to cross over the canal and continue along the road. Cross Ledwych Road and the road you have been following to take a footpath going gently up a slope to the left, then go right into the car park at **Droitwich Spa railway station**.

STAGE 2

Droitwich Spa to Bromsgrove

Start	Droitwich Spa railway station (SO 893 634)
Finish	Bromsgrove railway station (SO 967 692)
Time	3hr 45min
Distance	13.8km (8.6 miles)
Ascent	85m (280ft)
Descent	45m (150ft)
Terrain	Mainly flat canal towpaths, some slight slopes and a few steps
Refreshments	Several pubs in each town and along the route
Toilets	Priory Lane in Droitwich; Bromsgrove bus station, or Bromsgrove railway station for ticket holders
Parking	At either railway station
Accommodation	Several options close to start and finish

Leaving Droitwich via Netherwich Marina and Vines Park is a reminder of the town's deep historical and industrial past. The Romans came straight to Droitwich for salt, and it is certain that salt was exploited here for millennia beforehand. The canals helped boost salt production and distribution, with huge wealth being generated.

It's quite a symbolic moment to reach the junction of the Worcester and Birmingham Canal with the Droitwich Canal, after which the path heads north towards Bromsgrove, passing another industrial hub, Stoke Works. Interesting examples of water management can be seen as water is steered around locks and through property.

This section is particularly heavily populated by various dragonfly species and some beautiful pubs. The longest flight of locks in the UK awaits you at Tardebigge.

Leave the station on the north-west side and turn left into a wide alley which descends to Salwarpe Road. Cross over when safe, turn right and cross Ledwych Road. Continue down the road on the left-hand side. Cross over the canal and take the left-hand steps down to the canal. Pass under the bridge and continue alongside the canal, heading east.

Pass under the **railway line** and emerge onto a road. Head straight over to the left-hand side of the Railway Inn. Follow the path between the River Salwarpe and

Netherwich Basin. An interesting sign by the Netherwich Basin gives details of the longest navigable destinations from this point.

Continue on the path closest to the river until reaching a footbridge over a lock at the end of the park on the right. Cross over. There are some art pieces and historical features in the park. Stroll over to them on the right-hand side of the path.

Pass the Barley Mow pub on the right as you leave Droitwich town centre. As the sound of the M5 motorway becomes apparent, look out for a path leading up from the canal on your right. On joining the road, walk to the roundabout and cross straight over, heading for the tunnel under the **M5**. On the roundabout after the tunnel, take the footpath on the left through the wood. Go over the footbridge, just in front of the canal tunnel that passes under the motorway. Turn right after the bridge.

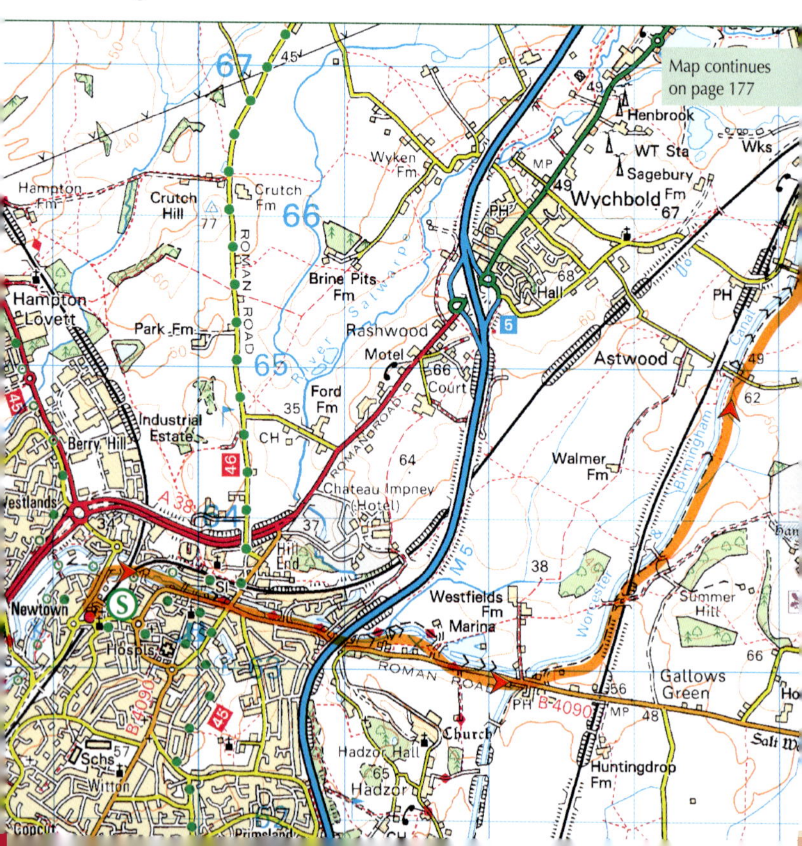

Map continues on page 177

The Worcester and Birmingham Canal as it passes under the railway to the west of Summer Hill

Pass two locks. At the next bridge, take the wooden steps up to the road. A good view of the marina and the locks is seen from here. Turn right for a short distance to the flight of steps down, on your left. Continue along a flight of locks.

The **locks** here have been rebuilt using sandstone capping blocks that weigh three tonnes each. The side basins are used to conserve water on the empty-and-fill cycle of the locks as boats move through. This is a short 'flight' of locks. On steeper gradients, they are built as 'staircases', which means there is no stretch of water between locks; the bottom gate of one is the top gate of the next.

After passing the three locks, take the path onto the road, cross over the bridge towards the Eagle and Sun, and then turn left immediately after the bridge back onto the towpath. Follow the right-hand side of the canal. You are right at the junction of the Worcester and Birmingham Canal and the Droitwich Canal.

After 4km, the Boat and Railway pub is positioned right on the canal at **Stoke Works**, an area combining centuries of industrial and residential structures. At Stoke top lock (number 28), take a moment to look across the fields, where you will see a windmill in the distance. A short distance further along, you pass the Queen's Head.

A narrowboat disappears into the distance

After another 3.5km, at Tardebigge bottom lock, the path starts to ascend the **Tardebigge Flight**, the longest flight of locks on the Birmingham and Worcester Canal and in the country.

This is a great place to spot a wide variety of **dragonflies**. Although dragonflies require water for their nymphs to live in, they do not spend their whole lives near water – for a week or so after emerging and metamorphosing from nymph to adult, they fly away from water before returning to mate. The main threats to dragonflies thriving are climate breakdown, water pollution, invasive species and habitat loss or degradation.

Go under bridge 51, then turn right up to the road. Cross over the bridge, following the road into **Upper Gambolds**. Bear right with the road in front of the first house, pass by and take the footpath on the left. Walk straight across the fields, keeping the hedge on your left, and continue on this line to a gate. Bear left on a diagonal across to the farm buildings. Cross the small stream and walk straight up through the farm buildings to join the road. Go straight on up the hill on St Godwald's Road.

Continue over the **railway bridge** and then turn left, passing the Travelodge and the Ladybird pub. After the pub, turn left down to **Bromsgrove railway station**.

For much of its history, **Bromsgrove** was a relatively small market town. Agricultural income was supplemented by the creation of cloth, and then nails. By the time of the Industrial Revolution, it was a nail-making centre, with individual households working on a piece-rate basis. As the industry declined due to mechanisation, nail makers struggled to make a living and poverty became rife. By the mid 20th century, residents were more likely to be working in Birmingham or one of the larger factories in the area.

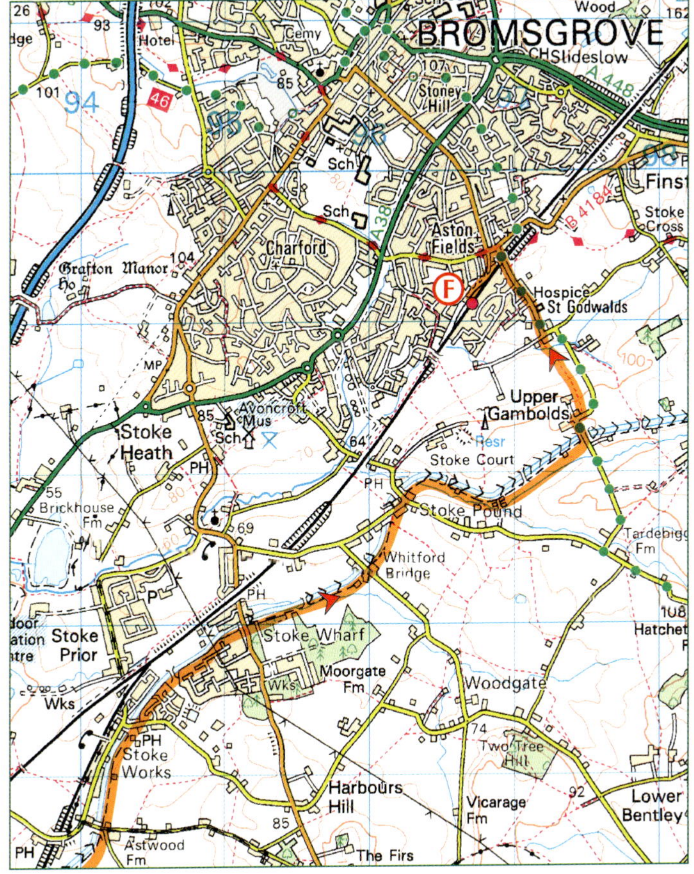

STAGE 3

Bromsgrove to Alvechurch

Start	Bromsgrove railway station (SO 967 692)
Finish	Alvechurch railway station (SP 023 720)
Time	2hr 45min
Distance	9.6km (5.9 miles)
Ascent	140m (470ft)
Descent	90m (280ft)
Terrain	Mainly canal towpaths, with a rise up the Tardebigge Flight
Refreshments	Several options in Bromsgrove and Alvechurch
Toilets	Bromsgrove bus station, or Bromsgrove railway station for ticket holders
Parking	At either railway station
Accommodation	Several options in Bromsgrove. There are no hotels in Alvechurch – the nearest accommodation is a couple of miles away, so it might be best to take the train to a larger place.

This stage regains the canal where the previous stage left off, then gently climbs the final locks of the Tardebigge Flight, passing the Tardebigge Reservoir on the way. This section of the walk has tremendous views.

The story of the investment into marinas, docks, elevators and pump engines is one of risk and enterprise, success and failure, illustrated through the sites you walk through on this fascinating historical route.

There are two tunnels en route, both of which are traversed overland. All the industrial activity and noise that once was gives way to one of the most tranquil spots on the canal network – the woodland setting of the northward end of Shortwood Tunnel, which almost seems as if fairies live there!

Leave Bromsgrove railway station, heading right onto New Road, then uphill to turn right at the Ladybird pub. Take the next right along St Godwald's Road. Continue to the junction with Lower Gambolds Lane. Head straight over into the farmyard. The path continues straight ahead over a low raised earth bund and crosses a small farm drain. Bear left on a diagonal to the field gate. Through this, proceed with the field boundary on your right-hand side until the path reaches a lane.

Part of the Tardebigge Flight

Turn right, then follow the lane left to cross then rejoin the canal, heading uphill. This is the second half of the **Tardebigge Flight** of locks. As you progress on the right-hand side of the canal, the banks of a canal water supply reservoir become visible. Take the flight of steps to view the **reservoir** and turn to see the long-distance views. Continue on the reservoir bank towards the lock house. Continue along the canal to lock 57.

TARDEBIGGE ENGINE HOUSE

Tardebigge Engine House is a former canal-pumping engine house near lock 57. It used to contain a steam-powered Newcomen-Watt beam engine, which was removed in 1915. The engine is significant as the first practical device to harness steam to produce mechanical work.

It was used to pump water from the adjacent Tardebigge feeder reservoir, which is 15m below the level of the top pound of the canal. At the top lock, it is still possible to see the balancing pit built for an experimental vertical boat lift. It was capable of moving 110 boats in 12 hours, with two men working the windlass and balances. Deemed too fragile, it was replaced by a larger-than-usual lock in 1815.

The Engine House above Tardebigge Reservoir

At the marina and docks, the footpath bears right up onto the road at the Tardebigge Tunnel. Turn left and, once over the canal, cross the road and take the path towards the **A448**. Cross the road. **Warning:** This is a dual carriageway, so you will need to cross to the island and then make the second stage of the crossing.

Climb the flight of steps on the far side of the road, cross the stile and follow the field boundary to another road. Cross and follow the small lane directly opposite. Continue to the end of the lane, turn left over the canal bridge and immediately right along Wharf Lane. Continue past the canalside buildings for a short distance, then take the footpath on the right to rejoin the canal. Follow the canal, now with the water on your right. Leave the canal at bridge 58.

CANAL TUNNELS

Canal tunnels were generally built by plotting the route above ground and sinking a series of shafts along the route. At the right depth, the tunnel was dug out from each shaft, in both directions. As you might imagine, this did not always result in a perfectly straight tunnel! Many longer tunnels were not dug wide enough for a towpath. In those cases, the horses that pulled the boats were led overground to the far end of the tunnel, and the boats were 'legged' through. This involved lying on the roof of the boat and pushing it forward by walking along the roof of the tunnel. This was a slow process and tended to create bottlenecks in the canal, with a backlog of boats each side.

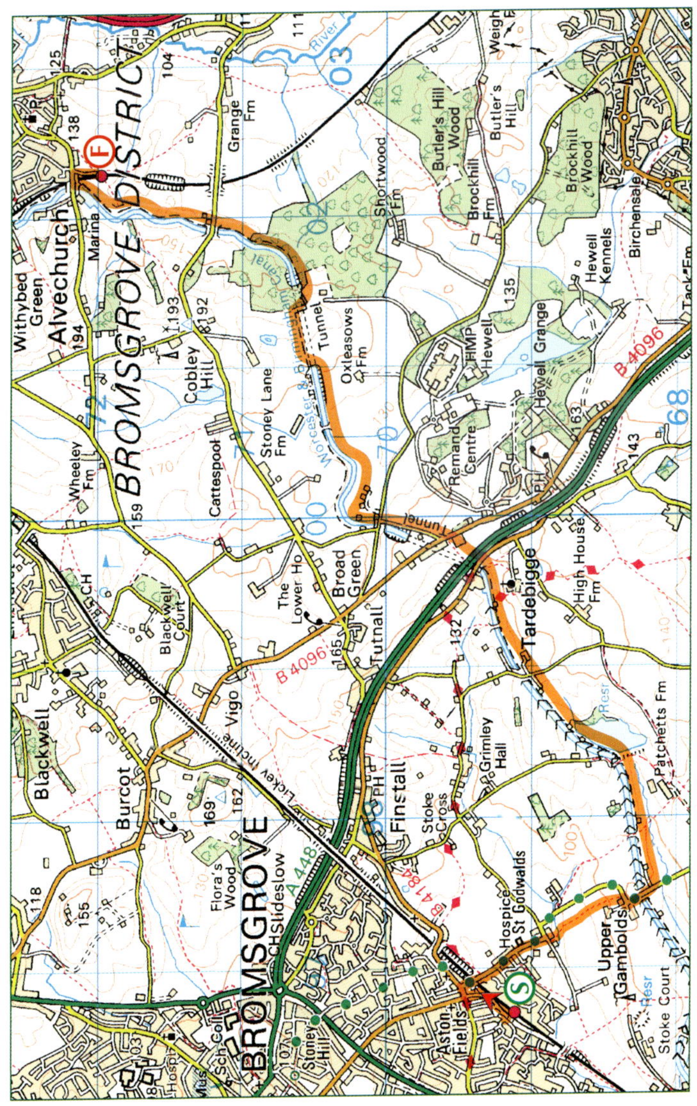

The woods after Shortwood Tunnel

Skirt the edge of the woodland that follows the course of **Shortwood Tunnel**, keeping an easterly direction to an open field with views up to a copse on the skyline. Head to the left of this copse and pick up the path that enters a hedged path, which then goes straight towards a large woodland. Follow the path into the woodland and bear right. The path gently descends and curves down back to the canal. This is a tranquil, beautiful stretch of woodland, even more so as the canal snakes its way out once more into open fields.

Continue along the canal for nearly 2km, past the **marina**. At the bridge, turn right and up to join the road. Cross over the **railway bridge** and turn right down to **Alvechurch railway station**.

STAGE 4

Alvechurch to Birmingham New Street

Start	Alvechurch railway station (SP 023 720)
Finish	Birmingham New Street railway station (SP 069 866)
Time	5hr
Distance	19.2km (11.9 miles)

Ascent	70m (240ft)
Descent	80m (270ft)
Terrain	Mainly canal towpath, which varies from tarmac to bare earth with occasional tripping hazards such as tree roots. One small ascent and descent where the canal goes through a tunnel and the path crosses the hill above.
Refreshments	Plenty of options in Alvechurch and Birmingham; the Crown Inn is on the canal close to Alvechurch
Toilets	The route passes a large Sainsbury's near the university campus; Birmingham New Street station for ticket holders
Public transport	Train to Alvechurch, return from Birmingham New Street
Access	Accessible for all-terrain buggies. There is one stile – it can be avoided by staying on the lane, which the route rejoins. Past King's Norton, there is a flight of 14 steps to descend that can't be avoided. There are also steps outside The Mailbox in Birmingham city centre: these can be avoided by using the lift.
Parking	Alvechurch railway station; central Birmingham
Accommodation	There are no hotels in Alvechurch – the nearest accommodation is a couple of miles away, so it might be best to take the train to a larger place. Plentiful options in Birmingham.

This part of the route is a real mix. Most is a green idyll, but as you would expect with a walk into the country's second largest city, it also passes housing, factory units, graffitied walls and under a motorway. Overall, it is a lovely, peaceful walk alongside the canal, which is now used by pretty narrowboats rather than industrial transportation. Most of the route is lined with trees, making it a cool walk on a hot day or a sheltered walk on a windy day. There are no locks on this stretch of the canal, so the walk is flat, except for an occasional bridge and where the canal passes through a 2.5km-long tunnel. Here, the walk climbs over the small hill above it, crossing fields and meadows and offering some views.

There are three opportunities to shorten the route if you are weary or short of time: at Bournville, University and Five Ways railway stations.

From the station, take the exit road up to the bridge. Turn left across the railway, then right before the canal, heading onto and along the towpath. At a junction of canals with booms across after 1.6km, turn left to keep the main canal on your

A narrowboat on the canal

left. After another 3.7km, the path approaches the **Wast Hill Tunnel**, where it rises to a lane.

> At the **Wast Hill Tunnel**, the route follows that which the horses would have taken while the canal boat owners lay on their backs and 'legged' the boat through the tunnel. This tunnel is 2.5km long; they must have been fit!

After 50m, cross the stile on the left into a field. To avoid the stile, continue along the lane. Head straight across the field to the right-hand side of an oak tree that is a little the worse for wear. The way ahead is clear along the right-hand edge of a meadow, right through a hedge, then diagonally left to a gate which returns you to the lane.

Turn left and follow the lane to a T-junction. Turn right, then left onto Bracken Way. At the T-junction, turn right down Longdales Road. At Thatchway Gardens, turn downhill, then left at the Sycamore tree. Take the straight path along this narrow stretch of green space. Continue ahead in approximately the same direction, crossing one road, until you reach a junction of paths with a circular stone mosaic built into the pavement.

Stay ahead, passing through a barrier. The wide, mown path continues across more open green space. A ventilation shaft indicates the point at which this path crosses the Wast Hill Tunnel. Follow this path ahead until the end of the park. Pass

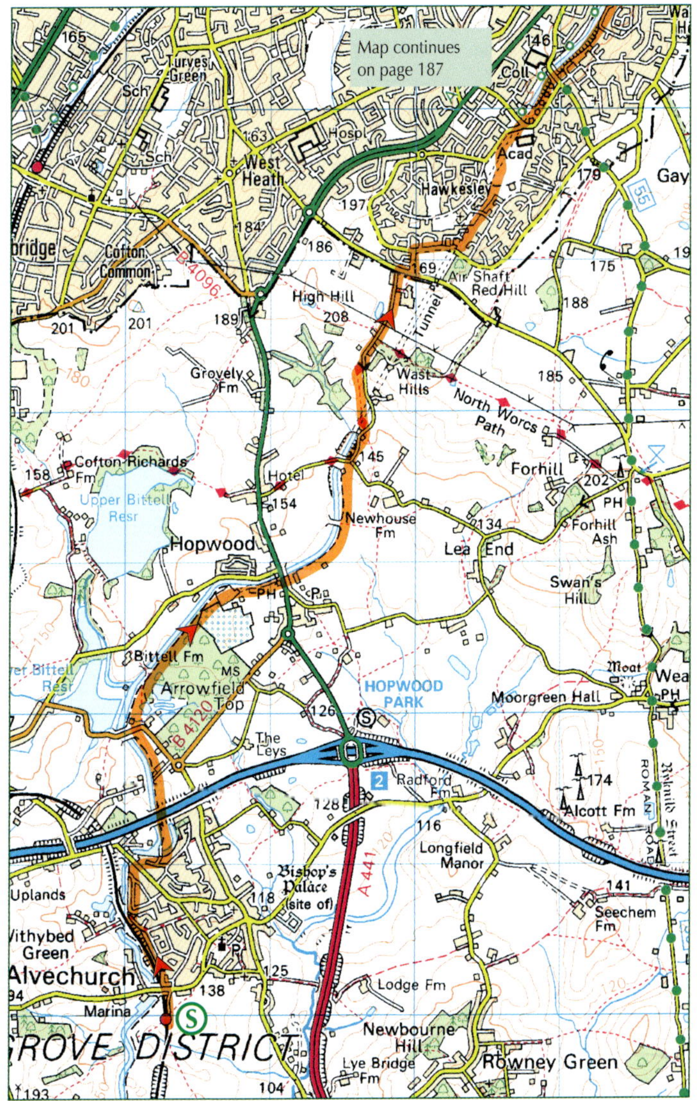

Map continues on page 187

the gates to a school, cross both pedestrian crossings and pass to the left of two white cottages, after which the route forks right and heads back down to the canal and along the towpath.

At the next junction of canals, stay ahead towards Bournville and Birmingham city centre. Where the towpath rises to a road (at **Lifford**), turn right over the bridge, and right again to return to the canal, this time with the water on your left. The next time the towpath rises, cross to the left, descend a flight of steps and turn right to continue under the **A441** with the canal on your right.

BOURNVILLE 'MODEL VILLAGE'

The Cadbury brothers, who were Quakers, were forward-thinking industrialists. When they needed a new factory, they found a site with a stream called the Bourn, and added 'ville' to name the site. Bournville was designed to enable their workers to enjoy a better quality of life, and as much as 30% of capital expenditure was spent on facilities for workers' welfare, such as tennis courts, a bowling green and swimming pools. The site was known as the 'factory within a garden'. Another radical idea they implemented was to give their workers a half day on a Saturday. Despite being told it would ruin the company, it is still going strong, although no longer family owned.

This section of towpath is popular with walkers, runners and cyclists

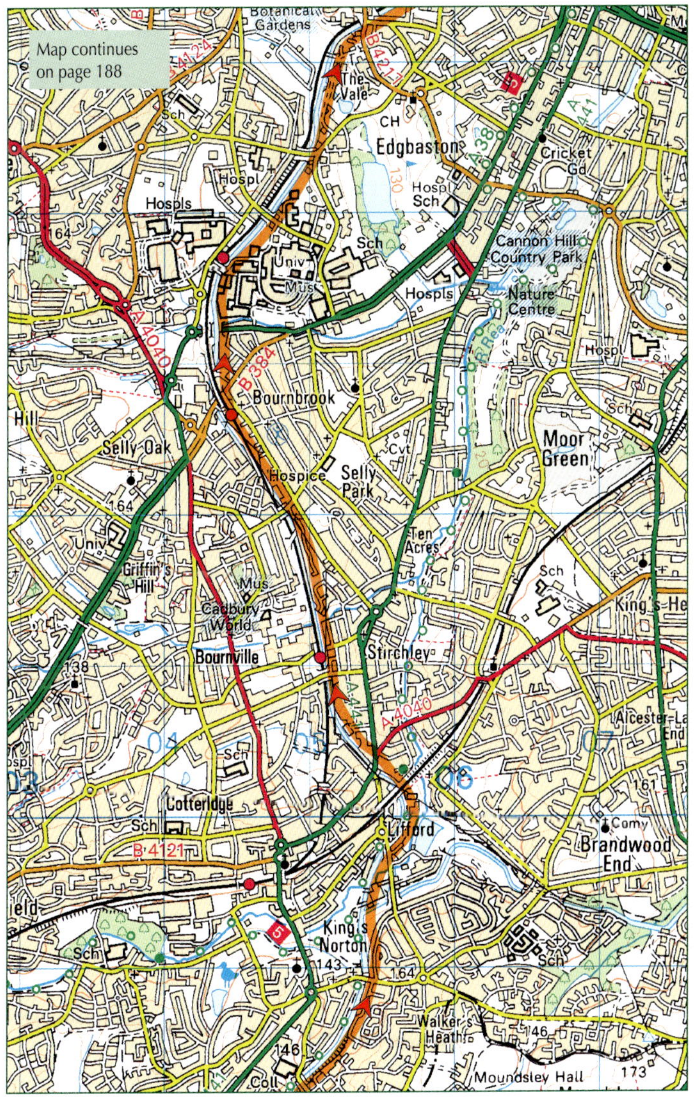
Map continues
on page 188
Botanical
Gardens
B 4217
B 4124
The
Vale
CH
Edgbaston
A 38
A 441
Cricket
Gd
Hospl
Hospls
Hospl
Sch
Sch
Sch
Univ
Mus
Cannon Hill
Country Park
Hospls
Nature
Centre
R Rea
A 4040
B 384
Bournbrook
Hospl
Sch
Hill
Selly Oak
Cvt
Moor
Green
Hospice
Selly
Park
Ten
Acres
Univ
Griffin's
Hill
Mus
Cadbury
World
Sch
King's Heath
Bournville
Stirchley
A 441
A 4040
Alcester La
End
Sch
Cotterldge
Sch
B 4121
Lifford
Comy
Brandwood
End
King's
Norton
Sch
Sch
Walker's
Heath
Moundsley Hall
Coll

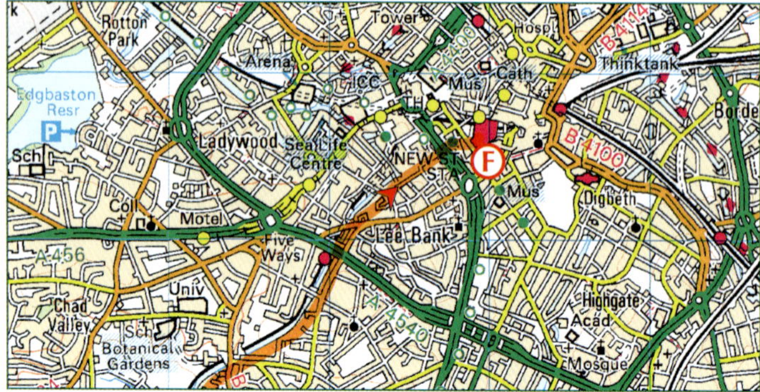

At the **end of the canal**, where it joins the Birmingham Canal at right angles, turn left and then sharp right up the ramp and along the walkway in front of The Mailbox. Continue ahead through The Mailbox Canalside building. This route is open from 6am to midnight. Head down two levels as you progress through the building to exit.

There are steps down to street level, or a lift to your left. Take these and cross under the bridge following the coloured stripes built into the pavement. Continue ahead, following the stripes, and before long, you will see the mirrored facade of **Birmingham New Street railway station**.

> **Birmingham** became a huge urban centre during the Industrial Revolution, and it is now known as Britain's second largest city – although Manchester might dispute the title. It has 56km (35 miles) of canals, which some suggest is more than Venice – so, arriving into this great city along the canal seems highly appropriate.

WALK 30

North Worcestershire Path

Start	Shirley
Finish	Bewdley
Time	2 days
Distance	57.4km (35.7 miles)
Terrain	Low rolling hills with some steeper ascents and descents

Starting close to the Birmingham suburbs, this route immediately leaves the busy city behind and wends its way across the northern reaches of the county. It starts with a warm-up over low hills, which are mainly laid to pasture, and which increase in size towards the end of the first day, then decrease in size again on the second day, to finish with a few kilometres along the banks of the River Severn.

It can only sensibly be split into two long days, or two short days and one long one. This route description opts for two long days, and as both stages start and end at public transport hubs, they can also be tackled as day walks.

The North Worcestershire Path ends at the start of the Worcestershire Way, so it is possible to continue for a longer multi-day walk (see Walk 31).

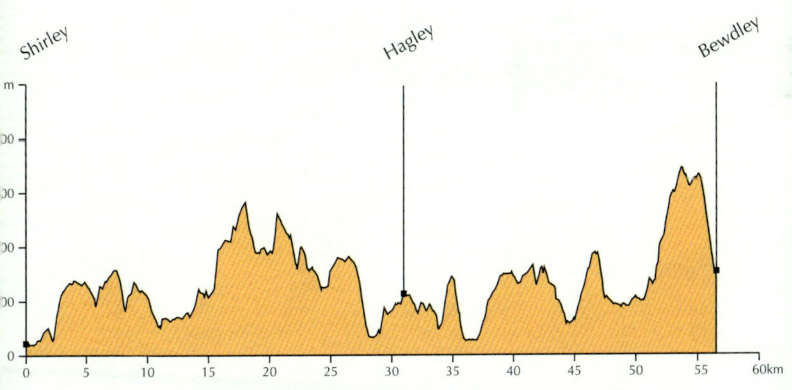

The view across neighbouring parkland

STAGE 1

Shirley to Hagley

Start	Peterbrook Road, Shirley (between Major's Green and Solihull Lodge) (SP 101 781)
Alternative start	Shirley railway station (SP 106 784)
Finish	Worcester Road (B4187), Hagley (SO 907 809)
Alternative finish	Hagley railway station (SO 901 805)
Time	9hr 30min
Distance	30.2km (18.8 miles)
Ascent	665m (2190ft)
Descent	680m (2240ft)
Terrain	From Shirley to the Lickey Hills, the route traverses low rolling hills, mostly on grassy paths and some on tarmac. From the Lickey Hills, the ascents and descents become higher and steeper, and there is more walking on woodland paths. There are multiple stiles in the early sections of this walk, many of which are not dog-friendly.
Refreshments	The Peacock pub, Forhill Ash (7.8km); Westmead Hotel, Hopwood (11.4km); Duckpond Café, Lickey (15.7km); several options close to start and finish
Toilets	Lickey Hills Visitor Centre (when open)
Public transport	Train to Shirley and from Hagley
Parking	At alternative start and alternative finish
Accommodation	Premier Inn Hagley Hotel is 3.2km from Hagley railway station; Westmead Hotel, Hopwood (on route at 11.4km); the Old Rose and Crown Hotel, Lickey (on route at 15.7km); several options in Solihull, around 4km from Shirley railway station
Note	This stage can be tackled as one long walking day, or with an overnight stay at the Westmead Hotel or the Old Rose and Crown Hotel. The path is frugally waymarked – you will need the map and instructions.

Walking this route across the north of Worcestershire, you would barely believe how close you are to the UK's second largest city – if it wasn't for the occasional view of its skyline from afar. The walk starts across charming pastoral countryside with low rolling hills, later climbing several hills shrouded in woodland. Although none of the summits are particularly high, collectively they offer a good workout for the legs and lungs and provide fabulous views across Birmingham and Worcestershire. When you reach the final summit at Four Stones, it seems as though the whole walk has been leading to this moment, crescendoing to a spectacular finale.

Alternative start at Shirley railway station

To start from Shirley railway station, turn right out of the station, take the first right, then turn left at the T-junction and right after crossing under the canal to reach the main route and start of the North Worcestershire Path. This adds about 1km to the route.

Main route

A subtle carving in the crossbar of a stile marks the start of the North Worcestershire Path. After crossing the stile, head diagonally left across the paddock, over a bridge, through a metal hand gate in the wooden fence ahead and into the woods.

On reaching a concrete slab, turn right along a track, then ahead at the junction, over another stile and along the left side of the meadow. Cross another stile, then head diagonally right across the next field. The waymarker post is visible ahead.

There is no fanfare at the trailhead – just a waymarked stile

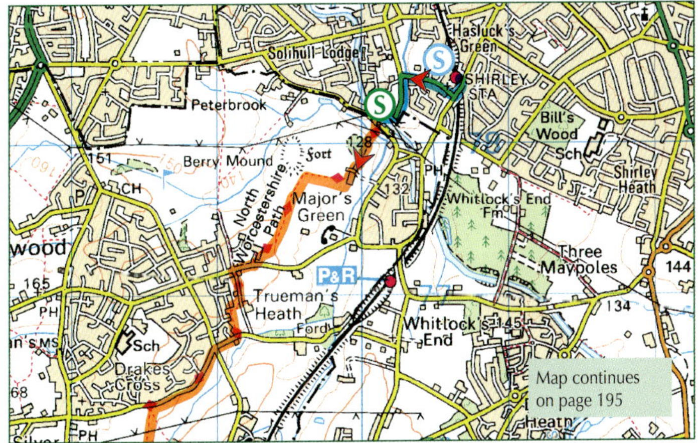

Map continues on page 195

RING-NECKED PARAKEETS

You may see Ring-necked Parakeets flying near the start of the walk. When you hear a harsh squawk, look out for green birds with pointed tails and wings, flying fast and straight as arrows, often seen in flocks. These are the only naturalised parrots in the UK, with the largest populations around the South East, but now seen all around the country. It is thought that the birds were once brought here as pets, and as they were captured from the wild in a similar climate to ours, they were able to fend for themselves when released, either accidentally or intentionally. They are opportunistic feeders, so love the variety of habitats and foodstuffs in our urban areas. Although they can be aggressive and compete with some of our native birds, they are also a favourite prey of Peregrine Falcons and other hunting birds.

Cross the next stile, then turn left along the edge of the field. After the kissing gates, turn left along a farm track. As some sheds come into view ahead and to the right, look to your left for a small bridge and take this path. Turn right to follow the concrete paving slabs and then, as they turn right into the stables, continue ahead along the right-hand edge of the paddock.

Turn right to follow the pavement along the road. Immediately past the first cottage (number 47), turn left along the tarmac drive. Pass Highfields Cottage, and immediately before the wrought iron gates to Little Trueman's Heath Farm at **Trueman's Heath**, turn right over another stile to a footpath along the edge of a

The path through a meadow near Major's Green

meadow. In the far corner, the path ducks through the hedgerow and over another stile and then along the right-hand edge of a paddock to a lane.

Turn right, and at the junction, continue ahead onto Houndsfield Lane along the edge of **Drakes Cross**. Opposite Houndsfield Court, take the waymarked track to the left. After a handful of metres, turn right through a kissing gate and then follow the path between paddocks. Through another kissing gate, continue along the right edge of the next paddock, past a gap in the hedge, to a further kissing gate.

Through the gate, continue to the right between some scrub and a fence, then briefly through woodland, and then ahead, this time between the fence on your right and scrub on your left. Pass through two gates and over a stile to reach a road.

Turn left, then almost immediately right along Brick Kiln Lane. Past the houses, turn left on Wilmore Lane to cross over the **A435**. Pass two houses on the right, and before the lane turns to the right, take a kissing gate into a field, and turn sharp right through the trees and along the right-hand edge of the field to a wooden hand gate. Through the gate, continue round the side of the field. Over a stile, stay on the path round the edge of the following field and across the next meadow to the corner of the hedge line. From here, continue with the hedge line on your left. With the **A435** on the far side of the hedge, turn left.

This takes you to a cottage. Turn left along its drive to a lane. Continue in the same direction through a small village and over a crossroads. At Malthouse Farm, turn diagonally left through a metal gate and on to a kissing gate on the far side of the yard. Take this to cross to the far right-hand corner of the paddock. Through a double gate, turn left to follow the left side of the next paddock. At the end, turn left over a small wooden bridge, then right along the right-hand edge of the following paddock. This takes you to the edge of an old **moat** that surrounds the house on the right.

Moats were not always built as a means of defence. Sometimes, they served as a status symbol for wealthy farmers, who would dig one around their farmstead.

Through a gate, turn right along the part of the moat that still retains water. Continue ahead through two gates, then diagonally right to a gate near the farm buildings. Through this, turn left through another gate and over a small bridge to follow a path that soon skirts the right-hand edge of a paddock and then a long hayfield. The route continues into the next field, where it crosses to the right of a solitary post in the middle to a waymarker on the far side. An alternative route heads diagonally across this field to the right, avoiding the need to walk along the lane.

On reaching the lane, turn right. About 20m short of the T-junction, turn left up some steps and across a **picnic site**. Cross the stone drive and continue ahead to a wooden hand gate. This leads to a lane, and the route continues ahead along the side of the **Peacock pub**, before turning right past the entrance to the pub car park, along a tarmac no-through road.

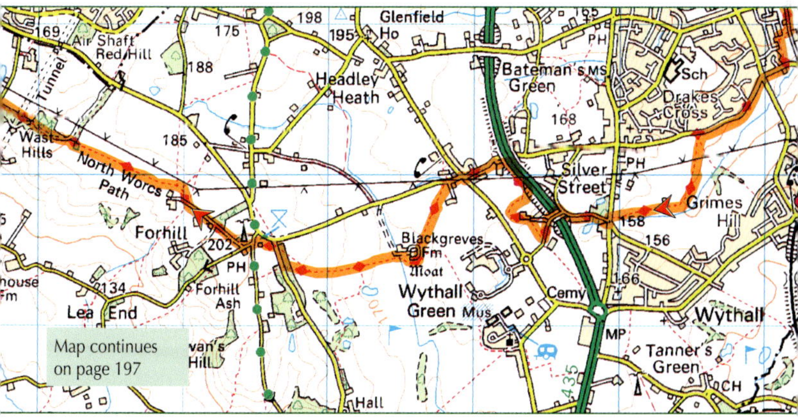

Map continues on page 197

Follow the path across a picnic site

There are many **mature oak trees** along this walk. The UK's two native species hybridise easily with each other and are very similar, so it is not always easy to identify the exact species. One way is to look at the acorns. *Quercus robur*, also known as the English Oak and the Pedunculate Oak, grows acorns at the end of a stalk (peduncle). *Quercus petraea*, on the other hand, grows its acorns directly from its twigs. Its other name is the Sessile (stalkless) Oak.

Where the tarmac drive turns left, continue ahead on a stone track past the sign for Little Forhill Farm. Just before the Big Forhill Farm sign, turn right at a waymark post, then proceed through a kissing gate and diagonally left, heading for the left side of the mature oak trees on the far side of the paddock. Through a gate, head for the next gate in the far left-hand corner. Pass through this and another in a hedge line. Cut diagonally right across the pasture to another gate.

Through this, the footpath follows the hedge on the right-hand side of two fields. At the end of the second, do not follow the track ahead. Instead, take the path on the right-hand side of a fence and continue in the same direction under trees. At a 'no trespassing' sign, bear right past a stile and along the left-hand edge of a meadow. From here, there is a view over the city of Birmingham.

After the next meadow, the route reaches a lane. Turn left and follow it for 200m to a double-width gate on the right. Enter the meadow here and take the clear route diagonally left, through the hedge, down the left-hand side of another meadow and across the middle of an arable field to a stile, where the path rejoins the lane. Turn right onto the lane and then right at the T-junction. This takes you to Birmingham Road at **Hopwood**.

Turn right, then left along the lane opposite **Westmead Hotel**, signposted St Michael's Church. At the end of the lane, continue straight ahead across the pasture and through a metal kissing gate that is visible in the far right-hand corner. The **Upper Bittell Reservoir** is on your left now and will briefly come into view.

After passing through a gate, the route continues along the left-hand edge of a field. Through another gate, the well-defined path soon crosses an arable field. At the far side, turn left to follow a hedge, with a view over the reservoir to the left.

In the corner of the field, the path continues between fences to a drive. Follow this drive to the left. Pass the reservoir drive on the left and continue ahead on the lane, under a **railway** and past a **church**. A few metres before Cofton Hall Cottage, turn right through a kissing gate along a clearly defined path on the right-hand edge of an arable field. Stay on this path as it bends to the left. At the crosspaths on the far side of the field, continue ahead. After a while, this brings you out onto a drive that leads to a road on the edge of **Cofton Hackett**.

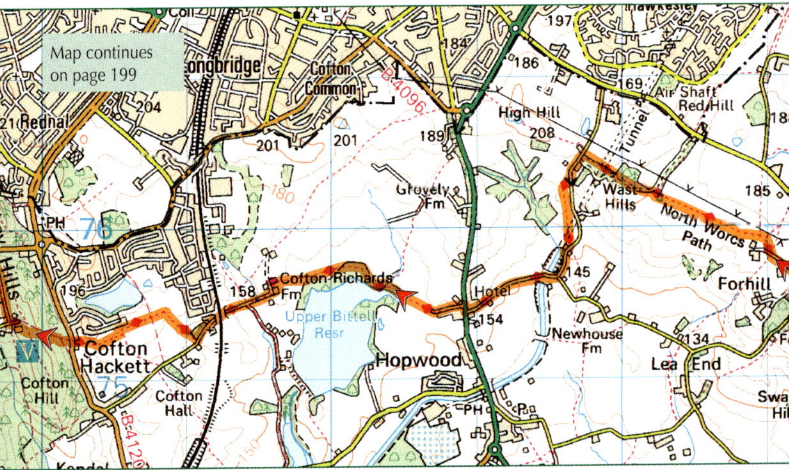

Cross the road and take the path directly uphill towards the **Lickey Hills Visitor Centre**. At the top of a flight of steps, turn right onto the bridlepath. At the car parks, stay ahead to the visitor centre, where you will find some interesting displays, public toilets and a water fountain.

Continue along the drive with the visitor centre on your left, and turn right at the school room, down a stone track. Past the cottage, continue in the same direction along a stone path through woodland and down to a road.

Cross and turn into the grounds of the **Old Rose and Crown Hotel**. Walk in front of the hotel, past a small pond and uphill to the right. Turn left to walk around the far side of the duck pond. This path rises alongside a stream. At a junction of paths, cross the stream and continue uphill on a stone track, following the green waymarkers. At the next junction of paths, turn right to continue uphill. At the next junction, it's a left turn to continue uphill. And at the next, turn right, then left. Don't worry too much if you lose track of all the left and right turns. As long as you head uphill, you will end up in the right place. Eventually, you will emerge from the trees within sight of the castellated toposcope on **Beacon Hill**.

From **Beacon Hill Toposcope**, there is a wide-ranging view that includes the skyscrapers of Birmingham city centre. This view is the reason that the site was first used for Tudor beacons, to warn of the impending Spanish Armada, and then in World War 2 for spotting fires and enemy aircraft.

The land was bought by the Cadbury family in 1907 and then gifted to the City of Birmingham for the benefit of the public. The toposcope was built to commemorate this gift, and rebuilt in 1988 into the 'castle' we see today. On a clear day, it is said that the view includes 13 of the old counties.

Beacon Hill Toposcope – climb the steps for a fabulous view over Birmingham

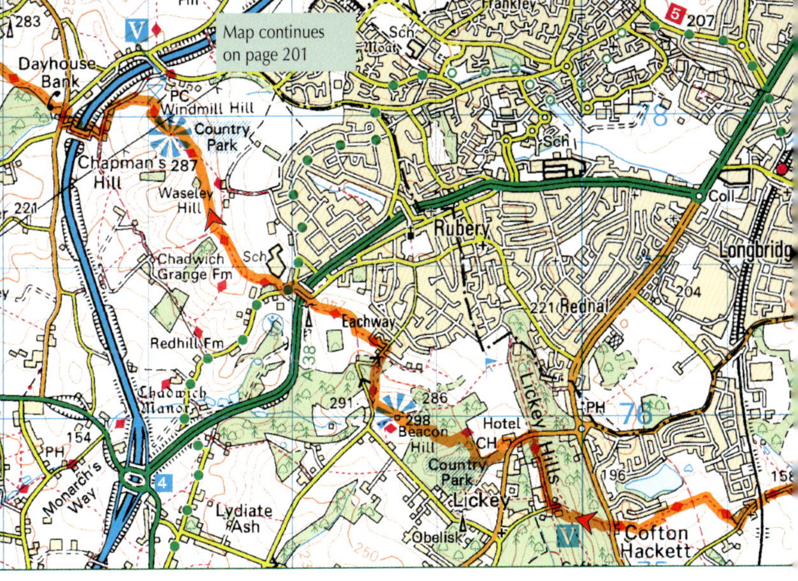

Turn left along the ridge until you almost reach a lane, where the path bends to the right downhill through woodland to one side of the golf course. On reaching Beacon Hill Road, cross and continue ahead. At a T-junction of paths, turn right.

At the road, turn left to cross over the **A38**. Turn left along Holywell Lane, then right through Waseley Hills Country Park south car park. Take the left-hand path, which is waymarked for the North Worcestershire Path and passes through a kissing gate on its way up the hill. The path does not quite reach the first summit. Stay right, with the summit on your left, and then ahead and down.

Continue ahead over **Waseley Hill**, to the right-hand side of a small woodland. At a series of gates, pass through the first one straight ahead towards Birmingham, through the second one and then turn diagonally left towards the pylon and the toposcope at the summit of **Windmill Hill**. From here, except for one bank of trees, there are 360-degree views extending to Cannock Chase (north), Daventry (east) and the Malvern Hills (south).

Exit this field by a kissing gate to the left of the pylon and turn right along the path down the right-hand side of the meadow. At the bottom of the meadow, turn right through the gate, left along the edge of the next meadow and left again at the waymark post. This route takes you along the lower edge of another meadow and then to a lane. Turn left to follow the lane through the hamlet, past a farm, over the **M5** and on to a road.

Turn right, then left immediately past the Olde Inn (no longer a pub), along a clear path across an arable field to a woodland. Resist the temptation to dive into the cool shade, as the route continues to the right on the field side of the woodland and remains heading in the same direction after leaving the trees behind, until it reaches a road.

Turn right onto the road. When the road bends to the right, turn left onto a lane. Follow this lane for around 1km to a T-junction with Shut Mill Lane. Turn right, then left up a footpath opposite the cottage gates. Head uphill through a couple of fields until you reach the top of the path. Turn right through the gate and follow the path, which undulates gently, meandering in and out of woodland, slowly climbing the ridge of Walton Hill. On leaving the woodland, another view over Birmingham city centre opens up. Over the course of the walk, it noticeably recedes.

When you reach the house driveway, turn diagonally left uphill, then follow the path round to the right. This will lead you to the trig point marking the summit of **Walton Hill**. Continue past the trig point on the wide path and take a left fork after about 100m.

Birmingham skyline as seen from the Clent Hills

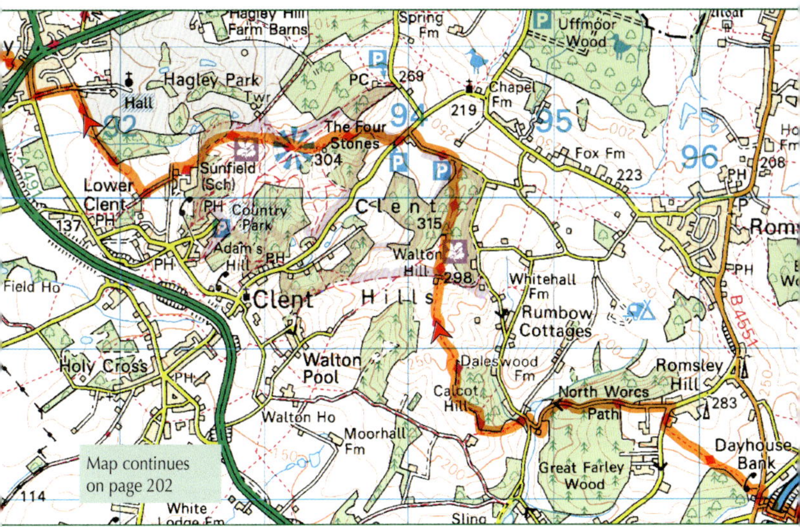

Map continues on page 202

Remain on this wide track as it meanders down the hill to a **car park**. Turn left along the lane; at the T-junction, turn left along St Kenelm's Pass. Head through the **car park** on the right and up a track. Continue on the main path, heading uphill. At the next junction, turn left, which will lead you to the summit of the hill, four standing stones and another view indicator. This view is stunning – it makes all the effort of the day worthwhile!

Walk past the **Four Stones** and along the spur ahead. Take the right fork at a stand of pine trees and continue ahead down a mown path after passing another viewpoint. Stick to the main path down through the woods, stay ahead at the crosspaths and again at the waymarker for the Buzzard Trail.

Where the slope flattens off, the route doglegs left, then right, to continue in the same direction, now descending gently. On reaching the track, turn left. At the security gate, turn right onto a track between hedgerows. At a junction of paths, turn right and continue in this direction until you reach the outskirts of **Hagley**, choosing either the path along the side of the meadow or that along the side of the woodland when you reach a stile. The paths rejoin at the end of the meadow.

When you reach a residential area, turn left along the street. At the end, turn right onto Bromsgrove Road. Cross the **dual carriageway** at the lights, then turn left, then almost immediately right along a narrow path between buildings.

The route drops off the Clent Hills through woodland

This path passes between fields and past paddocks, and eventually arrives at Worcester Road (**B4187**). Head straight over for the next stage of the walk.

Alternative finish at Hagley railway station

To finish at **Hagley railway station**, turn left along Worcester Road, then right at the traffic lights. This adds about 1km to the route.

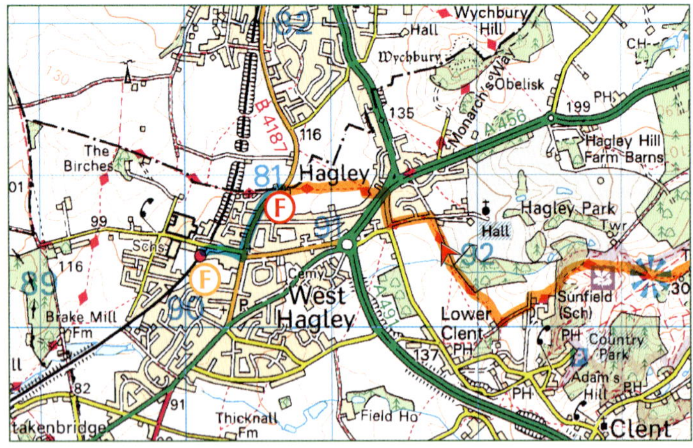

STAGE 2

Hagley to Bewdley

Start	199 Worcester Road, Hagley (SO 907 809)
Alternative start	Hagley railway station (SO 901 805)
Finish	Dog Lane car park, Bewdley (SO 785 756)
Time	8hr
Distance	27.2km (16.9 miles)
Ascent	505m (1660ft)
Descent	600m (1970ft)
Terrain	Tarmac, field paths and tracks; sandy bridleways. Gentle ascents and descents; only one significant ascent.
Refreshments	Hagley and Bewdley
Toilets	Bewdley
Public transport	Train to Hagley; buses from Load Street stop in Bewdley to Bridgnorth, Ludlow and Worcester
Parking	At alternative start and finish
Accommodation	Premier Inn Hagley Hotel is 3.2km from Hagley railway station; several options in Bewdley
Warning	There are no refreshment options along this route – you will need to carry enough food and drink for the whole day.

Circling round the north of Kidderminster, this stage of the North Worcestershire Path avoids passing through any towns or villages. It is a quiet, contemplative route that showcases local woodlands, ancient sunken lanes, meadow and pasture. There are plenty of small hills to cross in the early parts of the walk, and places where deep sand on uphill stretches makes it hard going. However, the final few kilometres flanking the River Severn are almost totally flat and offer a delightful finish to a long hike, and the route along open flood meadows is punctuated by a stretch of steep woodland reaching down to the banks. Continue a little beyond the end of the North Worcestershire Path towards the centre of town for riverside pubs and cafés.

As with the first stage of the North Worcestershire Path, the route is scantily waymarked, and you will need a map and/or directions to successfully navigate the walk.

Alternative start at Hagley railway station

To start from Hagley railway station, head east from the station, turn left at the traffic lights and walk to number 199 Worcester Road where Stage 2 starts.

Main route

Take the public footpath to the left of 199 Worcester Road. At the residential street, continue ahead past several side streets. At the end, take the footpath in the far right-hand corner. Continue in the same direction over the **railway** and a drainage channel, through a kissing gate and along the side of a meadow, steadily gaining height.

At a crosspaths, turn left through another kissing gate onto a gently descending path along the edge of woodland. When you reach the end of the path, turn right onto the lane and stay on it when it becomes a track. At a junction with a utility pole in the middle, turn left and follow the track to a lane. Cross and continue ahead on a footpath, which eventually rises to the **A451**.

Cross and take the path along the verge to the left, then turn right along a drive. Past Deerhurst, this becomes a shady track that leads to a lane. Follow the lane to the right until you reach some houses on the edge of **Iverley**. Opposite the third house, turn sharply left onto a bridleway.

On this route, several old tracks are lower than the surrounding land. One name for these is **holloways**. In some places, the level is lower due to compaction and erosion, and in others, ditches were dug to demarcate land ownership. The ditches were then used for transport. Either way, sunken lanes have usually been in use for a very long time.

The early parts of the walk are across low rolling hills

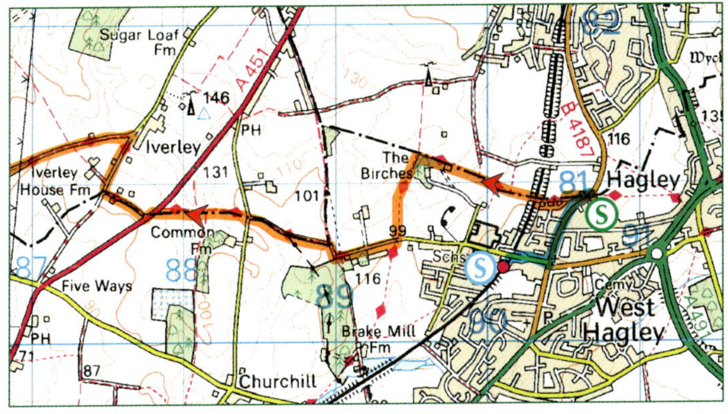

At a fork with a waymarker denoting the boundary between Worcestershire and Staffordshire, head right. Stay right at the next fork, which leads to a stile. Over this, the route continues along the right-hand edge of a meadow. Through a hedgerow, the path bears left up a slight rise, then down to a stile. After that, the route is clearly cut diagonally left across an arable field. Through a hedge, the route remains clear to the far corner of the hayfield ahead.

This leads to the **A449**. Cross and take the lane directly opposite, which soon crosses the **Staffordshire and Worcestershire Canal**, then the **River Stour**. Shortly after crossing the river, turn right onto a drive, then look for the path on the right between a hedge and a fence. A kissing gate leads to a long field, and the route continues along the right-hand edge. At the end, join the track to the power lines, then turn left to a lane. Follow the lane to the left to a junction.

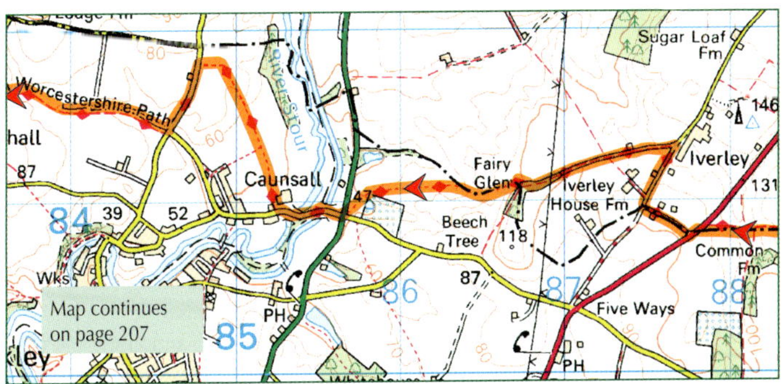

Map continues on page 207

There are some waymarks along the route, but not enough to rely on

Turn right along the bridleway immediately past the drive to the Sladd Estate. This passes paddocks and stables, and eventually arrives at a junction of paths and tracks. Turn right between hedges (not through the gate) and then right onto the lane. Immediately after Oakleigh, fork left along a track through woods.

This leads to a **picnic area**. Turn left through the **car park**, then turn left and proceed gently uphill. After a short distance, bear right at a junction to follow the bridlepath past Kinver Edge Farm. At a crosspaths, continue ahead; the two paths run parallel to each other to another crosspaths. Turn left. This is **Kingsford Forest Park**, a pine plantation with a border of broadleaf trees.

The route runs along the top of a steep wooded slope with occasional glimpses of a view. Where the main path turns away from the fence, fork right to keep the fence on your right. Just after the junction, there is a remembrance bench with a view.

The path soon skirts a fence surrounding a small, enclosed reservoir. Follow the fence to the left at the next junction, then take the broad track heading away from its gates. At a crosspaths, turn right downhill. At the next junction, turn left uphill. Still in the woods (now **Blakeshall Common**), the route forks to the left at the next waymarked junction, onto a footpath. At a minor fork, stay low. Cross the wide sandy bridlepath and continue ahead, taking the steps up the steep slope. The route continues between fields to a lane.

Turn right along the lane and stay ahead past several buildings. Fork right at a gate along another sunken track. This leads to a large house and a road at **Drakelow**. Cross and take Sladd Lane ahead.

Continue to the caravan park. The route heads straight up the main road through the park to another lane. Turn left, then after about 20 paces, turn right up some stone steps through a gate. A clear path leads along the edge of the field, across to a gate and then along the top edge of a small plantation.

At the end of this path, turn left through the kissing gate and along the right edge of the hayfield. Stay heading in the same direction until you reach a lane. Turn

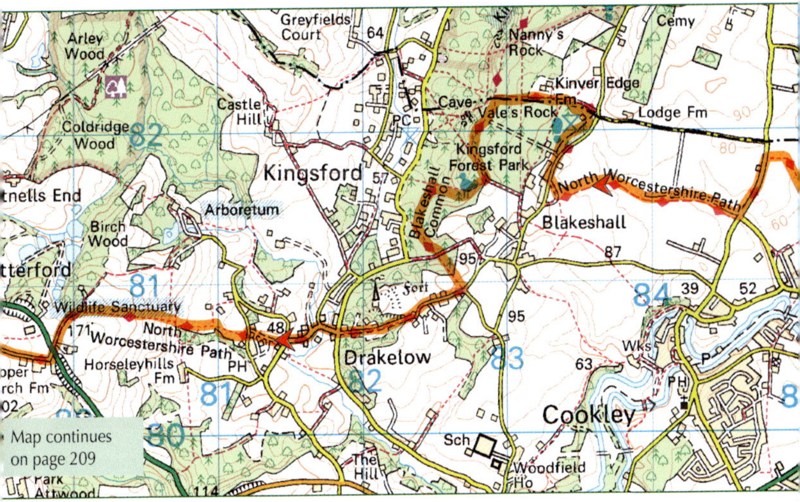

Map continues on page 209

around for a view across the neighbouring hills and valleys. It continues to improve as you climb. Cross the road to a kissing gate and continue uphill with the fence line on your left. When you reach a track, turn downhill and follow it to the **A442**.

The route rises through Eymore Wood before dropping to the river

The River Severn from the bridge at Upper Arley

Cross and take the lane ahead. At the end, turn right along another road. Opposite Bank Cottage, fork left off the road, then left again along a stone drive for Deer House and Woodcot Deep. Pass both houses and continue ahead, staying on the track to its end, then continue ahead along a clear path through Cox's Coppice and Gunhill Wood. Through a kissing gate, the route follows the outside edge of the woods for a short distance before heading back under trees, crossing a bridge and climbing, eventually reaching a T-junction of paths. You are now in **Eymore Wood**. Turn right. After a while, you will reach a wide junction of paths and tracks. Continue ahead on the stone track.

At the next junction, do not follow this track around to the right. Instead, continue ahead on a mown path. This leads to a T-junction of paths. Turn right, downhill, to cross a stream and then rise on the other side to a car park.

Turn right through the car park and then take the path in front of the noticeboard to the drive leading to Huntsfield Cottage. Follow the drive to the house. At the gates, turn right and follow the path to the left. Through a kissing gate, a clear route leads across the meadow and continues in this direction until the **River Severn** is just visible ahead. Turn right at the junction and keep the river on your left until you reach a pedestrian bridge at **Upper Arley**.

On this final stretch of the walk, you may well hear and even see a steam train on the **Severn Valley Railway**, and Arley Station can be seen from the footbridge. The railway was built in the late 19th century to transport coal, but its operations were always limited by having only one track, which made it challenging to run trains in both directions, even with passing places. By 1963,

it was considered unprofitable and was axed, but it only took a few years for railway enthusiasts to buy the track and start running services on it themselves.

Once you've crossed the bridge, turn right and then right again underneath it to follow the course of the river with the water on your left for almost 6km into **Bewdley**. On the approach to the town, the path passes a car park. Look for a waymarker post about two-thirds of the way along the car park: this marks the end of the North Worcestershire Path and the start of the Worcestershire Way.

WALK 31

Worcestershire Way

Start	Bewdley
Finish	Great Malvern
Time	2 days
Distance	49.1km (30.4 miles)
Terrain	Varied – from woodland, fields and river valleys to steep ascents and descents

The Worcestershire Way must be one of the most delightful multi-day walks in the world. It follows the ridge of the hills that march north from the end of the Malvern Hills, which is largely covered in mixed native woodlands. The route switches from east to west of the ridge, giving splendid views across the Severn Plain, across Herefordshire to the mountains of Wales and south to the Malvern Hills. It is also well signposted and well maintained, which makes it easy to follow.

The route is split into two stages of uneven length due to the lack of accommodation elsewhere. The first day is long but has a welcoming pub with rooms and campsite at the end. The second day is shorter, but with a steep climb to the top of the Malvern Hills towards the end.

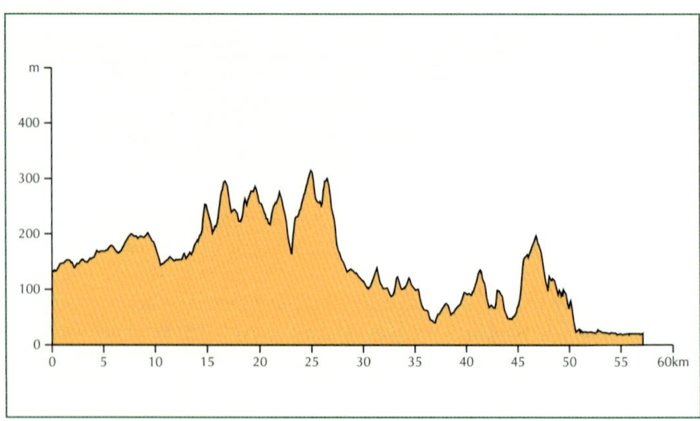

The view south along the Malvern Hills (Stage 2)

STAGE 1

Bewdley to Knightwick

Start	Dog Lane car park, Bewdley (SO 785 756)
Finish	The Talbot at Knightwick (SO 733 560)
Time	11hr
Distance	31.3km (19.4 miles)
Ascent	1065m (3490ft)
Descent	1060m (3470ft)
Terrain	Mainly woodland and field paths; lots of ascent and descent, sometimes steep
Refreshments	Plentiful options in Bewdley, including Bewdley Community Workshop and Café near the start; the Talbot at Knightwick
Toilets	At start and finish
Public transport	Buses to Load Street stop in Bewdley from Bridgnorth, Ludlow and Worcester; infrequent buses from Knightwick Surgery stop to Bromyard and Worcester
Parking	At start and finish
Accommodation	Several options in Bewdley; the Talbot at Knightwick
Note	This is a long walk with no refreshment stops or facilities once you have left Bewdley – take plenty of supplies with you.

Bewdley has a sense of belonging where it is, confirmed by the presence of the River Severn, local food markets and the Community Workshop and Café. Starting alongside the river and through the town, a pleasant woodland walk then leads to the historic St Leonard's Church in Ribbesford, with its unique carvings and very unusual 500-year-old oak octagonal pillars.

This well-waymarked path winds its way through rural agricultural areas and over woodland ridges, while also providing secretive stream valley settings and wide scenic views encompassing the Malverns to the south and as far as Wales to the west. The Talbot at Knightwick provides a welcome end point to a beautiful but hard day's walk.

Start along the banks of the River Severn, passing by the main bridge and turning right up Lax Lane. At the junction with Upper Street, turn right and then left at the first alleyway, which is just after the narrowing of the road, beside the 15th-century Little Pack Horse pub.

Continue past the Community Workshop and Café, straight on up into the woodland. Turn left at the first junction of paths. Pass the pond on your right and go through a gate, and then turn right following the chestnut-paling fence line. The path continues upslope through the cattle grazing pastures of Wyre Community Land Trust. Go through the gate, cross the road and continue along the lane on the opposite side.

The **Wyre Community Land Trust** is inspired by the work of John Ruskin, a Victorian writer, art critic and conservationist. He was given some land in the Wyre Forest in the 1870s, and it is now owned by the Guild of St George, the charity he founded that offers people an opportunity to reconnect with nature. The Wyre Community Land Trust offers educational and volunteering opportunities, courses, meat from the Dexter cattle they employ in conservation grazing, and wood and associated products from their sawmill and woodyard.

Fork left to follow the lane underneath the **A456**. Follow the track forking right, and at **Ribbesford Church** go into the grounds. Pass to the right-hand side of the church, climbing uphill. Stay ahead through the fields uphill. Continue through the woodland, keeping the boundary on your right-hand side. Exit the woods via the gate with a small paddock on your left. Continue through the next gate to join a quiet country lane. Turn left and continue along the lane.

Bewdley Bridge

The short stretch of road heading towards Horse Hill Farm

Turn right opposite **Horse Hill Farm barn**, signposted to the Frank Chapman Centre. Continue along the drive and as you enter the wonderful oak woodland, turn left onto a woodland track. Go through the next gate into a field with views now opening up to your left. Continue along the track for about a kilometre, at which point it bears left down a spur towards parkland.

On reaching **Little Lakes Holiday Park and Golf Club**, you may find that the land managers have cleared and mown walkways. The route descends to **Gladder Brook** in the valley bottom and then ascends following the hedge line. Turn left at the road in front of **Deasland Farm**.

Continue through the hamlet of Latchetts. Some 30m after the last building, the road bends sharply left; continue for another 40m to a footpath on the left. Cross the stile and go through the managed woodland to a small footbridge. Follow the path across the field, bearing right to the far corner towards the building. Turn left on Heightington Road through **Heightington** village. After passing a house on the right, the road begins to bear left. Take the path on the right.

Follow this path across the middle of the field. Go through the gate with a seat on your right. Bearing slightly right, descend across the field, heading towards a

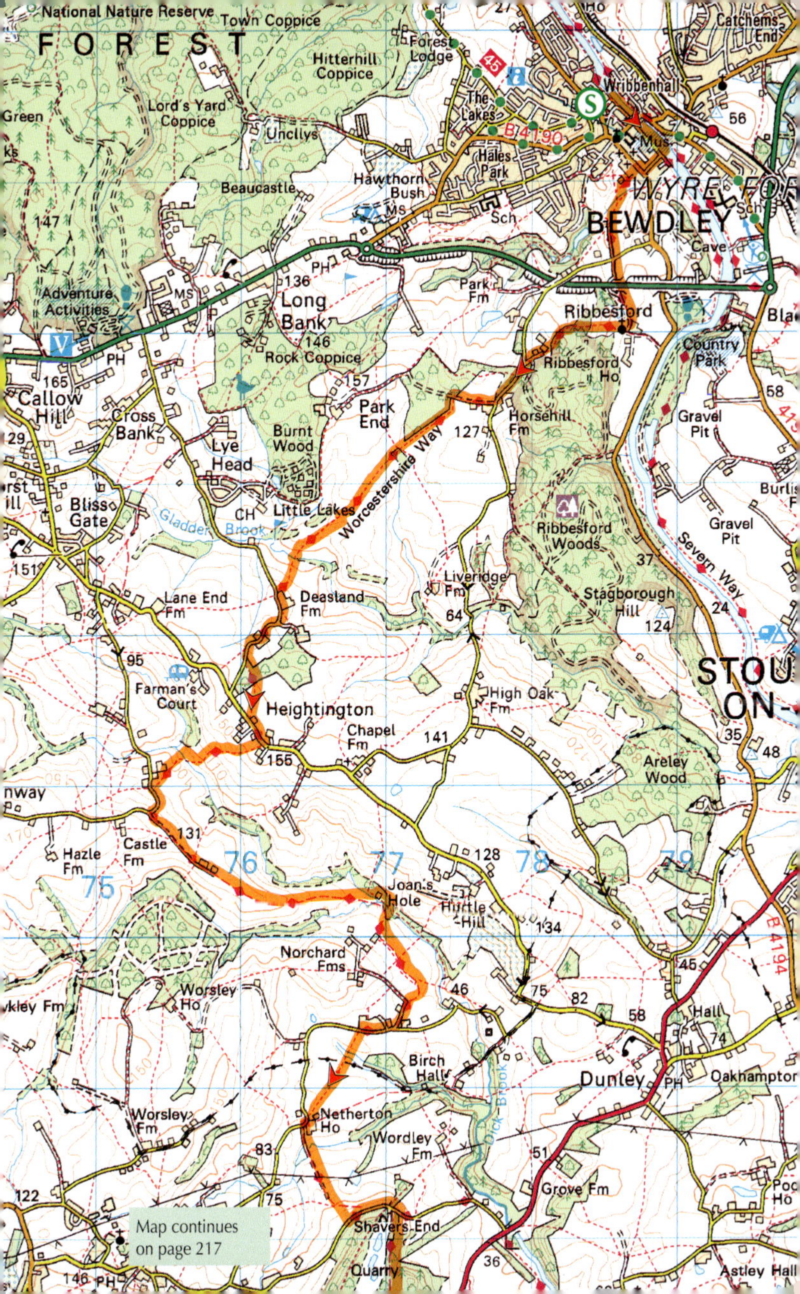

Map continues on page 217

gate in the woodland boundary. Turn right after the gate. Turn left across the middle bridge over the stream. Continue straight up over the next field into a horse paddock and bear left. At the next gate, bear right, keeping wooden rail fences to your right. Join the lane and turn left.

Continue uphill to take a gravel track on your left signed to Palmer's Farm. Continue past the farm. Off to the right you can see Abberley Clock Tower for the first time. After the descent alongside fields, go through the gate and continue straight on across the meadow, heading towards the woodland in the valley. Cross the footbridge where a bridleway continues down the stream bed. Bear right on the bankside, following the course of the stream; this is Dick Brook, which runs down to **Joan's Hole**. Cross another footbridge with the main stream on your right. Cross the third footbridge and turn left. The path follows a lovely deep holloway.

A **sunken lane** (hollow way or holloway) is a road or track that is significantly lower than the land on either side. This effect can be caused by use and compaction. In other places, it is where people walked along boundaries that had been demarcated with a ditch. Either way, they are generally ancient routes.

When the track opens up into a large meadow, continue along the defined and fenced route. Turn left at the lane leading to **Norchard Farms**. Continue to a narrow road and turn right. Passing Brockstone House on your right, continue for 230m and then take the footpath on your left.

Follow the field boundary to a tree-lined brook. Cross over the footbridge to continue on the same bearing across the next field. Bear right towards the field barn in the far corner of the field by **Netherton House**. Join the lane to the right of the barn. Turn left and follow it around the corner and then turn left onto a track, signposted 'Malvern 24 miles'. Continue towards the woods on the hill. On reaching the lane at the woodland edge, turn left.

The lane bears right and starts to drop downhill around **Shavers End**, going past an entrance to a **quarry**. The path is 20m further on, on the right. Follow it up through the woodland, merging into a small meadow. Cross diagonally left to the other side into the woodland. Look to your left for the first view of End Hill and Worcestershire Beacon, part of the Malvern Hills. Continue uphill, skirting the quarry and passing the Ramscombe Coppice sign. You are now on the ridge of **Abberley Hill**.

Very close to the summit, take the first green track on the left, continuing just below the ridge. Continue maintaining a pretty consistent contour line throughout. A sudden spectacular view to Abberley Clock Tower opens up, with a usefully placed seat – enjoy! Continue along the path to Flagstaff Wood Triangulation Point and then descend the wood to meet the lane. Turn left downhill.

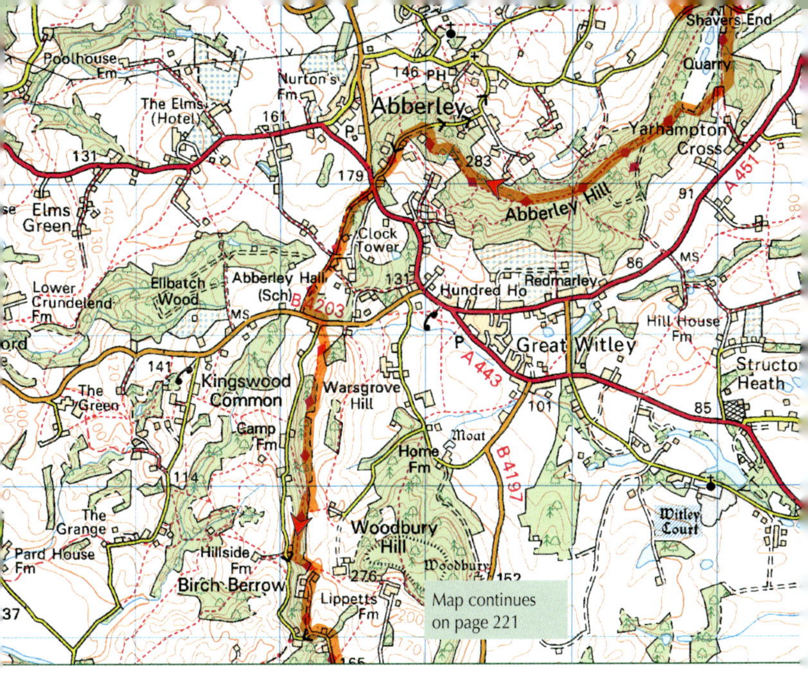

Map continues on page 221

At the junction with the **A443**, cross straight over onto the track opposite. Follow this to join the drive from Abberley School and continue downslope. Follow the gravel track with the tennis courts on your left. Leaving the school grounds, turn left onto the **B4203**. Cross the road when safe and take the first right-hand lane uphill. About 50m from the road junction, turn left onto the footpath. Bearing right, head for the path snaking up **Warsgrove Hill** and onto the ridge. The footpath now weaves between field and woodland, maintaining an approximate contour line along the ridge.

After going through the gate which exits Camp Hill, the path continues on the contour and bears left through a gate into the field. Follow the woodland boundary on your right, and re-enter the woodland further down the fence line. Alternatively, do not leave the woodland, but drop right on a smaller track which picks up the Worcestershire Way within 10m. A delightful downhill path then zigzags through the dappled forest.

On reaching the road, turn left. Within 30m the footpath goes left onto a residential drive. As the drive curves left to head to the house, there is a narrow path between Cypress trees heading upslope towards the wood. The path then swings steeply uphill to follow the valley to the ridge.

The view past Abberley Clock Tower

Bear right just before the summit into a little footpath beside a residential garden. Join the driveway and continue straight on. Maintain course roughly on the contour line. Pass by the houses and then enter the woodland ridge. Follow the path that curves round and descends the hill to join a lane. Turn left.

Continue along the lane, skirting a **quarry lake** with deep turquoise water. At the T-junction, turn right onto the road, signposted to Shelsley Beauchamp. Continue along the road as it starts to go downhill and bears right. Pass massive concrete barriers to prevent access to the quarry on your right, then take the footpath through the gate on your left slightly further downhill.

A short uphill slope leads to a contour path through the wood. At a junction of paths, bear left uphill. At the top, turn right and follow the green lane along the ridge of **Rodge Hill**. At a crossroads of paths (including the Martley Circular, Walk 4), continue ahead, signposted 'Malvern 17½ miles'. This stretch of contour path is on a wide grass track with tremendous views. On entering the woodland, take the right and then immediately go left, maintaining your position along the contour.

The view west from the ridge

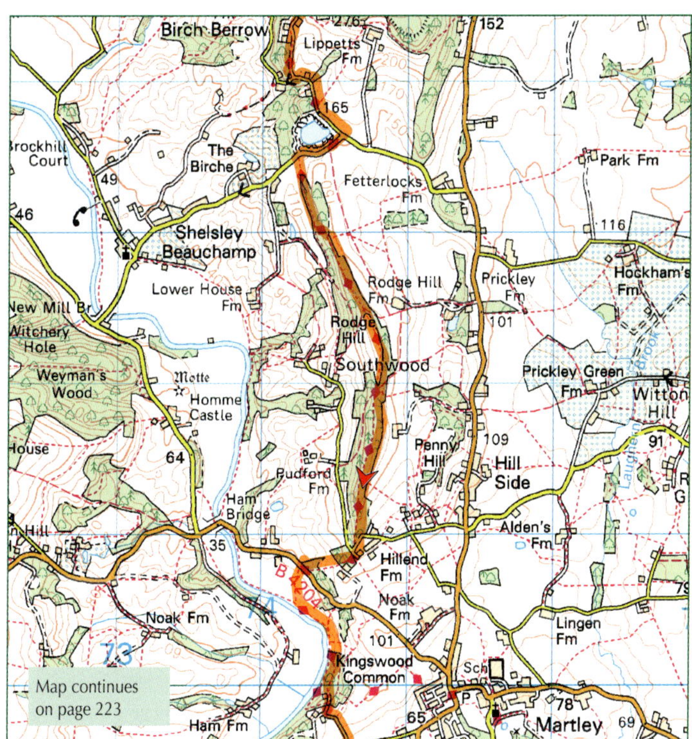

After a relaxing woodland ridge walk, go through a metal gate and start the descent to a lane. Go down the steps to the lane, turn right and then immediately left and then right through a gate into the coniferous wood. Cross over the stile and head right down the hill. The path joins the **B4204** at the bottom right-hand corner of this field. Turn right and then cross when safe to take the first footpath on the left through a metal gate. The path heads straight down the field and then towards the trees running along the **River Teme**.

Turn left with the river beside you on your right. Cross the footbridge and then follow the field boundary beside the river. As a fantastic view of the river opens up, continue for a short while and then branch left uphill, left of an Ash tree. The path enters the **Kingswood Common** woodland over a footbridge. Go through the gate and the path ascends through the wood.

The Malvern Hills from the north

Where the path reaches an area of excavation and a double gate, turn left uphill. Follow the narrow path alongside the wooden fence through the gate and onto the road. Head uphill. Just before the summit, take the footpath on your right, which closely follows the route of the road. Continue straight on to Berrow Farm.

On reaching the farm lane, turn left and then immediate right. The farm access track bears right and then there is a footpath ahead, straight across horse paddocks towards a white house set against the trees. Go through a narrow gate beside the white house onto a residential drive. Turn left and when you join the road, turn right and maintain your route on the road to **Berrow Green**.

Pass through the last buildings of Berrow Green to take the footpath on the left. Go through the gate and bear right following the right-hand side field boundary, with a spectacular view of the north end of the Malvern Hills. Within a few paces, take the right-hand footpath through the gate and then follow the path within the electric fence. Through the gate at the end of the horse paddock, turn left. Continue through the next gate and walk straight along the field boundary. Follow the boundary all the way round and up to the far corner of the field to a lane.

Cross the narrow farm lane through the gate and cross to the next gate visible across the field. Go straight across the next field, picking up the line of the power cables. At the bottom of the field, you'll see the exit onto the lane. Turn left. At the T-junction, turn left again.

Pass Hawks Nest Farm downhill and as the road bears left, take the path on the right. Go through the metal gate and continue across the field close to the left-hand boundary. Go through the next gate, turn right and head downslope towards the woods. Keep bearing right as you approach the woods then follow the woodland boundary until finding the gate. Turn left and enter the woodland. Cross the bridge and follow the woodland track uphill. On joining the main woodland track, turn right. Immediately before the track crosses several small dams, turn left and continue up the valley.

Follow the main track up and as it bears right into the new planting, head straight up on a narrow, faint path. Follow the path straight on up the hill until it

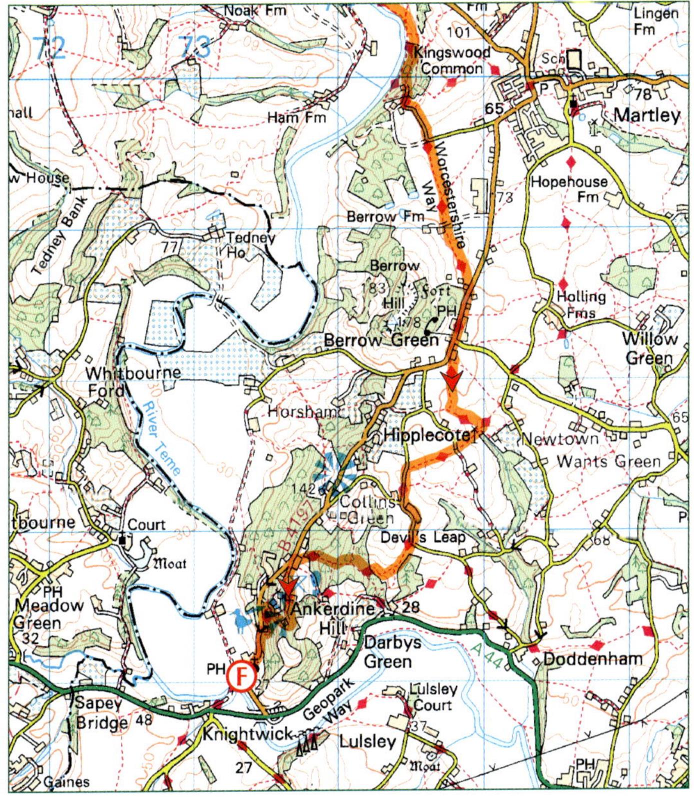

reaches a residential parking area. Turn left onto the driveway, heading along the ridge. Continue to the **Ankerdine Hill viewing point** via the brick-edged track. Continue along the gravel track towards Willow and Woodland Cottages. Bear right on the track into the woodland.

On reaching a residential drive, the footpath carries straight on and then turns sharp right downhill, skirting a residential garden. At the end of the wooden garden fence, take the left fork downhill. Follow this path as it zigzags downhill until it reaches the road. Turn left. Head down this road into **Knightwick**. Soon the Talbot will be visible – seats, drinks and food must now be top of the agenda!

STAGE 2

Knightwick to Great Malvern

Start	The Talbot at Knightwick (SO 733 560)
Finish	Bellevue Terrace, Great Malvern (SO 775 459)
Time	6hr
Distance	17.8km (11 miles)
Ascent	675m (2210ft)
Descent	560m (1830ft)
Terrain	Varied – from flat river valley to steep ascents to the Malvern Hills. One sudden confrontation with a fast road.
Refreshments	The Talbot at Knightwick; Great Malvern
Toilets	The Talbot at Knightwick; Great Malvern
Public transport	Infrequent buses to Knightwick Surgery stop from Bromyard and Worcester; trains from Great Malvern, 1km downhill from the finish
Accommodation	The Talbot Inn at Knightwick; several options in Great Malvern

A rare combination of landscapes awaits you on this route. The path soon rises from the valley of the River Teme to link woodlands, ridges, views and orchards, all the way to the magnificent Malvern Hills. The final stretch includes short but steep sections to gain 250m onto Lady Howard de Walden Drive, which winds around the hills with stunning views across the Severn Plain. The steep descent into Great Malvern passes dragons, cannons, pubs and more – the town is a real treat

The Talbot marks the end of Stage 1 and the beginning of Stage 2

THE TALBOT AT KNIGHTWICK

Meals, drinks, camping and accommodation are all available at the Talbot. This 15th-century inn was built to service those travelling between South Wales and the salt mines in Droitwich. The Talbot boasts of something unusual in its battle against spectral shenanigans – they found a dead cat in the chimney in the 1990s, possibly placed there to ward off evil spirits. Of more relevance perhaps to walkers, the pub takes local sourcing seriously. They have their own kitchen garden, on-site bakery and brewery – and if they don't produce it themselves, they do their best to find someone local who does.

With the pub on your right, cross the bridge over the River Teme. Cross the **A44** and take the left turn at the junction shortly afterwards, signposted to Lulsley, Alfrick and Leigh. Almost at the summit of the road, turn right onto a gravel and tarmac track that follows the route of the **old railway line**. Pass to the right of the farmhouse towards the end of the track and then straight through the gate onto the ridge. Magnificent views open up.

At a junction of paths, with large agricultural sheds to your left, continue bearing right on the wider of the paths. Go through the gate at the end of the fences and bear left along the ridge.

Alongside several sections of path, you will see **pits and quarries**. These are predominantly limestone, which was burnt in kilns to make lime. In some areas, lime was used for mortar for construction, but here it was mainly used as a soil improver. During the Agricultural Revolution, farmers started to use as much as four tons of lime per acre per year, so in an area like this, there was strong demand.

Continue along the summit through two gates, with the disused pits all around you. Joining a gravel track, turn right. **Ravenshill Wood Nature Reserve** is on your left. Walk down the slope to join the lane and turn right. Note the view towards the Malverns on your left. As the lane curves left, the footpath leaves it to the left into Crews Hill Wood nature reserve.

Crews Hill Wood is an ancient woodland, owned and managed by Worcestershire Wildlife Trust. It is incredibly diverse, including Oak, Ash, Beech, Lime, Wild Service, Hornbeam and Yew trees. The understorey is also thriving, along with ground flora that includes Native Bluebells and an impressive array of fungi. In turn, all this diversity provides food and shelter for a wide range of animal life. Keep your eyes peeled as you walk through!

After the ascent onto the summit ridge, keep heading along the ridgeline on the more distinct path. Continue into Black House Wood. As you begin the descent from the summit of Black House Wood, there is a crossroads of paths. The main track continues straight ahead, but the route follows the footpath downhill to the right. On reaching the lane, cross straight over to the footpath ascending along the side of an **orchard** into the wood on the opposite ridge. Climb the first slope and as the path levels, turn left to follow the route onto the summit of the ridge. Continue along the ridge.

At a crossroads of footpaths, continue straight ahead. At the next crossroads of paths, turn left downhill, then turn right onto the lower track, close to the fence line. Continue on this lower track inside the wood as it gently ascends into the field. Cross the stile, follow the field boundary to the right down to a gate in the bottom right-hand corner. Turn right along an alley beside residential gardens. Turn left at the road, proceed through the hamlet of **Longley Green**, cross the bridge and fork right.

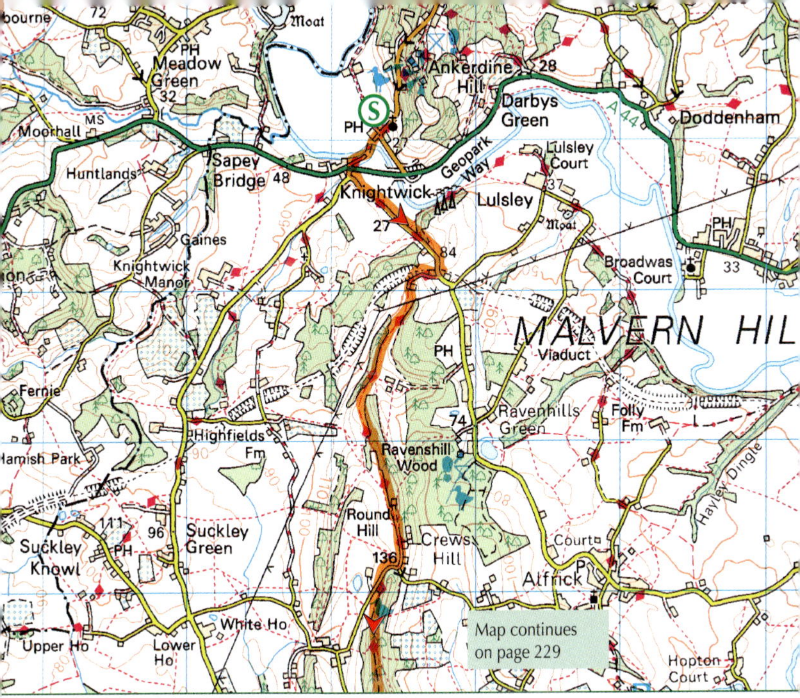

Map continues on page 229

View along the River Teme

Rolling grassland on the edge of the woods

Continue going uphill gently, passing a set of black-and-white roadside bollards, and as the road bears left uphill, take the footpath through the gate on the right. Exit the woodland through a gate and follow the left-hand boundary through the next field to the lane. Turn right.

Follow the lane uphill and just before the summit at a green triangle with a seat, take the track on the left. Follow the track as it bears right at a junction, along the edge of the woods on **Old Storridge Common**. The path diverts left at the end of the track just before a residence. Once you've completed the circuit of the residence and before reaching a gate leading into a field, turn left into the Long Coppice.

Bear gently right, continue downhill over the scrub and grassland to a track, and turn left at the bottom. Go through the gate into the orchard to circle round the residence. Pick up the track in front of the house. Continue along the lane, enjoying some lovely properties, **orchards** and views, until you reach a T-junction. Turn right. After 30m uphill, turn left and follow the field boundary on your right to the **A4103**. **Warning:** This is a busy road – please cross carefully.

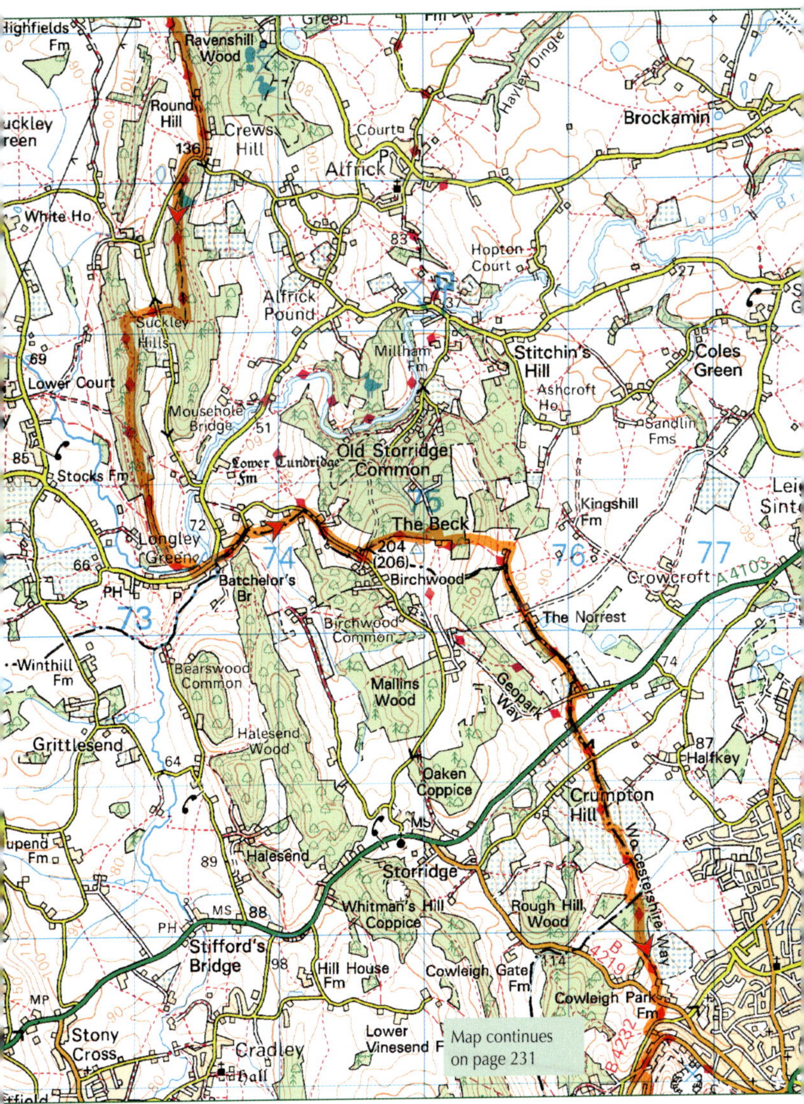

Map continues on page 231

Great Malvern with the Severn Plain and the Cotswold Hills in the distance

Once across the road, head straight through the gardens to the gate leading into horse paddocks. Continue straight ahead at the bottom of the post-and-wire fences. At the next lane, continue ahead. Pass by further horse paddocks and then enter an orchard at **Crumpton Hill**. Carry straight on through to newer orchards, enjoying views to the north Malvern Hills. Bear left and then right through the middle of the orchard. Go through the gate and follow the lowest of the three tracks in front of you. Bear left to cross the footbridge.

Bear left to head towards the metal gate and then to enter the orchard. Keep the wood on your left. After leaving the orchard, turn left at a track intersection past **Cowleigh Park Farm**. On reaching the road, turn left and then turn right just after the 30mph signs to view one of Malvern's famous springs – the Earl Beauchamp's Fountain.

A path continues up the steps just left of the fountain. The steep but short ascent emerges onto a lane. Turn right. Two paths intersect at the road as you come round the corner. Take the path on the left, up steps. On reaching the next road, turn right. Continue uphill until a left turn at Lamb Bank. The bank becomes a path, which continues straight up through a gap between houses. Go through a gate and turn right behind the gardens. At the first path intersection, continue uphill and behind the houses. At the next intersection, turn left and go uphill. Follow Lady Howard de Walden Drive, skirting round the summit of **North Hill**.

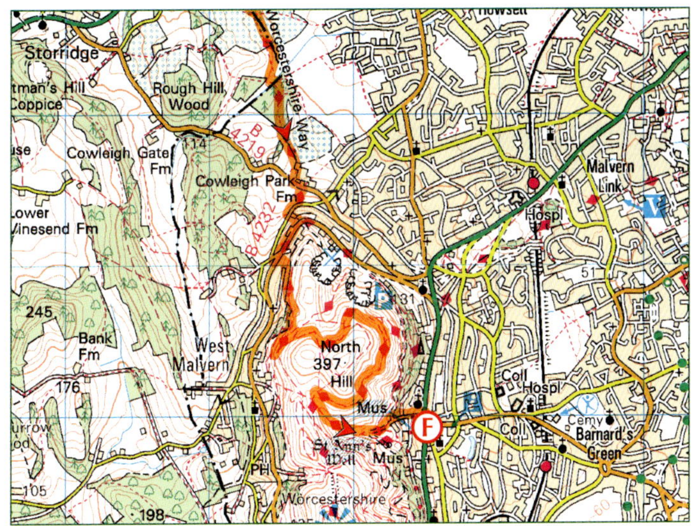

Most visitors to **Victorian Malvern** had to walk up to the clean air on the hills. Some who weren't well enough could hire a donkey for the ride up. Lady Howard de Walden was so wealthy that she had a carriageway cut around the top of the hill so she could access the clean air without having to expend any energy at all.

As you continue around on the drive, the views over Malvern Link and then Great Malvern open up. The valley that seems to run almost directly towards Malvern is the woodland area that you will descend into shortly. The drive bends around the top of Green Valley. Turn left down into this valley. Keep on walking straight down, saying hello to the donkeys at the donkey shed on the way past.

Continue down until you reach a T-junction on the edge of **Great Malvern**. Turn downhill, noticing the dragons on the entrance to number 36 – Happy Valley Cottage. Pass the Red Lion, then the famous Unicorn pub. Turning right onto Bellevue Terrace, your walk is complete. Use the pelican crossing, then take a few steps downhill to sip water from the only filtered fountain in Malvern, known as Malvhina. This is where the route ends, but perhaps the shops, bars and restaurants of Great Malvern will call you on for a few more steps.

APPENDIX A

Accommodation

Stage	Location	Name	Tel
Walk 29 – Worcester to Birmingham along the canal			
1	Worcester	The Worcester Whitehouse Hotel	+44 1905 24308
		The Old Infirmary	+44 1905 706786
		The Hop Merchant's House	+44 7912 691739
2	Droitwich Spa	St Andrews Hotel & Spa	+44 1905 779677
	Bromsgrove	Travelodge Bromsgrove	+44 871 9846625
3	Alvechurch		
	Hopwood	Westmead Hotel	+44 121 4451202
4	Birmingham	Holiday Inn Birmingham City	+44 800 405060
		Macdonald Burlington Hotel	+44 344 8799019
		Radisson Blu Hotel	+44 121 6546000
Walk 30 – North Worcestershire Path			
1	Shirley		
	Solihull	Crowne Plaza Solihull	+44 121 6239988
	Hopwood	Westmead Hotel	+44 121 4451202
	Lickey	Old Rose & Crown Hotel	+44 121 4533502
	Hagley	Premier Inn Hagley Hotel	+44 333 0031691
2	Bewdley	Mug House Inn	+44 1299 402543
		The Clockhouse	+44 1299 670027
		Horn & Trumpet	+44 1299 489547
Walk 31 – Worcestershire Way			
1	Bewdley	Mug House Inn	+44 1299 402543
		The Clockhouse	+44 1299 670027
		Horn & Trumpet	+44 1299 489547
	Knightwick	The Talbot	+44 1886 821235
2	Great Malvern	Mount Pleasant Hotel	+44 1684 561837
		Great Malvern Hotel	+44 1684 563411
		The Abbey	+44 1684 892332

all listings in the table below are hotels

Web/email	Comments
worcesterwhitehouse.co.uk / enquiries@worcswhitehouse.com	Close to Worcester Foregate Street station
worcesterluxuryapartments.co.uk / info@worcesterluxuryapartments.co.uk	Apartment-hotel close to Worcester Foregate Street station
thehopmerchantshouse.com / hello@thehopmerchantshouse.com	Close to Worcester Foregate Street station
standrewshotelandspa.com / enquiries@st-andrewshotel.com	Close to Droitwich Spa station
travelodge.co.uk	
westmeadhotel.co.uk / enquiry@westmeadhotel.co.uk	
ihg.com / reservations@hibirmingham.co.uk	Close to Birmingham New Street station
macdonaldhotels.co.uk/burlington	Close to Birmingham New Street station
radissonhotels.com / info.birmingham@radissonblu.com	Close to Birmingham New Street station
ihg.com / Reception@cpsolihull.com	4km off route
westmeadhotel.co.uk / enquiry@westmeadhotel.co.uk	
oldroseandcrown.com / book@oldroseandcrown.com	
premierinn.com	3.2km from Hagley station
mughousebewdley.co.uk	
clockhousebandb.co.uk / info@clockhousebandb.co.uk	
hornandtrumpet.mydirectstay.com / cookieathorn@gmail.com	
mughousebewdley.co.uk	
clockhousebandb.co.uk / info@clockhousebandb.co.uk	
hornandtrumpet.mydirectstay.com / cookieathorn@gmail.com	
the-talbot.co.uk / info@the-talbot.co.uk	
mountpleasanthotel.co.uk / reception@mountpleasanthotel.co.uk	
great-malvern-hotel.co.uk / sutton@great-malvern-hotel.co.uk	
sarova-abbeyhotel.com / abbey@sarova.com	

APPENDIX B

Useful information

Useful websites

Visit Worcestershire
visitworcestershire.org

Worcester Tourist Information
visitworcester.co.uk

Malvern Hills National Landscape
malvernhills-nl.org.uk

Cotswolds National Landscape
cotswoldsaonb.org.uk

Malvern Hills Trust
malvernhills.org.uk

Abberley and Malvern Hills Geopark
abberleymalvernhillsgeopark.org

Public transport

Rail services

Mainline rail services connect Worcestershire to Birmingham, London and other major cities. Stations within or close to the walking areas include:

- Worcester Foregate Street
- Worcester Shrub Hill
- Great Malvern
- Malvern Link
- Pershore
- Evesham
- Kidderminster
- Bromsgrove

West Midlands Railway
Regional train operator serving many Worcestershire routes.
westmidlandsrailway.co.uk

National Rail Enquiries
For train times, fares and service updates.
nationalrail.co.uk

Traveline
National journey planner covering bus, rail and other public transport options.
traveline.info

Bus Services

Bus services operate between many towns and villages in Worcestershire, though services may be limited in rural areas, especially on Sundays.

Bus operators include:

First Bus (Worcestershire)
firstbus.co.uk

Diamond Bus
diamondbuses.com

Stagecoach West
stagecoachbus.com

Nearing Birmingham (Walk 29, Stage 4)

Hello, and thank you for choosing a Cicerone guide!

It takes the combined dedication of many to create the book you now hold. Our authors explore the world to find the best routes; they research, write, record data and take stunning photos on the trail to inspire and guide new adventures. Then, our talented team work together with authors to create the best products for our readers, whether digital or printed. The final part of the picture is you; we deeply value hearing from Cicerone customers with ideas and updates from the trail. Your input helps us to improve and innovate across our guides.

Cicerone is proud to be a family business. Exploring the outdoors has always been central to our lives, and we are passionate about sharing our love of walking, trekking, cycling and climbing. If you have any feedback or just want to say hello, please get in touch – we would love to hear from you.

Happy adventuring,
Joe & Maddy

Joe Maddy

Contact us at

hello@cicerone.co.uk **cicerone.co.uk/contact**

The Cicerone story

1969 Cicerone is founded by Walt and Dorothy Unsworth and Brian and Aileen Evans, publishing Lakeland guides printed on a garage press.

1977 The *Tour of Mont Blanc* guidebook defines the modern trekking guide and establishes Cicerone internationally.

1999 Jonathan and Lesley Williams take over, bringing a deep love of the outdoors.

2011 Cicerone produces its first eBook.

2022 Joe and Maddy Williams take the helm, keeping Cicerone independent, family run and rooted in real adventure.

2026 The Cicerone App launches, bringing decades of trusted route knowledge, GPS-enabled maps and planning tools directly to your phone.

Discover more at **cicerone.co.uk/about-cicerone**

The Cicerone range

International walking & trekking

British walking & long distance

Pilgrimages

Short walks

Via ferrata, climbing & scrambling

Cycling, mountain biking & bikepacking

Winter climbs & snow sports

Trail & fell running

Our formats

Guidebook

The complete guidebook with detailed descriptions, route and maps, detailed facilities information and offline GPS navigation

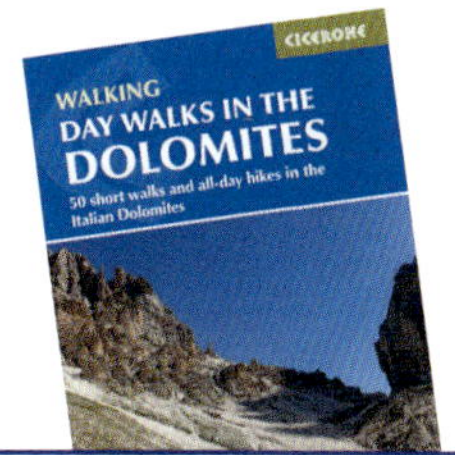

App

The complete guidebook with detailed descriptions, route and maps, detailed facilities information and offline GPS navigation

eBook

The digital edition of the guidebook with detailed descriptions, route and facilities information, profiles and maps, ready to use on any device

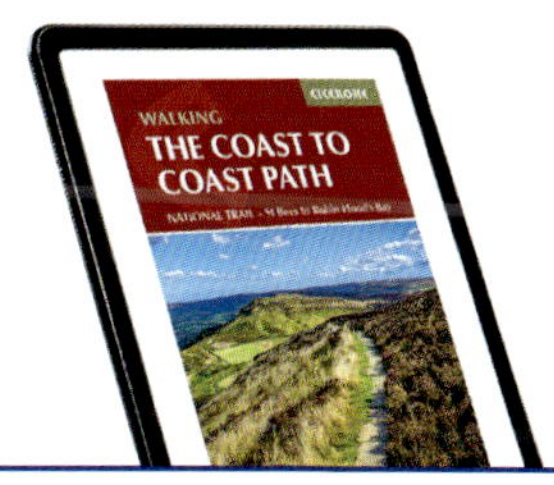

GPX files

Download GPX route files from your account to use on compatible devices for easy navigation and planning

See available formats for this book at **cicerone.co.uk/1244**

GPX files

Download free GPX files for this book

cicerone.co.uk/1244/GPX

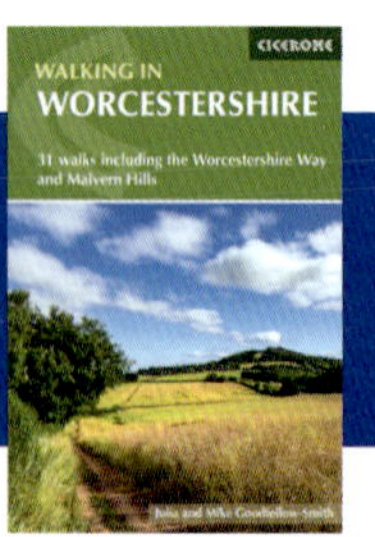

Other British walking guides

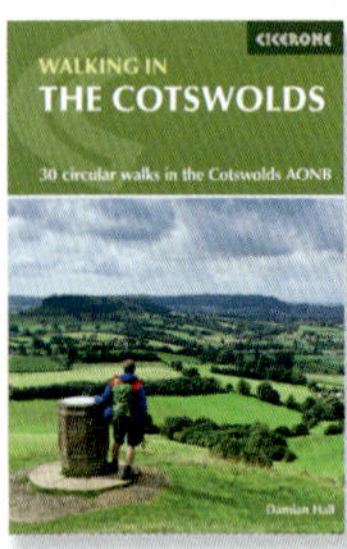

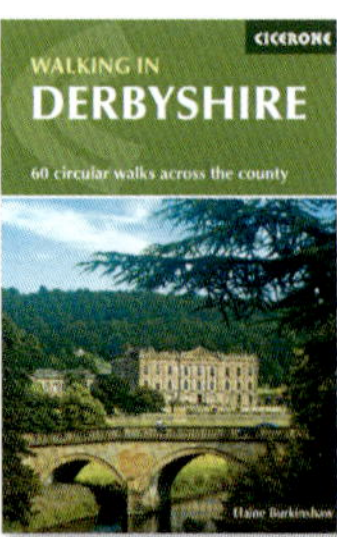

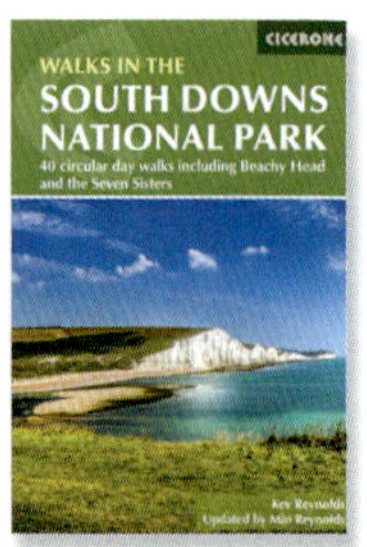

Other guides to this region

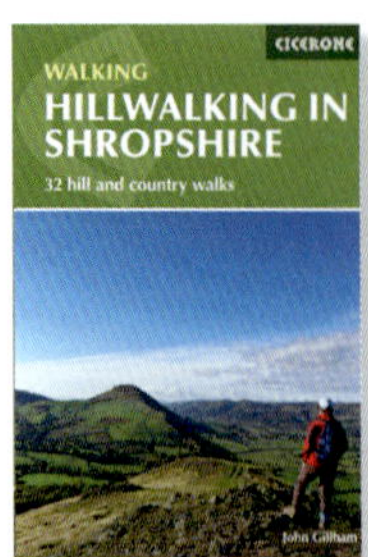

Trust Cicerone to guide your next adventure

cicerone.co.uk